THE PLOT AGAINST THE PEACE

Also by

MICHAEL SAYERS *and* ALBERT E. KAHN

SABOTAGE!—The Secret War Against America

AUTHORS' NOTE: *It should be borne in mind during the reading of* THE PLOT AGAINST THE PEACE *that the German General Staff has managed to involve many persons in all countries who were unaware they were being used in furtherance of Germany's secret plans. The inclusion of such persons in this book should not create the inference that they deliberately harmed the welfare of their own countries.*

THE PLOT AGAINST THE PEACE

A Warning to the Nation!

By

MICHAEL SAYERS and ALBERT E. KAHN

BOOK FIND CLUB, NEW YORK

George Braziller Director

BY ARRANGEMENT WITH THE DIAL PRESS, INC.

For Tana and Riette

This book is complete and unabridged in contents and is manufactured in strict conformity with Government regulations for saving paper.

PRINTED IN THE UNITED STATES OF AMERICA

CONTENTS

THE PLOT AGAINST THE PEACE

TO THE READER

This book is a warning to the nation. The secret rulers of Germany are already preparing for a new world war. They have vast hidden economic and political reserves for future use, not only inside Germany but throughout the world. Their Fifth Columns are active in the United States and every other country. Having suffered a military defeat in the Second World War, Germany's rulers are plotting to win the peace. They did it in 1918; they believe they can do it again today.

This book has been written to expose the German conspiracy aimed at undermining the peace, splitting the United Nations and resurrecting the military might of Germany. Much of this book will be deeply shocking to the average American. But the facts had to be recorded and they have to be read. The future peace and security of the American people and their Allies depend upon a full understanding of the character and plans of the secret rulers of Germany.

March 1945. THE AUTHORS.

PART I

CHAPTER ONE

THE HIDDEN RESERVES

"*Au revoir,* in twenty years!"

Colonel Hermann Kriebel of the German Armistice Commission, taking leave of the Allied representatives in 1919.

"One day we shall come back. Until then, *à bientôt!*"

The last words of an anonymous German military spokesman over the Nazi radio in Brussels on September 1, 1944.

I. *The Secret Plan: 1915-1945*

THE German General Staff has always regarded military defeat as merely a temporary phase of war. The war goes on. Battle strategy becomes underground conspiracy; artillery is replaced by propaganda; wartime espionage becomes post-war political intrigue, terror, assassination and secret preparation for new military attack.

"Even the final decision of war is not to be regarded as absolute," wrote Germany's former military theorist, General Karl von Clausewitz, in his celebrated treatise *Vom Kriege* (On War). "The conquered nation often sees it only as a passing phase, to be repaired in after times by political combinations."

These words have been deeply pondered by the German General Staff—the cabal of army officers, Junkers and industrialists who are the real rulers of Germany.* They provided the German General Staff with the basis of a secret plan by which it successfully operated after the First World War. Today Germany's rulers are again operating on the basis of this secret plan in Germany and throughout the world. . . .

The original form of this secret plan of the German General

* It should be remembered that throughout this book the phrase *German General Staff* does not mean the German military leadership alone, but describes the entire political, economic and military leadership of imperialist Germany. For a detailed characterization of the German General Staff, see Part II, Chapter Five.

Staff was discovered in 1915 by William Seamen Bainbridge, an American representative in Berlin. After the First World War, seeking to warn America, Bainbridge wrote a detailed report on Germany for the United States Government. It appears as *Document No. 26, Official Senate Documents, First Session of the 68th Congress of the United States.* This little-known American document contains the most sensational forecast ever made regarding German policy.

Here is the five-point secret German General Staff plan as revealed to Bainbridge in 1915, *three years before the end of the last war,* by a German officer in a room in the Hotel Adlon, Berlin:

> "(1) An armistice will come before any hostile army crosses Germany's frontier.
>
> (2) There will be no scars on the Fatherland after this war.
>
> (3) The immediate competitors in the economic and commercial world will be so crippled that, when it is all over, the Germans will be outselling them in the markets of the world long before they can get on their feet.
>
> (4) Following the war, there will be economic hell, industrial revolution. We will set class against class, individual against individual, until the nations will have pretty much all they can attend to at home and not bother with us.
>
> (5) If need be, the Fatherland may dissemble into component parts and reassemble at the strategic time."

In concluding this extraordinary revelation, the German officer turned to Bainbridge and said with deliberate emphasis:

> "The greatest struggle will come after the war. The weapon will be propaganda, the value of which we know. The Allies will be torn asunder, each will be put at the others' throats like a lot of howling, gnashing hounds. And when they are all separated from France, Germany will deal with her alone."

This German postwar plan was successfully carried out by the German General Staff after the First World War. The Armistice came before any hostile army could cross Germany's frontier. The war left Germany's economic might unimpaired, and Germany's plants, mills and mines unscathed. In the years following the war, Germany was able to challenge America, Britain and France for the markets of the world. German intrigue and propaganda set Britain against France, America against Europe and all countries against Soviet Russia. . . .

In the Second World War the German General Staff has been unable to prevent the invasion of Germany's home territory. But the German plan today is otherwise almost identical with the plan it carried out with such amazing success following the last German debacle. As Marshal Stalin pointed out in 1942, the German General Staff is methodical and efficient; but it is not very imaginative. Once it has conceived a plan, it follows it step by step, again and again and again, no matter what happens. Like burglars who continually leave their "signatures" behind them at the scenes of their robberies, the German General Staff conducts its conspiracy today precisely as it did thirty years ago.

On February 26, 1945, one of the most remarkable exposés of the Second World War appeared in the Soviet newspaper *Pravda*. It was an article revealing in full detail the plans of the German General Staff for converting the Nazi Party into an underground apparatus which would continue functioning after the military defeat of Nazi Germany and would carry on systematic preparations for a third world war.

Pravda reported that the German General Staff had already taken the following measures:

> "(1) Creation of a powerful financial base for extensive subsidizing of underground work.
> (2) Preservation of the main cadres of the party.
> (3) Preservation of the economic base of the German war machine.
> (4) The political preparation of revenge."

The article in *Pravda* stated that these activities were being carried on "both within and outside Germany," and that within Germany the Nazis were preparing to conduct their underground work chiefly along three lines: organization of sabotage and terrorist bands; setting up of a widely ramified clandestine fascist organization; and sabotage of peace terms between Germany and the United Nations.

The article continued:

"At the present time, the German General Staff feverishly prepares plans for the operations of the fascist underground army, which must be centered chiefly in the hilly and wooded terrain of East Prussia, southern and southwestern Germany, in Tyrol and in Austria."

A special secret staff had already been selected to direct the operations of the Nazi underground machine. *Pravda* revealed the names of the men on the staff:

"To direct these operations, a special headquarters has been set up in Munich under Wilhelm Schepmann—one of the organizers of anti-Allied sabotage in the Ruhr in 1923. The members of Schepmann's staff are Ernst Kaltenbrünner, Gestapo chief and chief of the Military Intelligence Service; Hitler's personal friend, Werner von Alwensleben; senior officers of the Security Service and Obergruppen Fuehrer Schellenberg* and Melle."

The terrorist detachments of the Nazi underground army, stated the Soviet newspaper, "will consist of picked fascist cutthroats from SS units," which "at present . . . are studying future theatres of operations in the areas assigned to them."

Pravda went on to give a detailed description of the vast and intricate apparatus that had already been organized by the German General Staff:

"Simultaneously a ramified network of secret caches of arms, ammunition, clothing, provisions, secret signals and communication lines is being laid out.

"Along with the preparation of terrorist bands, a huge underground apparatus is being set up to conduct various underground work and fascist propaganda—the so-called sixth column.

"The territory of Germany, divided into sectors and areas, is being covered with a dense network of clandestine Nazi party organizations, consisting of many thousands of secret cells. . . .

"This clandestine organization will serve to build up cadres for the future German Army."

The overall postwar strategy and tactics of this elaborate Nazi underground organization, concluded *Pravda,* were to be supervised from abroad by a "special secret General Staff" residing "in one of the neutral countries."

*Obergruppen Fuehrer Schellenberg was previously active as a secret Nazi agent in the United States. See page 169.

II. *Conspiracies and Confessions*

In the spring of 1943 the German General Staff started its contemporary application of the secret German postwar plan. Nazi Germany was face to face with catastrophe. The entire German Sixth Army under General von Paulus had been surrounded and annihilated by the Red Army at Stalingrad. That was the historic turning point of the Second World War.

In November 1943 the French resistance weekly, *Combat,* published in Algiers, printed the text of a secret German General Staff memorandum which had fallen into Allied hands after the German debacle in North Africa. The author of memorandum was General Otto von Stuelpnagel who ruled France for Hitler from 1940 to 1944.

This is what the German General wrote:

> "What does a provisional defeat matter to us if because of the destruction of manpower and material which we will have been able to inflict on our enemies and neighboring territories, we have obtained a margin of economic and demographic superiority greater than before 1939? The conquest of the world will require numerous stages, but the essential is that the end of each stage brings us an economic and industrial essential greater than that of our enemies. With the war booty which we have accumulated, the enfeebling of two generations of the manpower, the destruction of the industries of our neighbors and that which we can save of our own, we shall be better placed to conquer in twenty-five years than we were in 1939. The interval of twenty-five years is a limited interval, for that is the time which will be required for Russia to repair the destruction we have visited on her."

The memorandum mentioned some of the elaborate devices by which the rulers of Germany would seek to evade a just peace:

> "We do not have to fear peace conditions analogous to those which we would have imposed because our adversaries will always be divided and disunited. Our enemies recognize already that the 1919 formula, 'Germany will pay,' lacked sense and worth. We will furnish them some brigades of workers, we will restore

some art objects or out-of-date machines, and we can always say that those which we do not restore were destroyed by enemy bombardments. We should immediately prepare as camouflage a list of such objects destroyed by Anglo-American bombs."

The basic aim of the German plan, now as in 1918, is to secure a final peace settlement, no matter how severe it may appear on the surface, or how hard on the German people, which will leave German economic power intact.

With amazing consistency Germany's rulers are repeating the same strategy they employed in the past to obtain the kind of peace settlement suitable to their aims. In both instances, this strategy was mapped out long in advance. . . .

In his war memoirs, General Erich Ludendorff revealed that as early as 1916 the German General Staff decided that it could not win the First World War and that it then began its campaign for a negotiated peace. The peace intrigues went on steadily throughout 1916, 1917 and were intensified after the failure of Ludendorff's spring offensive in 1918.

Ludendorff tells of the hopes he placed in the Vatican as an intermediary for a negotiated peace. "I also entertained some hopes," continued Ludendorff, "of the efforts being made by the representative of the Foreign Office in Brussels, Herr von der Lancken, who sought to get in touch with French statesmen. He went to Switzerland, but the gentlemen from France stayed away."

Ludendorff reveals that the German General Staff was confident it could divide the Allied nations, play one against the other, and so secure the kind of final peace settlement that Germany wanted.

In August 1918, Ludendorff told the Kaiser: "The war must be ended."

But the Kaiser, like Hitler twenty years later, was unwilling to surrender his power and demanded the continuation of the hostilities.

At this juncture, when the German General Staff was frantically seeking peace so as to forestall complete Allied victory, the famous German steel magnate, August Thyssen, published an extraordinary "Confession" for all the world to read. It was the most sensational document of the last war.

August Thyssen, stating that German industrialists were prepared to sacrifice the Kaiser in return for peace, wrote:

> "In 1912 the Hohenzollerns saw that the war had become a necessity to the preservation of the military system upon which their power depends . . . they, therefore, in 1912, decided to embark on a great war of conquest.
>
> "But to do this they had to get the commercial community to support them in their aims. They did this by holding out to them hopes of great personal gain as a result of the war. . . .
>
> "I was personally promised a free grant of 30,000 acres in Australia and a loan from the Deutsche Bank of £150,000 at 3 per cent . . . to enable me to develop my business in Australia. Several other firms were promised special trading facilities in India, which was to be conquered by Germany . . . a syndicate was formed for the exploitation of Canada. This syndicate consisted of the heads of twelve great firms; the working capital being fixed at £20,000,000, half of which was to be found by the German government.
>
> "There were, I have heard, promises made of a more personal character . . ."

This astonishing document reached the United States in the early spring of 1918. It was published as a pamphlet entitled *The Hohenzollern Plot* by August Thyssen. It was reprinted many times, quoted in newspapers, inserted into the *Congressional Record,* and publicized especially in American business circles. It did much towards convincing American public opinion that peace could be made with the "sound, business interests" in Germany.

Meanwhile, although Thyssen's "Confession" had openly called for the removal of the Kaiser and the conclusion of the war, nothing was done by the Kaiser's Government to arrest Thyssen or stop the publication of his document. The steel magnate continued to live in Germany, unmolested and in full control of his vast industrial interests.

After the war, August Thyssen died, and the famous "Confession" was forgotten.

But the German plan had worked. The peace left German industry intact and in the hands of Fritz Thyssen, Krupp,

Kirdorff, Stinnes and their associates, the industrial representatives of the German General Staff.

Twenty years later, in the summer of 1940, another astonishing and sensational "Confession" was made public by a German industrialist. With Poland conquered and France in its last throes, the German General Staff was again ready for peace in the West, so that it could prepare the next stage of the war: the invasion of Soviet Russia. This time the German "Confession" denounced Hitler, and stated that German industry was prepared to sacrifice Hitler in return for a favorable peace with the nations of the West.

The 1940 "Confession" was written by Fritz Thyssen, son of August Thyssen, and inheritor of his father's steel trust.

Fritz Thyssen wrote:

> "I undertook to finance the N.S.D.A.P. (Nazi Party), together with von Papen, von Schroeder, Kirdorff, Krupp von Bohlen und Halbach. We are, so to speak, the guarantors to Germany and the world for Hitler's good conduct . . .
>
> "Hitler promised us the things we most wanted: to von Papen, power and honor; to Krupp, commissions and money, mountains of money; and to me, in particular, a peaceful period of German politics at home and abroad; and understanding with England; and understanding with the working classes who, through far-reaching social reforms, should be compensated for the loss of all political rights; the abolition of trade unions and the appropriation of their property. He promised us a sort of Christian state whose authority should be supported by the Church. . . ."

This second Thyssen "Confession" which burst like a bombshell in the summer of 1940 was immediately circulated throughout Europe and America, just as the first Thyssen "Confession" had been in 1918. The words of Fritz Thyssen were printed in various forms in the United States by *Life,* the New York *Times,* the *American* magazine, *Time, Newsweek,* were quoted on the radio, referred to in Congress, and, in general, given the widest possible publicity. Fritz Thyssen was reported to be a fugitive from the Gestapo, hiding somewhere as a miserable refugee in southern France.

Thyssen was actually living in a luxurious private villa at

Cannes. On one side of his villa was the home of Pierre Etienne Flandin, the notorious French pro-Nazi politician and advocate of a Franco-German alliance against Soviet Russia. Flanking Thyssen's villa on the other side was the prewar residence of Sir Neville Henderson, former British Ambassador to Berlin, one-time friend of Goering and Ribbentrop, and ardent member of the British Cliveden Set.

After the Nazi occupation of France, Fritz Thyssen continued to live in his luxurious villa at Cannes surrounded on all sides by Nazi officials and high-ranking Nazi generals.

In 1943, as Hitler's armies faced disaster in Russia, Fritz Thyssen returned to Germany. He was last seen by a Swedish correspondent early in 1944 residing at the Hotel Adlon in Berlin, still ready to make peace with Britain and America "to save Europe from Bolshevism."

Fritz Thyssen wrote in his famous "Confession":

> "Peace is to be had. The price is not high. It is easy to arrange. . . . *We still have men who hold the reins.*"

In January 1945, when the Red Army smashed through the crucial German defenses east of Berlin, German peace emissaries rushed frantically into Sweden, Switzerland, Spain and Portugal. Edmund Hugo Stinnes showed up in Stockholm. Franz von Papen appeared in Madrid. Dr. Hjalmar Schacht was in Switzerland. The Vatican was besieged by German couriers. In every case the reported peace offers were identical: Germany would get rid of Hitler; Germany would repay what she had stolen; Germany would disarm; Germany would disband the Nazi organizations and abolish the Nazi laws; Germany would transform herself, just as Thyssen had promised in 1940, into a "Christian state." So long as Germany could keep her economic power intact, Germany's rulers were ready to come to almost any terms with their enemies.

But precautionary steps had already been taken by the German General Staff and its Nazi and industrialist representatives to build hidden reserves of capital, cash and investments in foreign countries.

III. *Camouflaged Capital*

In the fall of 1918, within a few months of the General Staff's decision to sue for peace, billions of marks had been smuggled out of Germany to Sweden, Holland, Switzerland, Spain, Argentina, Brazil and other foreign centers of German commercial activity. The *Neue Zuercher Zeitung* in June 1919, estimated the figure of "emigrated capital" which German interests had cached in Switzerland at 35 billion marks. The Dutch aviation designer, Fokker, describes in his memoirs *The Flying Dutchman* how an entire military aviation plant in Germany was dismembered and secretly transported to Holland. The Dornier Airplane Company, with headquarters in Friedrichshafen, was moved across Lake Constance to Switzerland. The Rohrbach plant was transferred to Denmark; Heinkel and Junkers established themselves in Sweden. All these transfers were done at the request of the General Staff and accomplished with the aid of the German Army.

Admiral Canaris, of the Imperial Naval Intelligence, and subsequently of the Nazi Naval Intelligence, went to Spain to supervise German-controlled shipyards and submarine plants at Vigo.

Baron Manfred von Killinger, Imperial Army officer and subsequent Nazi Consul in the United States, established a company in Echevarria, Spain, to experiment with new types of submarines for Krupp.

The same thing is happening today.

A dispatch from Stockholm, Sweden, to the New York *Times,* January 30, 1945, revealed that German industrialists were placing huge capital foundations in Sweden by registering their patents at the Swedish State Patent Office to elude seizure by the United Nations. The *Times* dispatch read:

> "A perusal of patent applications, which must be recorded in the Swedish Official Journal, reveals that a good 50 per cent of all patent applications hail from German firms. The latest ones

come from such major German concerns as I.G.Farben, Zeiss-Ikon, Boch and the Daimler-Bainz companies, besides the A.E.G. and Siemens."

This flight of German capital into neutral Sweden represents only a fraction of the capital investments which Germany had already secreted abroad.

As of February 1945 there were no less than 987 joint stock companies in Spain controlled completely by German capital. Two thousand Spanish companies, many of them with branches and affiliates in North and South America, have German directors on their boards.

As late as the summer of 1944, as the American journalist Ted Allan revealed in *Collier's* Magazine on February 3, 1945, the international German trust, I.G.Farben, built four new chemical plants in Madrid. In March 1944, I.G.Farben completed a synthetic oil plant in Pueblonuevo del Terrible near Córdoba. This plant had a Spanish name, Calvo Sotelo, and was supposedly controlled by Spaniards. It was owned completely by I.G.Farben. Also in the summer of 1944, I.G.Farben built a magnesium plant in Santander, Spanish northern port. Other German plants, steel, textile, munitions and mines, exist in Catalonia, the Asturias, the Basque country and in Galicia.

The Spanish multi-millionaire Juan March, who financed Franco's Fascist *Falange* to the tune of $60,000,000, was a German spy in the First World War, a Krupp agent and collaborator with Admiral Canaris, chief of the German Naval Intelligence. Today, March is providing commercial fronts for German capital smuggled into Spain and, through Spanish outlets, into South America.

Portugal is another center of German financial and industrial activity. An uncensored report printed in the New York *Times* on January 12, 1944, disclosed: "Like Spain, Portugal teems with German agents and in Lisbon they are as ubiquitous as bootleggers were during prohibition in America. Their red necks gleam in every bar and fine restaurant . . ." Through Portuguese commercial fronts, the Germans have also been able to penetrate South America.

Throughout the Americas, especially in Argentina, German agents have built important new plants, and gained control of mines, banks, railroads, aviation lines, chemicals and steel works. Fritz Mandl virtually controlled the munitions industry in Argentina on behalf of I.G.Farben. Axel Wenner-Gren, the Swedish multi-millionaire adventurer, and intimate friend of Marshal Hermann Goering, has set up Krupp and I.G.Farben fronts throughout South America, and especially in Argentina. Alfredo Moll, who has been described as the "gray eminence" of the Nazis in Buenos Aires, is the son-in-law of the president of the Central Bank of Argentina. Moll is director of the firm of Anilinas Alemenas, branch of the I.G.Farben trust in Argentina.

Testifying before the Kilgore Committee on September 12, 1944, Sims Carter, Assistant Chief of the Economic Warfare Section of the U. S. Department of Justice, revealed:

> "When the German guns are silenced in Europe, the principal German industrial combines plan renewed activity from bases in Argentina. Organizations and outlets of distribution have been maintained. Profits from sales at wartime prices made ample means available. All the machinery is ready for safeguarding German supremacy in the steadily expanding South American market."

The plan by which the German General Staff has operated in South America was drawn up many years before Hitler took power in Germany. If the German plan prevails, it will continue to operate many years after the smashing of the Hitler regime. This plan is directly aimed at the eventual German conquest of the United States.

Immediately after the First World War, the German secret infiltration of the Latin American countries by economic, political and military agents went into high gear in preparation for the Second World War. Captain Ernst Roehm, organizer of the Nazi Storm Troops, showed up in Bolivia in 1925 as "special adviser" to the Bolivian Army. The German aviation officer Fritz Hammer went to Colombia, where he later organized Nazi espionage and economic infiltration under cover of Nazi aviation concerns. General Bohnstedt became head of the military academy in Salvador and official instructor to the Salvadorean Army. General Reinecke, General Kundt and many other officer-agents of the German General Staff became active in Chile, Paraguay, Peru, where they sought to influence the officers' corps and spread hatred of the United States.

Besides the German army men, there were the economic agents of the German General Staff. After the last war, hosts of these German economic agents swarmed into the South American republics. The international octopus of German intrigue, I.G.Farben, spread its tentacles far and wide. In 1941-42, official investigations disclosed that:

In Brazil, the chief centers of Nazi activities were the Farben concerns of Allianca Commercial de Anilinas Ltda. and A. Quimica Bayer of Rio de Janeiro. The Brazilian Farben executive, Hammers, was a leading agent of the German Military Intelligence.

In Peru, Dr. Friedrich Bank and Guillermo Corvejo, executives of the Farben Compania General de Anilinas, were both key agents of the German Military Intelligence.

In Chile, Werner Siering, manager of the Farben Bayer concern, reorganized the German Military Intelligence Service in Chile in 1935 and was Secretary of the Chilean Nazi Party.

In Venezuela, Alfred Becker and Arnold Margerie, executives of the Farben La Quimica Bayer in Caracas, supervised German Military Intelligence and Nazi Party operations throughout the Caribbean area.

In Ecuador, L. E. Brueckmann, head of the Farben concern of Brueckmann and Company of Guayaquil, doubled as Nazi Consul; and his fellow Farben executives, the manager Herr Tetke and the treasurer Herr Ruperti, were the leading Nazi Party organizers in Ecuador.

In Mexico, chief executive of the Farben concerns Compana General de Anilinas, La Union Quimica and Casa Bayer, was Baron von Humboldt, who was also chief of the Mexican Nazi Gestapo. . . .

On February 22, 1945, Edward R. Stettinius, United States Secretary of State, called on the leaders of the American republics to "stamp out utterly every vestige of Nazi influence in this hemisphere" and warned that the Western Hemisphere still faces "the danger of secret Nazi-Fascist infiltration" into its economic and political life. Addressing the Inter-American Conference at Mexico City, Secretary of State Stettinius said:

> "The Axis leaders will, of course, attempt to escape the consequences of their crimes. We must be constantly on the alert for the flight to this hemisphere of Nazi funds and Nazi underground leaders who will seek to find a refuge here as a base for an ultimate comeback."

IV. *Appeasement International*

During the last war a prominent neutral diplomat asked a member of the German General Staff, "What will you do if you lose?"

The German officer replied, "We will organize sympathy."

Throughout the Second World War Germany's rulers have never lost contact with certain circles in Europe and America which openly sympathized with Germany's aggression and advocated support of Nazism as a "bulwark against Communism." A convenient meeting place for secret negotiations was established by the German Government in Basle, Switzerland, at the headquarters of the Bank of International Settlements.

An article in the New York *Times,* on May 19, 1943, commented on the existence of this German-controlled institution in Switzerland:

> "Allied preparations for an invasion of the European continent make the Bank for International Settlements at Basle, Switzerland, look still more incongruous than it ever looked since the outbreak of the war in September, 1939. In the seclusion of a Swiss city, American, German, French and Italian bankers, not to mention Swedish, Swiss and Netherland representatives, are still at work side by side and attend to common business. . . .
>
> "Does it mean that, in this world of today, so hopelessly torn asunder, all belligerents are tacitly agreed to preserve a unique shelter for what was formerly called international finance—a

shelter to be eventually used at will for the purpose of a policy of appeasement?"

The directors of the Bank of International Settlements are men of great influence, and they include three directors of the Bank of England; the powerful Nazi financiers—Baron K. F. von Schroeder of Cologne, Reichsbank President Walther Funk and Dr. Hermann Schmitz, President of I.G.Farben; and the American Wall Street banker, Thomas H. McKittrick, Director of the First National Bank of New York and President and General Manager of the Bank of International Settlements.

On November 23, 1943, Harry White, special adviser to the U. S. Treasury Department, told Washington correspondents: "It [the Bank of International Settlements] is German-controlled. Germany is being very nice and hopes to use it to get back into financial power. There's an American president doing business with the Germans while our American boys are fighting Germans."

Throughout the war, the Nazis permitted payment of dividends to the international members of the Bank of International Settlements. On May 22, 1944, a United Press dispatch from Basle, Switzerland, reported:

> "The Bank of International Settlements declared a dividend of 4 per cent today when Swiss Board Chairman Ernest Weber called the annual meeting to order . . . Weber previously had obtained approval of today's decisions from the chairmen of the national banks in owning nations—the U. S. A., Britain, Germany, France, Belgium, Holland, Sweden, Italy and Japan.
>
> "With last year's business closed, the American, French, German, Italian and Dutch executives of the bank now face another year of daily meetings. . . .
>
> "General Manager of the BIS is the American representative, Thomas H. McKittrick. His colleagues include a German, a Frenchman, an Italian and a Dutchman . . ."

The American banker McKittrick told the United Press correspondent, "We keep the machine ticking . . . because when the Armistice comes the formerly hostile powers will need an efficient instrument such as the BIS."

By means of this unique apparatus, German industrialists have been able to maintain contact with their prewar sympathizers and economic associates in every country in the world. The French, Dutch, Belgian, Italian and Finnish directors were Nazi appointees. Two active British directors on the BIS are Sir Otto Niemeyer and Frank Tiarks, both of whom are directors of the Bank of England. Before the war, Niemeyer and Tiarks were prominent members of the notorious Anglo-German Fellowship, key center of pro-Nazi and anti-Soviet agitation in Britain. The German General Staff's postwar plan counts heavily on the continued friendship of these international financial circles.*

Throughout Europe, German economic agents are active as propagandists for German postwar ends. Not all of these agents are Germans. Some are former collaborationists, who have evaded arrest and imprisonment or execution for treason. These men are still linked to the international German economic empire. They are now safeguarding German interests and promoting the General Staff plan by attempting to foment agitation against the anti-Nazi governments of the liberated countries.

By painting the new governments in Europe as "Communist," the Germans and their agents seek to disrupt the United Nations and to make the world forget the German crimes.

Former collaborationists in Europe make a point of contacting any American businessmen and officials who will listen to them. Some Americans bring back fascist propaganda to the United States under the impression that they are simply repeating the opinions of "conservative elements" in Europe.

Early in 1945 Frederick C. Crawford, former President of the National Association of Manufacturers, returned from a trip to

* As of February 1945, Dr. Hjalmar Schacht was residing in Switzerland. Dr. Schacht, who, like Fritz Thyssen, was reported to have broken with the Nazis, held the post of Minister without Portfolio in the Nazi Government. In Switzerland, Dr. Schacht was in constant touch with the German directors of the Bank of International Settlements.

Europe and reported to the New York Chamber of Commerce that Frenchmen were saying that, if let alone, the Nazi rule in France would have become acceptable to the French people. On January 5, 1945, Mr. Crawford stated:

"A fine conservative Frenchman I had known for years told me that if it [the Nazi occupation] had gone on for a year and a half more, he believed the French working people would have settled for things as they were."

The French anti-Nazi underground, according to Mr. Crawford, was composed of "Communists" and "underworld ex-convicts." On the other hand, Mr. Crawford had this to say regarding the collaborationists who had sold out their country to Hitler:

"What is a collaborationist? I will tell you. If you operated your business for the Germans and didn't expand it, you were a patriotic citizen. If you operated your business for the Germans and expanded it to any substantial amount, you were a collaborationist. And, lastly, if you got into trouble with labor, you are a collaborationist with Germany."*

But even more important than building pro-German sentiment in the United States, from the viewpoint of the German General Staff, is the attempt to maintain German capital and investment in America through the connivance of certain American citizens.

* "One of the boldest reports from Europe is Mr. F. C. Crawford's," declared Elizabeth Dilling, in the January 1945 issue of her *Patriotic Research Bulletin*. At the time, Elizabeth Dilling was under Federal indictment for allegedly conspiring with Nazi Germany against the United States Government.

A few years before this, on his return from a previous European trip in June 1939, Mr. Crawford had praised Benito Mussolini and dismissed the threat of a Nazi-fascist war as "newspaper talk." He also stated at that time: "What difference does it make if the dictatorship of Germany is consuming one-fourth of production for military grandeur or whether the bureaucracy of the New Deal is consuming one-fourth of production to maintain itself?"

V. *Business as Usual*

Almost immediately after the First World War, agents of German industrialists flocked to the United States. They became American citizens and built up American affiliates of German firms. Many of them were exposed by U. S. government agencies after 1941. Many fled back to Germany or into South America. Others are still operating in the United States. Some American businessmen, attracted by the profits, have maintained their connections with Germany, aided the Germans in their plan to protect their American investments, and are prepared to resume open business dealings with Germany as soon as they possibly can.

The German General Staff is counting on this.

The German steel trust, headed by the number one Nazi peace emissary Fritz Thyssen, controls from its Dusseldorf headquarters at least 175 known branches and agencies in nearly every country in the world. Other branches are concealed behind various false names and ownership-titles.

Edward Barreau, German-born president of the Thyssen steel-trust's New York branch, Steel Union-Sheet Piling, Inc., wrote to the head of the Brazilian branch on December 1, 1939, in a confidential letter later seized by the U. S. Department of Justice:

> "You are aware of the fact that you are on the Black List and if anyone unqualified should get hold of your letter, which evidences a direct relationship between you and us the next thing that would happen would be that we would also be on the Black List. This being the case, we trust that you will understand when we caution you to use the utmost care in regard to your correspondence with Germany."

In 1940, Kurt Orbanowski, who had headed the Bulgarian branch of the Thyssen steel-trust, was sent to the United States to become director of the Steel Union-Sheet Piling, Inc., and its successor, the North River Steel Corporation. Orbanowski had been born in the United States. When the Department of

Justice began cracking down on economic agents in the United States after 1941, Orbanowski changed his name to Orban. On January 25, 1942, he wrote in a confidential message to the head of the Argentine Thyssen branch that Edward Barreau "who is a very newly naturalized citizen" planned to retire to a farm in the United States for the duration of the war, but he, Orban, because of his American birth, was "much less subject to criticism in the present time" and he "may even take over or become the successor to the North River Steel Corporation."

Commenting on these facts, Sims Carter of the Department of Justice told the Kilgore Committee on September 12, 1944:

> "By the time the present war broke out, most of Germany's leading industrial, commercial and banking firms had American connections. Even after hostilities had begun, key figures continued to arrive in the United States and other parts of the hemisphere from Germany."

Mr. Carter added a final note of warning:

> "German activities have not been confined to the steel industry. There is every indication that all German industry intends to resume its activities in the Western Hemisphere after the present war. As the second World War draws to a close, military warfare can be expected once more to assume the form of economic warfare."

There are American businessmen, aware of Germany's secret preparations for the postwar period, who believe that Germany will succeed in repeating her successful intrigues following the last war . . .

On November 24, 1943, a startling item was published in the Financial Section of the New York *Times*. The item was part of a report of a meeting held by the Export Managers Club at the Hotel Pennsylvania in New York. The highlight of the meeting was a survey on postwar conditions. The survey disclosed that America's leading export managers believed the United States would be faced with two principal world competitors after the defeat of Germany and Japan.

The first in importance would be Great Britain.

The second would be—*Germany!*

While this remarkable opinion as to the continued economic power of Germany after the war was being expressed by businessmen in New York, Allied planes were pounding German industrial centers, the Red Army was encircling and annihilating German armies, and the United Nations leaders were on record as stating that German power, both military and economic, would be totally smashed as a result of the war.

Thanks to clever German manipulation of cartels, a few powerful American industrialists still have a vested interest in the preservation of the German economic and industrial power, the backbone of German militarism.

Through cartel arrangements, certain American businessmen are under agreement to collaborate with German industrialists after the war. Cartels still in operation, or temporarily "suspended" until the war ends, cover chemicals, rubber, magnesium, zinc, aluminum and many other vital products. Many of these cartel contracts are legally valid until 1948, 1956 and even 1968. At least one great American company, Standard Oil of New Jersey, has flatly refused to cancel its postwar cartel deals with Germany.

"The Standard Oil Company of New Jersey directors were asked by certain stockholders to cut off all relations with Farben after the war, but it was refused," Homer T. Bone, Chairman of the Senate Patents Committee, informed the Senate Military Affairs Committee on June 4, 1943. "One official said such a request was 'an affront.' There is clear indication that after this unpleasant interlude of war they will hold hands again and resume their very harmonious and beautiful arrangement with the cartels."

Within one week of May 1942, the U. S. Department of Justice uncovered no less than 162 cartel agreements between the German I.G.Farben trust and American business firms.

"The secret influence of the international cartel is going to be thrown in favor of peace without victory when the first opportunity arises—just as it was thrown in that direction at

Munich," declared Thurman Arnold, Assistant Attorney General of the United States, in a speech before the Illinois Bar Association on June 3, 1942.

Assistant Attorney General Arnold further warned in the same speech:

> "The small group of American businessmen who are parties to these international rings are not unpatriotic, but they still think of the war as a temporary recess from business-as-usual with a strong Germany. They expect to begin the game all over again after the war.
>
> "It is significant that all these cartel leaders still talk and think as if the war would end in a stalemate, and that, therefore, they must be in a position to continue their arrangements with a strong Germany after the war. This is not shown by their speeches, but by the actual documents and memoranda of business policy which we find in their files."

In October 1939, one month after Hitler invaded Poland, the Standard Oil executive, Frank A. Howard, undertook a mission to Europe on behalf of his company. His travels took him from Paris to London to The Hague and, finally, to Vichy. In a confidential report to W. S. Farish, then president of Standard Oil, Mr. Howard outlined the difficulties of his mission. He stated that he had met with French army and industrial leaders in Paris and had certain discussions with them concerning oil supplies for the French war machine. Mr. Howard's report then proceeds:

> "I was somewhat concerned when it was discovered that I had left these discussions to undertake discussions in Holland with Germans interested in the same problems."

Howard's passport for Holland was finally cleared by the British, and Howard was able to report:

> ". . . I was able to keep my appointments in Holland where I had three days of discussion with the representatives of the I.G. . . . We did our best to work out plans for a modus vivendi which would operate through the terms of the war, whether or not the U. S. came in."

A number of American businessmen who have stakes in Germany take the view, much encouraged by German economic agents, that they are not concerned with politics. Thus corporations like Standard Oil, Ford Motor Company and General Motors, which have done business with Nazi Germany, state that the political character of the German regime is none of their business.

A remarkable letter written to a stockholder by Alfred P. Sloan, chairman of General Motors, expresses this attitude. The letter is dated April 6, 1939, and reads in part:

> "General Motors is an international organization. It operates in practically every country in the world . . . many years ago, General Motors—before the present regime in Germany—invested a large amount of money in Adam Opel A.G. It has been a very profitable investment, and I think outside of the political phase, its future potentiality from the standpoint of development and profit, is equal to, if not greater than many other investments which the Corporation has made. It enjoys about 50% of the business in Germany—a little less than that to be exact. It employs German workers and consumes German materials. . . .
>
> "Having attained the position which we have, through evolution, hard work, and, I believe, intelligent management, of approaching 50% of one of the most important industries in Germany, I feel that we must conduct ourselves as a German organization, involving German capital . . ."

In the same letter Mr. Sloan acknowledges that an American corporation should govern its operations "in accordance with the foreign policy of the United States." But the notion that profits and politics can be rigidly separated is a dangerous one, and certainly one that the Germans have in the past known how to utilize for their own sinister ends. . . .

During the First World War, the financing of the German espionage and sabotage ring in the United States was in the hands of the German commercial attaché, Dr. Heinrich Albert. In 1919, following a Senate investigation, Senator Nelson characterizes him as the "Machiavelli of the whole thing . . . the mildest mannered man that ever scuttled ship or cut a throat." Dr. Albert worked smoothly and with amazing success. Intimate with scores of American bankers, manufacturers and traders, he regularly conveyed vital espionage material to the German Government. At the same time, Dr. Albert was the paymaster of the secret sabotage ring which von Papen organized to blow up American ships, infect American cattle with disease germs, set fire to American war plants and docks, wreck American bridges and stir up anti-Allied sentiment throughout the country. Through Dr. Albert's hands passed at least $40,000,000 for the secret organization of sabotage, sedition and conspiracy in the United States. In 1917, Dr. Heinrich Albert was forced to leave the United States and return to Germany. . . .

Little was heard of Dr. Albert during the ensuing years. Nevertheless, he was still extremely active on behalf of the German General Staff. When the colossal international German trust, I.G.Farben, was organized in 1925, Dr. Albert was called in to advise on how to deal with America. Through Dr. Albert's advice, scores of well-mannered young German business agents arrived in the United States during the 1920's and early 1930's, took out naturalization papers, and organized "American" firms in which the controlling interest was always held by I.G.Farben. Typical of the I.G.Farben agents sent into America, on Dr. Albert's advice, were William von Rath, subsequently chief of Nazi intelligence in Switzerland, and director of several American fronts for I.G.Farben, and Werner von Clemm, who married a cousin of Joachim von Ribbentrop, set up the Pioneer Import and Export Company in New York, and was arrested and imprisoned in 1943 as a Nazi agent engaged in smuggling diamonds to finance espionage in America.

Dr. Albert remained in Germany, residing at Viktoria-Strasse 8, Berlin. As of February 1945 he still held the important post of Director of the Ford Motor Company, Cologne, Germany. The Cologne Ford Company is partly controlled by I.G.Farben. . . .

The case of Rudolph Hutz also exemplifies how German industry works in the service of the German General Staff.

On August 21, 1918, toward the end of the First World War, Rudolph Hutz was arrested by U. S. Secret Service agents in his summer home at Meredith, New Hampshire. Hutz was charged with espionage on behalf of the German Government, specifically with trying "to deliver to the German government or its representatives certain documents, writings, code books, photographs, blueprints, models, plans, maps, instruments, appliances and information relating to the United States national defense."

Hutz was interned as a German spy.

Twenty-three years later, on December 12, 1941, U. S. Treasury agents raided the offices of the General Aniline Corporation at 230 Park Avenue, New York. General Aniline was a front for I.G.Farben. Chairman of the Aniline board was William von Rath of Germany. Directors included Henry Ford's son, Edsel Ford. Standard Oil's Walter C. Teagle had resigned in 1938. The American vice-president of the company was—Rudolph Hutz.

CHAPTER TWO

THE NAZI UNDERGROUND

I. *"Universal Chaos"*

THE Nazi Party, as the chief political instrument of the German General Staff, has the task of fulfilling the political phase of the secret German postwar plan to sabotage United Nations' victory and peace.

In 1915, Point Four of the German General Staff's secret plan called for the stirring up of postwar international political and economic "hell," so that "the nations will have pretty much all they can attend to at home and not bother with us."

On January 30, 1945, in his speech commemorating the twelfth anniversary of the Nazi power, Adolf Hitler prophesied that after the Second World War "universal chaos" will consume the world.

The Nazi task is to set individual against individual, class against class, nation against nation, and thus to make impossible the consolidation of Allied victory and give the German General Staff an opportunity to rise again as a military threat to the world for a third time in this century.

On November 6, 1944 Marshal Josef Stalin warned the Soviet people and the world:

> "After the defeat of Germany she will, of course, be disarmed, both in the economic and military-political respects. However, it would be naive to think that she will not attempt to restore her power and develop new aggression. It is known to all that the German leaders are already now preparing for a new war . . ."

Like German industry, the Nazi Party also has its hidden economic and political reserves for the postwar struggle against the peace. Statistics recently issued by the British Ministry of

Economic Warfare estimate that the Nazis looted close to $27,000,000,000 from the conquered European nations. Most of this loot was appropriated by the Nazi Party, providing a massive secret fund for the financing of international Nazi underground activities for years to come. Besides this, the Nazi leaders have their personal financial caches. Since 1943, Nazi money, jewels and other valuables have been streaming across the Reich frontiers and finding their way by clandestine channels into Spain, Switzerland, Sweden and North and South America. In Switzerland alone, more than 300,000,000 gold francs, or approximately sixty million dollars, are known to have been banked to the private accounts of Nazi leaders. . . .

With these vast hidden sums at their disposal, the Nazis have already reconstituted and reorganized their wartime international Fifth Columns and set up new propaganda agencies and terrorist leagues for the postwar period. Already, in all countries of the United Nations, Nazi-financed and Nazi-inspired agitators are at work seeking to create the "chaos" which Hitler called for in January 1945. Terrorist attempts have been made on the lives of General Charles de Gaulle of France, Marshal Tito of Yugoslavia and other United Nations leaders. Race riots, separatist movements, wildcat strikes, *putsches* and political disorders of every kind are being deliberately incited by Nazi Fifth Column agents in an attempt to break the national and world unity of the United Nations.

In France, Paul Ghali revealed in a European dispatch to the Chicago *Daily News* on September 28, 1944, Joseph Darnand's notorious *Militia* and other French fascist organizations have been "reconstructed and rearmed" under the personal supervision of Heinrich Himmler to carry on underground "terrorism and fifth column activities in France after the war."

In Italy, former agents of the Fascist OVRA, trained by the Nazis, have been smuggled back into the liberated areas to build propaganda and terrorist agencies, to plot assassinations of anti-fascist Italian leaders and to spread anti-United Nations and other Nazi propaganda. A Rome dispatch to the New York *Herald Tribune* on February 10, 1945, by John Chabot Smith, warned of "the alarming degree of Fascist sympathy and Fascist underground organization which still exists in liberated Rome."

In Greece, Leland Stowe reported in February 1945, certain Nazi agents and Greek Fifth Columnists posing as "anti-Communists" and Greek "nationalists" had taken advantage of the confusion following the campaign against the Elas resistance movements to penetrate the Intelligence services, special police units and even Greek government offices, and to carry on widespread terrorism and Nazi-fascist agitation.

In Finland, a few weeks after the German Army withdrew and the Finnish government signed peace with Soviet Russia, two Red Army officers were assassinated in a Helsinki park. Investigation by the Allied Control Commission revealed, according to a statement by Soviet officials in January 1945, that Nazi agents and Finnish Lappo fascists were spreading their propaganda throughout Finland and fomenting widespread underground "opposition to the United Nations and particularly the Soviet Union."

In Norway, in February 1945, Nazi leaders and Quislingites prepared for future underground struggle by destroying all records of their past activities and concealing their identities with false birth certificates. Lord Vansittart, spokesman for the British Intelligence Service, told the House of Lords on February 7, 1945, that he knew "the names of a good few of the worst Gestapo butchers and torturers in Norway who have their false papers ready," and who were planning to go underground in Norway after the Allied armies liberated that country "to organize sabotage and political assassination."

Similar Nazi-fascist terrorist and propaganda activities, or preparations for underground struggle, were going on in Bulgaria, Yugoslavia, Rumania, Sweden, Denmark, Belgium, Holland, Czechoslovakia and elsewhere.

On February 24, 1945, at a session of the Egyptian Chamber of Deputies, during which Egypt declared war on the Axis, four fascist terrorists fired ten shots at Premier Ahmed Maher Pasha, fatally wounding the Egyptian leader. One of the assassins, Mahmond Essawy, had been previously interned for pro-Nazi activities.

In Spain, the Soviet newspaper *Red Fleet* revealed on February 7, 1945, German planes from Stuttgart and other German airports were arriving "every day in Barcelona with Hitlerites." From Spain, the Nazi agents were moving on to other countries in Europe and especially to South America, bringing with them funds and instructions for the potent Nazi Fifth Columns already operating in the Western Hemisphere.

In January 1945, J. Edgar Hoover, Director of the U. S. Federal Bureau of Investigation, sent out a nationwide alarm for three key German agents believed to have been secretly landed in the United States to make contacts with other agents already operating in the country. Each of these three German agents had previously been active in South America. Here are their records:

Max Christian Johannes Schneeman: forty-four years old; former resident of Pereira, Colombia, South America, born in Hoeehst, Germany; expert linguist, fluent in French, Portuguese, Spanish and German; agent of the Nazi SS (Schutz Staffel or Elite Guards).

Hans Rudolf Zuehlsdorff: twenty-five years old; former resident of Bogotá, Colombia, where he was a commercial advertiser and sales representative for a German firm; born in Guestrov, Meke, Germany; expert linguist, fluent in German, English and Spanish; described by the FBI as being "more American than German in his mannerisms"; agent of the Nazi Propaganda Ministry.

Oscar Max Wilms: thirty-seven years old; former resident of Managua, Nicaragua; fluent in Spanish, German and English; born in Hamburg, Germany; former partner in a German export-import firm at Managua; agent of Nazi Propaganda Ministry.

The most important of all the German agents in South America has been General Wilhelm von Faupel, the German General Staff's leading expert on Argentina.

Faupel's work in the Americas has not been interrupted as a result of the defeat of the German Army in Europe. In fact, Faupel's work was specially designed by the General Staff to continue long after the end of the present war. Faupel's task has been to prepare the ground in South America for a third world war. If Germany's plans succeed, next time the United States will not be able to fight Germany in Europe; it will be fighting for its own existence in the Western Hemisphere.

Faupel's entire career as an agent of the German General Staff is in itself a revelation of the long-range planning of Germany's rulers. Before the First World War, from 1911-1913, Faupel was active in Argentina as a "professor" at the Military Academy in Buenos Aires. Thoroughly familiar with Latin American and Spanish affairs, he was recalled at the outbreak of war and sent into Spain to become chief of the German espionage and sabotage activities in the Mediterranean area. Then, immediately after Germany's defeat in 1918, Faupel was sent back to Argentina. Until 1927, he held the post of "chief adviser" to the Argentine General Staff. On the eve of the Nazi seizure of power, Faupel returned to Germany. He next appeared to public view as Director of the Nazi Ibero-American Institute, central clearing-house for German espionage and conspiracy in the Western Hemisphere.

Under Faupel's command, at the headquarters of the Ibero-American Institute, which Hitler housed in an imposing mansion at Number 7 Fuerenstrasse, Zehlendorff, Berlin, hundreds of German agents and American, Canadian and South American fifth columnists were trained for work. The Spanish Fascist *Falange* was born in Faupel's headquarters, and Faupel personally organized the Nazi Condor Division which invaded Spain to suppress the Republican Government and help put Generalissimo Franco in power. In 1938, with *Falangist* Spain as a springboard, Faupel began his final preparations for the German conquest of South America.

The plan by which Faupel operated was not new. It had been the dream of the General Staff for generations to establish Pan-German hegemony over the South American republics as a prelude to the invasion and conquest of the United States. As far back as 1904, Ernst Hasse, precursor of Hitler, and President of the notorious Pan-German League in Berlin, wrote in a widely-publicized article:

> "The Argentine and Brazilian republics and all the other seedy South American states will accept our advice and listen to reason,

voluntarily or under coercion. In a hundred years, both South and North America will be conquered by the German Geist, and the German Emperor will perhaps transfer his residence to New York."

Like his successor, Hitler, Hasse was at first regarded outside of Germany as a crackpot. But the German General Staff, whose agent he was, considered Hasse a leading authority on German world policy, and soon acted directly on his advice regarding South America. At the outbreak of the First World War, all of Central and South America was infiltrated by German agents inciting hatred against the United States. German activities in the United States were chiefly designed to keep America out of the war, but in the event that effort failed the German General Staff had another plan.

In 1917 the German General Staff sought to involve Latin America, especially Mexico, in a secret military pact with Germany and Japan aimed at the invasion and conquest of the United States. At 3 A.M., Berlin time, on January 19, 1917, the following secret message was sent by wireless to Count von Bernstorff, German Ambassador in Washington, from the German Foreign Office in Berlin:

Berlin, January 19, 1917

"On the first of February we intend to begin submarine warfare unrestricted. In spite of this it is our endeavor to keep neutral the United States of America. If this is not successful we propose an alliance on the following basis with Mexico: That we shall make war together and together shall make peace. We shall give general financial support and it is understood that Mexico is to recover the lost territory in New Mexico, Texas and Arizona. The details are left to you for settlement. You are also instructed to inform the President of Mexico of the above in the greatest confidence as soon as it is certain that there will be an outbreak of war with the United States and suggest that the President of Mexico on his own initiative should communicate with Japan suggesting adherence at once to this plan; at the same time offer to mediate between Germany and Japan.

"Please call to the attention of the President of Mexico that the employment of ruthless submarine warfare now promises to compel England to make peace in a few months.

"(signed) Zimmerman."

Today, the German intrigue in Mexico goes on under cover of the Nazi-inspired *Sinarquist* movement which, intimately related to the *Falange*, has been devised by the German General Staff as a means of continuing German political influence in Mexico after this war. But the chief focus of German intrigue in South America today is in Argentina. Under German influence, Argentina has become a source of continuous unrest and anti-United States conspiracy in the Western Hemisphere.

In concentrating on Argentina, the German General Staff has again followed a plan which it elaborated many years ago. Before the First World War, Otto Tannenberg, the famous Pan-German propagandist and agent of the General Staff, wrote:

> "Germany will take under its protection the republics of Argentina, Chile, Paraguay and Uruguay; furthermore, the southern third of Bolivia and the southern portion of Brazil."

On March 26, 1944, in his personal publication *Das Reich*, the Nazi Propaganda Minister Dr. Paul Joseph Goebbels wrote:

> "Argentina will one day be at the head of a tariff union comprising the nations in the southern half of South America. Such a focus of opposition against the United States of America will, together with Bolivia, Chile, Paraguay and Uruguay, form a powerful economic bloc; and eventually, by way of Peru, it will spread northward to place the dollar colony of Brazil in a difficult position."

On June 10, 1944, ten weeks after Goebbels' pronouncement, Colonel Juan Peron, Vice-President and War Minister of Argentina, delivered his pro-Nazi speech which led to the breaking off of relations between the United States and Argentina. Here is what the Argentine War Minister said:

> "In South America, it is our mission to make the leadership of Argentina not only possible but indisputable. . . . Hitler's fight in peace and war will guide us. Alliances will be the next step. We will get Bolivia and Chile. Then it will be easy to exert pressure on Uruguay. These five nations will attract Brazil, due to its type of government and its important group of Germans. Once Brazil has fallen, the South American continent will be ours. Following the German example, we will inculcate the masses with the necessary military spirit. . . ."

The voice was the voice of Colonel Peron, but the plan was that of the German General Staff. . . .

"Everywhere, in both Americas," reported the well-known American foreign correspondent, Sigrid Schultz, in 1944 in her significantly titled book *Germany Will Try It Again*, "they [the Nazis] have incited racial groups, anti-Semitic groups, university professors and students, and the numberless, formless, frustrated people who hope for advancement with Nazi help. American newspapers have recorded case after case of arrests of Nazi and Japanese sympathizers in this country—air-raid wardens, professors' wives, heads of manufacturing concerns. But these were simply the individuals who were careless or reckless. We must anticipate that they are only a small part of the big whole. The Germans confidently count on their political influence increasing in the United States . . . Thus, the total-war strategists of Germany plan ahead not only for tomorrow but for generations to come."

The Nazi Fifth Column in the Americas remains a powerful, active and lavishly financed instrument of the German General Staff's postwar conspiracy against the peace.*

II. *Inside Germany*

Speaking over the Berlin radio, on February 13, 1945, Dr. Paul Schmidt, spokesman of the Nazi Foreign Office, said:

> "Millions of us will wage guerilla warfare; every German before he dies will try to take five or ten enemies with him to the grave. . . . There have been worse situations in history than the one in which Germany is today. Eighty million people know how to defend themselves. We have gathered experience in smaller countries. Millions of Germans will pay back murder with murder."

Preparations for Nazi underground warfare against the United Nations' military authorities in occupied Germany were

* See Part III of this book for details concerning the operations of the Nazi Fifth Column in the United States.

started long before the first Allied armies crossed the Reich frontiers.

As far back as July 1943, the little-known but important Nazi leader, Konstantin Hierl, chief of the *Reichsarbeitsdienst* (Reich Labor Corps) began organizing Nazi guerilla units for postwar operations in Germany. Hierl was experienced at organizing such conspiracies. In 1923 he wrote a book entitled *The Conduct of War with Improvised Armies.* Hierl was one of the chief organizers of the German General Staff's Black Reichswehr and the Nazi SS.

In the summer of 1943, Hierl addressed a secret Munich convention of Nazi leaders of the Reich Labor Corps. A copy of his speech later fell into the hands of Allied Intelligence agents. Hierl outlined the future underground organization of the Nazi Party in Germany in the event of German military defeat as follows:

> "The [Nazi] party achieved its utmost power and its greatest influence during its legal period when it was centrally ruled. Never was a party more efficiently centralized than ours. The principle for the illegal period which will come after the war must, however, be utmost decentralization. In fact, we must decentralize to such a degree that we must seem to have disappeared. The one hundred men who formerly marched through the street or attended a meeting will then be found in one hundred different plants or offices in one hundred different cities. Only thus can we survive."

By the time the Allied armies crossed the Reich frontiers, there were few Nazi party leaders to be found in Germany. They had gone underground. Most of them had false identity papers taken from obscure Germans killed in air-raids. Others had been planted in concentration camps to pose as anti-Nazis.

When American troops first occupied towns in western Germany in 1944, scores of "anti-Nazi" Germans immediately approached the American military authorities with offers of important information and cooperation. In the occupied town of Aachen, fifty-seven camouflaged Nazis secured posts in the American-directed city administration in the first weeks of the occupation. In the occupied town of Stolberg, eighty-five of the eighty-seven "anti-Nazi" city officials cooperating with the Americans turned out to be camouflaged Nazis. These agents secretly sabotaged the American military occupation, and in many cases directly supervised and protected underground Nazi terrorist and propaganda cells in the vicinity.

The case of Otto Meyer, heard before an American military court in Aachen in February 1945, indicated the thoroughness with which the Nazi leaders had prepared in advance for the Allied occupation of German towns. When American troops first entered Aachen, a short, fat, narrow-faced German came to the American military authorities, showed his identity papers, and introduced himself as Otto Meyer, a millionaire businessman and long-time secret opponent of the Nazi regime.

"Only through the Americans could we be delivered from the yoke of Hitlerism!" said Otto Meyer. He gave information to the American authorities concerning underground Nazi activities in Aachen. The information led to the arrest of Nazi agents in the neighborhood. Meyer said he could obtain further information. He was given a special pass entitling him to circulate freely at any time in American-held territory . . .

Then American Intelligence officers began bringing in their reports. From the lips of recently liberated, maimed and sick prisoners of the Aachen Nazi concentration camp, and from other sources, the American authorities established the true character of the "anti-Nazi" businessman, Otto Meyer. They found that Meyer was a leading underground officer of Himmler's SS; that he had actually founded the Nazi Party organization in Aachen in 1928; that, previously, he had headed a terrorist fascist gang in Aachen which robbed and murdered German democrats; and that in 1933, after the Nazis seized power, Meyer became Burgomaster of Aachen and made himself a millionaire through seizure of properties belonging to Jews, Catholics and Communists whom Meyer personally sent into the Aachen concentration camp.

Disclosures at Otto Meyer's trial further revealed that before the American Army entered Aachen, Meyer had received special instructions from his SS superiors on how to behave himself "when the gullible Americans should occupy the area." His assignment was to supervise the Nazi underground in the occupied Aachen area. The few Nazi agents who had been arrested by the Americans as a result of his information turned out to be persons of no real importance to the Nazi underground. The SS officer Meyer had deliberately sacrificed them to establish himself in the eyes of the American authorities as a genuine "anti-Nazi. . . ."

Otto Meyer was only one among many such cases. Other camouflaged Nazis in Aachen sought to take control of the local school system so as to retain the Nazi hold on the mind of the children and the youth. In February 1945, when American authorities were trying to get the Aachen schools functioning, three "anti-Nazi" Germans, a businessman, a lawyer and a teacher offered to cooperate with the Americans in reorganizing the education system and purging it of Nazi doctrines and methods. A subsequent report from American headquarters in Aachen stated: "The Allied official, although pleased that such an idea came from the Germans themselves, investigated the trio. They discovered that the teacher had been a leading member of the Brown Shirts. . . ."

Maintaining their grip on the German younger generation remains one of the chief aims of the Nazi underground inside Germany. In recent years, special training centers were set up throughout Germany by the Nazi Party to create youth cadres for the coming postwar struggle. Hitler Youth leaders were trained for sabotage and guerilla warfare at *Heimschulen* (Resident Schools). Other training centers called *Adolf Hitlerschulen* instructed young Nazi Party members in underground techniques, including terrorism and propaganda. Picked youth cadres for the future Nazi underground and guerilla warfare units were trained at *Fuehrerschulen* in Bavaria, East Prussia and Pomerania. Under the supervision of Heinrich Himmler, Konstantin Hierl, Walter Schellenberg, Wilhelm Schepmann and other key Nazi underground leaders, secret caches of explosives, arms, ammunition, and valuables to be converted into money were hidden throughout the country for future use.

"If our antagonists defeat us but spare our lives," the Nazi propaganda organ *Rheinisch-Westphaelische Zeitung* declared on September 24, 1944, "they will thereby give rise to a generation of German fanatics, to millions of youths like Horst Wessel."

This was not Nazi bombast. A dispatch from the United States First Army Headquarters in Germany on January 11, 1945, revealed that fanatical Hitler-Jugend elements were carrying on underground campaigns of sabotage, espionage and terrorism in all American-occupied German towns. Attacks had been made on American soldiers. American weapons, ammunition, arms and hand grenades had been stolen. Military information had been conveyed to the Nazi Army.

On February 15, 1945, a dispatch from the American Ninth Army reported that an extensive underground Nazi progaganda and terrorist ring had been discovered in the German town of Monschau. Among the members of the ring was a seventeen-year-old Hitler Youth girl named Maria. When this girl was arrested, she said, "I've done nothing, absolutely nothing to the Americans. What do I know of military operations? I am a woman!"

But American Intelligence officers intercepted some of the girl's secret letters addressed to Peter, an SS man, who was the girl's lover. Written shortly after American soldiers took Monschau, these letters clearly show the extent to which the Hitler Youth propaganda has influenced the German youth.

In one letter to her SS lover, Maria wrote:

> "I feel it clearly that we, the youth, are a sorely tried but also a steeled youth and as hard as iron, destined to fight on for the ideal of our indispensable Fuehrer. When everybody deserts the Leader he shall be able to depend on his real youth. They will never betray him . . ."

In her letters the girl wrote that an American major had given her permission for her family to move into a better home. She added, "The Hitler Youth have been taught to make a good impression." The Americans were "easy to deal with," she wrote, because "they are not soldiers . . . 'fight' and 'advance' are foreign words to them."

Another of her letters read:

> "I hate the Americans! One thing they cannot take away from us. We will start our new life under the old principle that we have been taught—to live means to fight. Wait and see who laughs last. . . . These pigs are afraid of us!"

III. *The Secret Order*

Only after the Allied armies penetrated German soil did the world begin to realize the almost incredible lengths to which the Nazis had gone in their maniacal ambition to create a secret order of German world rulers prepared to wage continuous warfare, underground or as open military hostilities, for generations to come, until the final goal of German world conquest has been achieved.

In Vogelsang, Germany, in the first week of February 1945, one of the most extraordinary monuments of Nazi fanaticism was captured after a brief, bloody battle by the Ninth Infantry Division of the United States Army. Located on the sides of a serried mountain overlooking a great lake, American troops found a vast establishment of weird brownstone masonry buildings, towered halls, huge dormitories, spectacular palaces and terraces, all grouped around spacious courts and walks adorned with stone fountains and massive statuaries of German eagles and mounted Teutonic knights.

These grandiose buildings, spreading over hundreds of acres, with walls four feet thick, and undermined by endless mysterious passages and chambers, were built in recent years by order of the Nazi Party. They comprised an *Ordensburg*, a special academy for the training of future German rulers of the world; and, since 1943, for the training of the future underground Nazi leaders of the German General Staff.

Every device of architecture and exploitation of the landscape were utilized by the Nazi leaders to invest this *Ordensburg* at Vogelsang with an overwhelming atmosphere of splendor, mystery and awe-inspiring power.

"From the palaces and terraces of this school for Fuehrers, which Adolf Hitler founded to train future generations of world masters, one could look out today on a Wagnerian scene," reported the American correspondent Harold Denny on February 6, 1945.

". . . It was a rainy, cloudy day and fog arose in writhing plumes from those other mountain tops. This slowly twisting fog gave a mysterious and almost horrible tone to the scene's beauty —a scene worthy of a twilight of the gods and into which Valkyries might fittingly ride . . . This school is so big that one could spend many days exploring its dozens of great buildings . . . Our bombs destroyed or badly damaged at most a third of the school's many structures. . . . But most of this astonishing monument to ruthlessness remains."

In the dark ages in Europe, the secret Order of Teutonic Knights lodged its neophytes in central fortresses or Burgs of the Order. Here they learned the secrets of the Order and were instructed in the arts of ruling over "inferior men" by conspiracy and terror. The new *Ordensburgen* built by the Nazis represented a deliberate attempt by twentieth-century fanatics to bring back the dark ages and revive the sinister mysteries of the Teutonic Order. Five of these Nazi academies were erected in various parts of Germany. Before the war, Hitler told Hermann Rauschning, who later recorded Hitler's words in *Voice of Destruction:*

"In my *Ordensburgen,* a youth will grow up before which the world will shrink back. A violently active, dominating, intrepid, brutal youth—that is what I am after!"

In the archives at *Ordensburg-Vogelsang,* American authorities found a document entitled *Der Weg zur Ordensburg.* It was signed by Dr. Robert Ley, Reich organization leader of the Nazi Party and it explained the purpose of these Nazi academies. They were not ordinary Nazi Party propaganda seminaries or espionage schools such as had been established by the Nazis throughout Germany after 1933 for the instruction of rank-and-file Nazi Party members. The *Ordensburgen* were restricted to those destined to become the leaders—the Ortsgruppensleiters, Kreisleiters, Gauleiters and Reichsleiters—of the future German world state.

Among the subjects taught at the *Ordensburgen* were Race, History, Languages, Economics, Philosophy and Social Sciences. Special attention was paid to gymnastics and sports. Students had to prove, like the medieval Teutonic Knights, that they would not shrink from any act of daring, cruelty or resolution. Every graduate had to jump from a plane with a parachute, dive from a thirty-foot board, box, fence and shoot. "We want to know whether these men have the will to lead and rule," wrote Dr. Robert Ley. Horsemanship was taught so that each student would know how "to rule the living animal with his iron will."

After the Nazi defeat at Stalingrad, early in 1943, the *Ordensburgen* were entirely devoted to the training of selected political leaders, army officers, scientific experts and industrialists who were to constitute the picked cadres of the future underground German General Staff directing the postwar German conspiracy throughout the world. Graduates of the *Ordensburgen* were supplied with elaborate false records by the Intelligence Division of Himmler's SS and sent into foreign countries, not for immediate action in most cases, but as long-range secret representatives of the German General Staff. They constituted an Elite Order of Nazi Germans dedicated to the maintenance of the General Staff's secret economic, political and military power, no matter what happened to the Nazi state as the result of a United Nations' victory.

"These men," stated the document signed by Dr. Ley, "to whom the National Socialist Party now gives everything that a real man can hope for from life, must realize and keep in the bottom of their hearts that they are now dedicated to the Order for life and death and that they must obey it without question. . . . These men must know that there is no road back for them. He who fails or would betray the part of the leaders will be destroyed by this Order. . . . Such are the hard and inexorable laws of the Order. Every National Socialist leader must know that he is climbing a steep grade. You can walk here only if you have the sleepwalker's sure touch. You can have this assurance only if you are inspired by an absolute belief in and unshakable loyalty to Adolf Hitler and his idea."

During 1944, at least 2,000 Nazi leaders are known to have been trained for postwar conspiracy at the *Ordensburg* in Vogelsang. And this was only one of five such schools in Germany.

CHAPTER THREE

THE CONSPIRACY OF THE OFFICERS

I. *The German Officers' Corps*

AFTER the First World War, German army officers boasted in Berlin: "The Allies lost the most important battle of the War!"

They were referring to the peace. . . .

Late in 1917, a year before the Armistice which ended the First World War, General Hugo von Freytag-Loringhoven of the German General Staff wrote his voluminous *Lessons of the World War*. In this book, General von Freytag-Loringhoven was already outlining German strategy for a second World War.

"The next war," wrote General von Freytag-Loringhoven, "will be a war of movement." Hence the Kaiser's Army would have to be demobilized, re-trained and completely re-equipped. But this would only be possible, wrote the German General, if the General Staff succeeded in preserving its inner corps of fanatical and indoctrinated officers.

As General von Freytag-Loringhoven put it:

> "The spirit of German militarism with which our world position stands or falls rests ultimately on an officers' corps which must be thoroughly efficient for the purposes of war."

Preservation of its corps of fanatical, trained officers was the master-stroke of the German General Staff after the First World War.

In 1918-1919 there was revolution in Germany. Millions of German people rose in revolt against the unholy ruling trinity of Junkers, industrialists and army officers which had tyrannized over Germany for so long. In Berlin, the workers and soldiers built street barricades and stormed the administration centers of the Imperial power. In the Rhineland-Westphalia, a workers' revolutionary committee arrested Fritz Thyssen and other big German industrialists as war criminals. In Bavaria, the rule of the General Staff was overthrown and a revolutionary Republic declared. For a time it seemed that the German revolution which Heinrich Heine and Carl Schurz had dreamed of and which had been so bloodily suppressed in 1848, was going to be victorious at last and the final end of German militarism and imperialism was at hand. General Erich Ludendorff, the military leader of the General Staff, fled to Sweden. The Kaiser had already fled to Holland. Throughout Germany, the Junkers, industrialists and generals were collecting their valuables and packing their bags for hasty flight.

A few months later, Ludendorff returned to Berlin. The Thyssens, Krupps and Stinnes again had resumed absolute control over their war plants and mines. Germany was once more safe for the Junker barons. The General Staff resumed its temporarily interrupted preparations for a new world war. . . .

It was the German officers' corps which crushed the German revolution and re-established the rule of the General Staff.

Within twenty-four hours of the German decision to sue for an Armistice in 1918, the General Staff had concluded a secret agreement with the new, supposedly anti-militarist German Social Democratic regime. By this secret agreement the German officers' corps was to be preserved under cover of a struggle against Bolshevism in Germany, and used against the German democratic revolution.

The German Social Democratic President Ebert later testified in 1924 before a court in Magdeburg: "At the time I recommended to Hindenburg a pact between the Supreme Army Command and the Social Democratic Party."

General Walther Groener of the German General Staff testified at Munich in 1925:

> "On November 10, 1918, I had a telephone conversation with Ebert, and we concluded an alliance to fight Bolshevism and Sovietism and restore law and order. . . . Every day between

11 p.m. and 1 a.m. the Staff of the High Command talked to Ebert on a special secret telephone. From November 10 our immediate object was to wrest power in Berlin out of the hands of the Councils of Workers' and Soldiers' Deputies. For that purpose it was planned to have ten divisions march into Berlin. Ebert agreed that they should be heavily armed. According to our schedule, Berlin was to be purged after the entrance of our divisions. . . . Everything was discussed with Ebert."

Immediately after the signing of the Armistice, the German officers' corps went underground. In the name of "national defense against Bolshevism," so-called Freikorps or terrorist guerilla bands of officers were formed under the clandestine supervision of the General Staff. In 1918-1919, with incredible ferocity these Freikorps units of fanatical officer-guerillas stormed through the German cities and provinces, burning, looting, torturing, raping and murdering. The democratic German revolution was stamped out in an orgy of terrorism and atrocity. Other Freikorps units, armed to the teeth, roamed the Baltic states and Polish Silesia where they slaughtered and plundered for two years after the Armistice.

Not all the freebooters of the Freikorps bands were native-born Germans. Many of them were international adventurers previously employed by the German General Staff as paid agents, propagandists, spies, saboteurs and assassins. Leaders of the Freikorps included terrorist White Guards from Finland and the Baltic states, ex-Ochrana agents and Black Hundred pogromists from Czarist Russia, as well as thieves, cutthroats and degenerates from the military jails of Europe. The Freikorps were the prototypes of the mass army of murderers which Nazi Germany eventually let loose upon the free nations of the world. Without exception, the leaders of the Freikorps were the founders of the Nazi Storm Troop and SS formations. After Hitler came to power, these men became top SS officials, high-ranking diplomats, and generals of the Nazi *Wehrmacht.*

Here are some of their names:

Lieutenant Colonel Konstantin Hierl: Freikorps lieutenant in Berlin area; officer of the Bavarian General Staff; author of treatise in 1923 entitled *Conduct of War with Improvised Armies;* captain in the Black Reichswehr and organizer of the Nazi SS; in

1939, became chief of Nazi Labor Service *(Reichsarbeitsdienst);* since July 1943, in control of underground Nazi Party organization in Germany for postwar period.

Heinrich Heydrich: Freikorps leader in Berlin and the Baltic states; subsequently SS leader and, finally, the notorious Nazi Hangman of Prague.

General Franz von Epp: founder of the von Epp Freikorps which suppressed the Bavarian revolution and then marched into the Ruhr to carry out wholesale massacres of the Ruhr workers; as of February 1945, head of the Nazi Military Political Bureau and Governor *(Reichsstatthalter)* of Bavaria.

Baron Manfred von Killinger: leading member of the Erhardt Freikorps and the von Epp Freikorps; organizer of the murder of the Catholic Minister Matthias Erzberger; convicted of complicity in various other assassinations and sentenced to eight months' imprisonment, which he never served; author of *Ernstes und Heiteres aus dem Putschleben* [Gay and Serious Moments in the Life of a Putschist], which contained the typical passage describing the whipping of a trade union girl—"I gave the signal and the brigadiers laid the she-goat over a wagon shaft and stroke by stroke with a horse-whip painted her back red till not a streak of white showed"; early Nazi Storm Troop leader; appointed by Hitler in 1937 to be Consul General of the West Coast region in the United States; organized Nazi sabotage-espionage ring in America; appointed German Ambassador to Rumania in 1940; ran amuck when Red Army was approaching Bucharest in 1943, killing a number of members of his staff and then shooting himself.

Ritter von Leeb: leading staff officer of the von Epp Freikorps; organizer of Black Reichswehr unit in Bavaria; as of February 1945, Field Marshal of the Nazi *Wehrmacht.*

Lieutenant Hauser: Freikorps leader in Berlin area; subsequently high-ranking SS officer; as of February 1945, Colonel-General of the Waffen-SS.

Bernhard Ramcke: Freikorps lieutenant in Eastern Germany; subsequently Reichswehr officer; then Major General of Nazi paratroopers and, in 1944, Commander of the French fortress of Brest; now a prisoner of war in the United States.

Heinz Guderian: Freikorps officer who participated in the 1919 German officers' attack on Riga; leading Nazi officer in Reichswehr; Hitler's famous "*panzer*-General"; as of February 1945, Chief of the German General Staff.

Captain von Kleist: Freikorps leader of the June 1919 assault on Riga; subsequently notorious Nazi officer; as of February 1945, Field Marshal of the *Wehrmacht*.

Captain Felix Pfeffer von Salomon: organizer of the Pfeffer Free Corps which suppressed the Ruhr workers' revolt; subsequently, Surpreme Leader of the Nazi S.A.

Von Scheubner-Richter: Baltic Russian adventurer and Freikorps captain in the Baltic states; became Hitler's second-in-command in 1921 and died at Hitler's side in the Munich *putsch* on November 8, 1923.

General von der Goltz: Eastern European leader of the Freikorps; aided Mannerheim in the suppression of the 1918-1919 Finnish workers' revolt; became chairman of the National Association for German Officers and Nazi Reichstag deputy; his son was made Prussian State Counsellor by Goering.

Avaloff-Bermondt: White Russian Freikorps leader in the Baltic states; adviser to Alfred Rosenberg on Nazi intrigue in Russia; accompanied the Nazi invading armies in 1941 as would-be Russian Gauleiter.

Lieutenant Gerhard Rossbach: Freikorps leader and organizer of the notorious Rossbach Organization, a secret officers' murder gang which terrorized Pomerania for years after the war; subsequently became Hitler's personal representative in Northern Germany.

Captain Ernst Roehm: organizer of the Freikorps *Reichsflagge* in Bavaria; founder and head of the Nazi Storm Troopers; purged in 1934.

Captain Hermann Erhardt: Admiralty staff officer and organizer of the Marine Erhardt Brigade, also called the Consul Organization, an officers' terrorist league; the first Freikorps organizer to adopt the symbol of the Swastika as a sign of anti-Semitism and "Aryan" supremacy; the symbol was taken up by other Freikorps leaders and became the official symbol of the Nazi Party in 1921.

Financed by German industry, protected by the German Government, these guerilla Freikorps officers' units were soon united into the so-called Black Reichswehr, an entire underground German officers' army fully prepared for the Second World War.

The chief of the Black Reichswehr was Fedor von Bock. He later became a Nazi Field Marshal.

The liaison officer between the Black Reichswehr and the official Reichswehr, under the command of General Hans von Seeckt, was Major Kurt von Schleicher. In 1932, Schleicher conducted the backstairs negotiations by which Thyssen, Krupp, Schroeder and Papen handed over German state power to Adolf Hitler.

The chief of the Intelligence Division of the Black Reichswehr was Captain Eugen Ott, former assistant to Colonel Walther Nicolai of the Kaiser's Military Intelligence. In 1933, Hitler sent Ott to Tokyo to negotiate secretly with Japanese army officers for what was subsequently to become the Berlin-Rome-Tokyo Axis, and, when this was accomplished, Hitler made Ott Ambassador to Japan. . . .

Today, a new Black Reichswehr of German officers and Nazi Party leaders has been formed inside Germany. Elaborate plans for its organization, financing, discipline and maintenance were drawn up by the Supreme Command of the Nazi *Wehrmacht* long before the Allied armies crossed the German frontiers.

In September 1944, an important document bearing the imprimatur of the Supreme Command of the Nazi *Wehrmacht* fell into American hands when the United States forces penetrated German territory on the Western Front. This Nazi army document contained official instructions to Nazi officers to save their own lives at all costs "in an emergency" even if it meant deserting their own troops. The document stated:

> ". . . the German officer is too valuable to be sacrificed. It was the German officers' corps which most promoted Germany to be the world power in the first attempt in 1914-1918. It was the same officers' corps which reconstructed Germany for the second attempt to lead the world. It has been foreseen that the second attempt would also fail. This time our final and complete victory was so certain even a short while ago that we can prepare ourselves with fresh courage for a new later fight. We need our officers. At all times we have found troops in sufficient quantities. . . ."

On September 29, 1944, British Foreign Secretary Anthony

Eden told the House of Commons that the Allied Intelligence Services had obtained further evidence of the Nazi determination to organize a new Black Reichswehr. Secretary Eden declared:

> "The Gestapo, together with the SS and a nucleus of high army officers, have created a secret organization of young Nazis and Reichswehr officers in order to continue resistance in Germany after Allied occupation and to wait and prepare for the opportunity of starting another war."

Like German industry and the Nazi Party, the Supreme Command of the *Wehrmacht* also has hidden economic reserves with which to finance its postwar underground operations. On its final retreat through the countries of Europe, the *Wehrmacht* pillaged and looted whatever it could take back to Germany and convert into hidden cash. This was done by order of the Supreme Command. A confidential order to brigade commanders issued by Field Marshal Fritz Erich von Mannstein on September 17, 1943, read:

> ". . . our pillage should be methodical and organized. It is necessary to import above all commodities of little weight representing great value, such as jewelry, precious metals and stones, cultural objects, books, linen, stamps, et cetera, in order to sell them easily and transform them into monetary deposits in inviolable places."

Much of this loot was set aside as a secret fund for the maintenance of a postwar underground Nazi officers' corps. The leaders of this underground Nazi officers' corps are mostly officers and non-commissioned officers of the SS regiments. These men are the picked inner guard of the German military Supreme Command. Since 1934, after the purge of dissident Nazi elements under Roehm, ordinary Nazi Party members were not permitted to join the SS. The rank-and-file of the SS was recruited only from the most fanatical and resolute members of the Nazi Party. Under the personal supervision of Heinrich Himmler, the SS was completely reorganized and converted into a Nazi military élite. The uniform of the SS was remodeled to resemble that of the Death's Head Hussars, the notorious cavalry élite guard of the Kaiser. Senior SS officers were selected from the upper circles of the German General Staff itself. Leading German industrialists, army men and Junkers, and their sons, became SS officers. For example, Baron von Schroeder, director of the Bank of International Settlements, became a General of the SS.

The Intelligence Division of the SS currently directs Nazi underground activities not only in Germany but throughout the world.

"We shall build our lives as in past years," Heinrich Himmler, chief of the SS and Plenipotentiary General of the Third Reich, instructed SS officers in the winter of 1944. "Sooner or later, we shall make it so that the territory vital to Germany will become her forefield."

II. *The Fehme*

The first task of the underground Nazi officers' corps is to prevent at all costs the rise of a strong anti-Nazi and genuinely democratic German leadership.

To accomplish this the Nazi officers' corps relies on its characteristic weapon of secret terror—the same weapon by which the German officers' corps preserved itself and stamped out democratic opposition in Germany after the First World War.

On January 18, 1945, the American correspondent Charles Shaw reported by CBS shortwave radio from Europe that a mysterious Nazi officers' terrorist organization named "the Fehme" was operating in American-occupied western Germany. The purpose of this terrorist organization, which was under the direction of the Horst von Pflugk-Hartung of the SS, was "to conduct a postwar reign of terror against anti-Nazi Germans who might coöperate with the United Nations." The Fehme had already claimed a number of victims in western Germany. . . .

In Germany, for centuries the name of the Fehme has inspired fear and horror. Originally a secret terrorist society of the medieval Teutonic Knights, forebears of the present-day German General Staff, the Fehme was used by the ancient "manorial lords" of Germany to stamp out peasant rebellion and to preserve the privileges of the feudal ruling caste. The Fehme operated in secrecy and by night. Its victims were kidnaped, taken before the *Fehmgericht,* the Secret Fehme Court of Vengeance, formally "excluded from the Teutonic community," and then hanged or beaten to death. The bodies were left in public view as a warning to all. The assassins remained immune, anonymous, protected by the Emperor whose absolute will they were alleged to represent. The killings were known only to be the work of the mysterious Fehme.

After the last war, the dreaded Fehme was revived in Germany—as the secret weapon of the underground officers' corps of the General Staff, financed by the Junkers and industrialists.

"When the Fehme returned to Germany following the 1918 Armistice," writes the European journalist Paul Winkler in his book, *The Thousand-Year Conspiracy,* "its reappearance was due to the initiative of two groups of interests, the Junkers and the leaders of heavy industry in Westphalia. In any event, every clue to the crimes of the revived Fehme uncovered by German tribunals or contemporary newspapers in their exposures led directly to either the Junkers or to heavy industry . . . The principal aim was to execute, one by one, the leaders of the young German Republic."

The Fehme directly paved the way for Nazism in Germany.

Within three years after the signing of the peace, no less than 354 Fehmic assassinations were perpetrated in Germany against Germans interested in upholding German democracy and world peace. One by one, in the name of the vengeance of the Fehme, the best leaders of the German democracy were wiped out.

The assassinations occurred with baffling regularity. In every case, as the various trials and investigations disclosed, the killers were German army officers, generally staff officers and only rarely non-commissioned officers. All of these officers belonged to the underground military organizations of the General Staff, the so-called Freikorps and Black Reichswehr. Each Freikorps and Black Reichswehr unit had its own Fehme. By the law of the Fehme, the "bloody task," the actual killing, was considered to be the privilege of the higher-ranking officers.

Protected by the German General Staff whose will they executed, the officer-murderers of the Fehme acted with incredible boldness. They openly warned of their intention to kill and boasted of the killings.

Almost without exception, the Fehme killers went unpunished. Usually, they simply vanished after the murder. When arrested and brought to trial before the German courts, they were acquitted, or subjected to fines or ridiculously small prison terms, and then pardoned or permitted to escape. In the innumerable cases of "minor" political murders, where the victims of the Fehme killings were Communists, Catholics or Jews, no punishment at all was meted out by the German courts.

"A German murderer is not a murderer when the victim is a Jew, a Catholic or a Communist," indignantly reported E. A. Mowrer in a dispatch to *The Nation* on March 11, 1925. "Who decides? The courts."

That was written by an American correspondent in Germany eight years before Hitler came to power.

In 1918, the first victims of the officers' Fehme were the famous leaders of the German workers' revolution, Karl Liebknecht and Rosa Luxumberg.

"Had there been enough Karl Liebknechts, the future of Germany and of the world might have been different," wrote the former American Under-Secretary of State, Sumner Welles, in 1944 in his book, *Time for Decision.*

An official statement of the German Government announced that Karl Liebknecht had been shot "while trying to escape" and that Rosa Luxumberg had been lynched by an "infuriated mob of citizens" after her police guard had been "overpowered."

Both statements were official lies.

Karl Liebknecht and Rosa Luxumberg were murdered by the Fehme unit of the Garde Kavallerie Schützen Division, a special counter-revolutionary officers' regiment under the command of Major Pabst. The following year Major Pabst participated in the General Staff's Kapp *putsch.* Later, he became an important Nazi. In 1938, after the annexation of Czechoslovakia, Hitler appointed Pabst as head of the Nazi-controlled West Bohemian Mines (*West Boehm. Bergbau Aktienverein*).

Officers under Pabst's command kidnapped Karl Liebknecht and Rosa Luxumberg on the night of January 15, 1919. They were brought to the fashionable Adlon Hotel, on Berlin's west side which had been converted into the headquarters of the Garde Kavallerie Schützen Division. After a summary "hearing" Karl Liebknecht was taken outside by six armed officers. A non-commissioned officer, Runge, posted as sentry at the hotel entrance, hit Liebknecht twice with the butt of his gun. Liebknecht fell to the ground. The officers then grabbed him, pushed him into a waiting car, and drove rapidly to an isolated spot along the Neuer See in the Tiergarten. The car stopped and Liebknecht was pushed out and murdered by several shots in the back. The first shot was fired by Captain Horst von Pflugk-Hartung. . . .

The murder of Rosa Luxumberg was carried out in a similar fashion. She was brought out of the hotel by officers. The same sentry, non-commissioned officer Runge, smashed at her head with his gun-butt. Rosa Luxumberg was flung into a car which drove rapidly away. Inside the car, First Lieutenant Vogel and another officer murdered her with two shots in the back of the head. Rosa Luxumberg's body was thrown into the Landwehr-Canal in the Tiergarten.

The murders aroused the democratic elements in Germany. Mass public protests compelled the German Government to arrest and order a trial of the assassins. A special prosecutor named Joerns was put in charge of the case. From the outset, the trial was a farce. While the trial was in progress, the prosecutor Joerns attended supper-parties with the accused officers in prison. At his orders, the cell doors were kept open all day, and the "imprisoned" officers had permission to leave their cells at night to frequent night clubs and beerhalls. On May 17, 1919, the court handed down its decision.

Captain Horst von Pflugk-Hartung, the murderer of Liebknecht, and other superior officers were acquitted. Soon after Pflugk-Hartung became one of the leaders of Himmler's SS.

Himmler sent him to Denmark to head the Nazi spy service in that country. Today, Pflugk-Hartung is directing the operations of the new Fehme inside Germany. . . .

The other assassins also got off without punishment. First Lieutenant Vogel, the murderer of Rosa Luxumberg, was formally sentenced to 28 months' imprisonment. A few days later, Vogel received false identification papers from the German Foreign Office and "escaped" to Holland. Subsequently, Vogel became a leading officer in the SS.

The brutal sentry, non-commissioned officer Runge, was formally sentenced to two years' imprisonment. A few days later, Runge mysteriously "vanished." The German authorities said they could not find him. Subsequently, Runge showed up in a brown shirt uniform as one of the leaders of the Nazi Storm Troops.

The special prosecutor Joerns, on May 20, 1919, was appointed Chief Prosecutor *(Oberreichsenwalt)* of the German Social Democratic Republic. As of February 1945, he was holding the same post under Hitler.

That is how the Fehme terror was launched in Germany—by officer-agents of the General Staff under the protection of the German courts and the German Government. . . .

The next Fehme victim was Kurt Eisner, Prime Minister of the short-lived revolutionary Bavarian Republic which was ruthlessly suppressed by the officers' regiments of the General Staff. On February 21, 1919, Kurt Eisner was waylaid near his home and murdered by two shots in his head. The killer was the high-ranking army officer, Count Arco-Valley.

Again, public clamor forced official action. Arco was arrested, tried and found guilty and sentenced to death. Then the Fehme went into operation to protect its agent. An ultimatum from Captain Dietl of the Bavarian Reichswehr to the Bavarian Government read: "Either Arco will be pardoned or you will all be hanged by tomorrow." Arco's sentence was promptly commuted to "confinement in a fortress." Later, Arco's sentence was suspended and he was appointed by the German Social Democratic Government as director of the *Sueddeutsche Lufthansa,* a major state-controlled aviation concern. By 1929, Arco was a key liaison between the Nazi Party and German industry. When Hitler came to power, the assassin of Kurt Eisner became one of the heads of the Nazi commercial aviation, key instrument of German intrigue and espionage throughout the world. Arco's protector, Captain Dietl of the Bavarian Reichswehr, became the first open Nazi officer in the German Army. In 1943, Hitler delivered a special funeral oration for Dietl who, as commander of the Nazi *Wehrmacht* on the Murmansk front, had met with an unexpected death in Russia. . . .

In 1919, revolutionary Bavaria was a concentration-point for Fehme operations. On the estates of Bavarian Junkers the underground officers' corps maintained their secret arms caches and military training centers. By 1921, Adolf Hitler's Nazi Party had its headquarters in Munich, capital of Bavaria.

One by one, the leaders of the Bavarian democratic revolution were systematically eliminated by the Fehme.

On May 2, 1919, Gustav Landauer, famous German Shakespearean authority and philologist, former Minister of Education in the Bavarian Republic, was kidnapped, beaten, and shot to death by a Fehme unit of German officers led by Major Baron von Gagen. Eye-witnesses to the crime testified that Baron von Gagen knocked Landauer down with a club and he and other officers trampled on the elderly scholar and kicked him. Amid shouts and applause, non-commissioned officer Digele yelled, "Won't the pig die at all?" (*"Will denn das Schwein gar nicht sterben?"*) and fired a shot through Landauer's back which killed him. At the trial, the court fined Baron von Gagen 300 marks. Non-commissioned officer Digele was accused of "manslaughter"; but acquitted on the grounds that "he could have been under the impression that he was acting under orders." Proceedings against all other officers involved were suspended.

During a session of the Bavarian Landtag, in the summer of 1921, Deputy Karl Gareis exhibited a pile of documents and announced: "I have here the evidence of a thousand years' conspiracy—evidence which I shall present to you shortly." Gareis was understood to be referring to the operations of the Fehme and its notorious connection with the Junkers, but

Gareis' evidence was never made public. A few days after his speech in the Landtag, Deputy Gareis was accosted by two men in the street and shot to death. The assassins escaped and were never apprehended. The Bavarian police did not even try to find them.

The Fehme killings went on. After their successes in Bavaria, the killers became bolder.

On August 26, 1921, Fehme killers of the Freikorps unit commanded by Baron Manfred von Killinger assassinated Reich Secretary of the Treasury Matthias Erzberger, leader of the German Catholic Centrist Party, who had proposed a tax plan contrary to the wishes of the Junkers and industrialists. Erzberger was waylaid while on vacation in the Black Forest by two armed officers, Lieutenants Heinrich Tillessen and Heinrich Schulz, and shot in the back. As Erzberger lay on the ground, Tillessen and Schulz fired eleven more shots into his body. A few days later, aided by German government officials, the assassins escaped into Hungary. Subsequently, Tillessen became a high-ranking Nazi and married the daughter of the pro-Nazi Hungarian Prime Minister Goemboes. His accomplice, Schulz, became a lieutenant of the SS.

The Fehme terror reached a climax with the daylight assassination on a Berlin street of the German Foreign Minister Walther Rathenau who had dared to oppose the secret war plans of the General Staff and had outraged the Nazis by signing the Rapallo Treaty of friendship with Soviet Russia. Rathenau was publicly marked for Fehmic execution. In beerhalls throughout Germany, fanatical officers sang:

> *"Knallt ab den Walther Rathenau,*
> *Die gottverdammte Judensau!"*
> ("Crack down Walther Rathenau,
> The goddamned Jewish sow!")

On June 23, 1922, Rathenau was assassinated in his car at the corner of Wallott Street, Berlin. As Rathenau's automobile slowed down, a black sports car drew up alongside it. Two men stood up in the black car and one of them fired several shots at Rathenau with a tommy-gun. The other man flung a hand-grenade.

Subsequent investigation established that the black car had been placed at the disposal of the assassins by the Saxonian Nazi industrialists, the brothers Johann and Franz Kuechenmeister of Freiberg. The Fehme leader, and originator of the assassination plot, was Lieutenant Willy Guenther, key agent of the General Staff and temporary private secretary to Ludendorff. Many other high-ranking officers were directly implicated. The two killers, First Lieutenants Erwin Kern and Hermann Fischer, were chased by police who trailed them to the Saaleck Castle near Koesel where they had their hideout. The police opened fire and Kern was killed, Fischer committed suicide. The driver of the murder car, Ernst Werner Techow, was arrested and sentenced to a term of imprisonment; but was later pardoned and joined the Nazi Party. Another accomplice in the crime, Ernst von Salomon, became one of the most famous Nazi propagandists, writing regularly in Goebbels' weekly newspaper, *Das Reich.*

After Hitler came to power, the bodies of the two killers who died at Saaleck Castle were exhumed and reburied with great ceremony and, at Hitler's order, a monument was erected to their memory as "Germany's national heroes."

The murder of Rathenau eliminated the last prominent personality in Germany capable of obstructing the plans of the General Staff. The public Fehmic assassinations were halted. German newspapers reported that the Fehme had been disbanded.

But the Fehme terror throughout Germany had not stopped. It operated continuously against the German populace. Week after week, the German local newspapers reported cases of bodies found in ditches, workers beaten to death, farmers hanged, merchants and intellectuals tortured and shot.

Throughout the 1920's the Fehme was used to silence German citizens who happened to stumble on evidence of the secret war preparations of the General Staff, and against members of the Black Reichswehr itself who had incurred the wrath of the underground officers' corps.

In later years, with the rise of organized Nazi murder gangs, the officers' Fehme temporarily vanished from the German scene. The work of the Fehme was carried on by the Gestapo and the SS, most of whose leaders had originally been leaders of the Fehme.

Today, as the Nazi regime disintegrates, the Fehme has been revived to serve the same purpose it fulfilled in 1918.

The new Fehme of the Nazi officers' corps is not only operating in Europe. It is also operating in America.

III. *The Fehme in America*

In January 1945, the United States War Department made public some of the facts concerning the reign of terror which German army officers and Gestapo agents had instituted in German war-prison camps in America.

In 1943, within a few months after the thousands of German prisoners taken by the American Army in North Africa began streaming into the United States, the official War Department report disclosed, small groups of fanatical officers began to impose themselves as dominating factors on the German prison camp committees. In many camps, these men elected their own choices as "camp spokesmen." Figureheads were chosen while the ringleaders remained in the background in order to conceal their identity from the American authorities. Propaganda was circulated that it was the duty of the prisoners to remain "pure Germans" and to return to Germany after the war to carry on the work of the Nazi cause. All those suspected of anti-Nazism or distaste for German militarism were subjected to intimidation and terror. Beatings of anti-Nazi prisoners were frequent. A series of violent deaths finally exposed the systematic character of this terrorism.

The New York *Times* reported on January 16, 1945: "Six murders and two forced suicides have occurred in German prisoner-of-war camps in the United States, and investigation by the War Department has indicated that in all but one of these eight cases the victims were anti-Nazis who had been accused of treason by fellow-prisoners. Some were charged with giving information to the American authorities, others with speaking or writing anti-Nazi views."

Prompt action was promised by the War Department to put a stop to this reign of terror. According to American officials, the terrorism had been instituted by a *Fehmgericht,* or Secret Court of Vengeance, which German army officers and Gestapo agents had set up in war-prisoner camps in America. The *Fehmgericht* was the name of the secret court-martial of the Fehme.

All of the incidents reported by the War Department followed the typical pattern of Fehmic murders. German Army officers carried out the killings. The victim was visited, usually at night, brutally beaten and murdered. In two cases, the victims were forced to commit suicide.

At the German War Prisoner Camp Concordia, Kansas, on the night of October 18, 1943, Captain Felix Tropschuh, thirty-year-old engineer from the Sudetenland, committed suicide by hanging himself. Investigation showed that he had been suspected by the Fehme unit operating in the camp of being anti-Nazi. On the morning of October 18, Gestapo agents in the camp found his diary in which he had written down his disillusionment with the Nazi ideology. That afternoon, a German colonel denounced Captain Tropschuh as a "traitor" and demanded his "trial." In a secret assembly of the *Fehmgericht,* Captain Tropschuh was found guilty of "treason to the Fatherland." He was stripped of his insignia of rank and expelled from the "German community of fellowship." The victim tried to escape to American protection, and asked for an interview with the American compound commander; but the German colonel persuaded the American commander that the matter was so trivial it could wait until the next day. That night, after the American camp personnel had been withdrawn from the interior of the prisoners' barracks, Captain Tropschuh was taken from his room by German officers. He was forced to sign a note, written by a German lieutenant, which stated: "I voluntarily take leave of my life." Then he was taken back to his room and left alone with a table, a chair and a piece of strong rope. Two German lieutenants stood on guard outside the room. The official investigation, as reported by the New York *Times* on January 17, 1945, continues:

> "This was about nine o'clock. Captain Tropschuh was heard pacing the floor for about an hour, when a noise was heard, and one of the German lieutenants opened the door and found him hanging from an overhead beam. This was reported to higher German officers, who notified the camp authorities. When an American medical officer arrived he found the body still hanging and ordered it cut down, saying that if this had been done at once it might have been possible to save the man's life. The medical officer had been delayed in reaching the scene by a German guide who said he had trouble locating it."

On January 11, 1944, the Fehme again went into action at Camp Concordia. This time the victim was Private Franz Kettner, a thirty-nine-year-old Austrian truck driver who had been captured in Tunisia as a member of the German Air Force. He, too, had been ostracized from the "German community of fellowship" and sentenced to Fehme execution because he was anti-Nazi. At his own request, Kettner was placed in the guard house under custody of American soldiers; but he developed hysteria from fear. He was discovered at four o'clock in the morning, lying face down on his bunk, his wrists slashed with a razor.

The Fehme unit at Camp Hearne, Texas, was less subtle in its methods. It beat its victim to death. He was Corporal Hugo Krauss, age twenty-five. Born in Germany in 1919, Krauss came to the United States with his parents in 1928, and returned to Germany in 1939 as a result of his friendship with a German-American Bund member, who arranged for payment of part of his travel expenses. Krauss was captured by the American Army in North Africa, and brought to Camp Hearne as a war-prisoner. He began to criticize the German Army and Nazi regime. He predicted that America would win the war and said he considered himself an American citizen and intended to stay in the United States after the war. Krauss was summoned before the *Fehmgericht*. On the night of December 17, 1943, from six to ten German officers entered the compound, where Krauss was confined, through a hole which they had cut in a wire fence separating it from another compound, invaded Krauss's barracks, and dragged him from his bunk and beat him with clubs. Krauss screamed for help, but no one came to his aid. His barracks mates looked on while his skull was fractured, both arms broken and his body battered from head to foot. Krauss died as a result of this beating on December 23, 1943.

At Camp Tonkawa, Oklahoma, on November 4, 1943, the Fehme unit murdered Corporal Johann S. Kunze of Leipzig. Kunze was beaten to death. After the murder a meeting was called in the mess hall. A German officer said that Kunze had been accused of "high treason" in transmitting information to the American camp authorities. The German officer stated that the killing had been done in "self-defense" and that it would be so reported later to a German military court.

At Camp Papago Park, Arizona, on the morning of March 13, 1944, another Fehme victim, Werner Dreschler, enlisted man of the German Navy, was found hanged in a washroom six hours after his arrival at the camp. An Army court-martial uncovered the fact that six men, former members of his own submarine crew, had beaten him in his barracks and later hanged him, on the ground that he had given information about his U-boat to American interrogators. A German submarine captain in the camp was quoted as saying that all anti-Nazis were traitors and should be put out of the way.

At Camp Chaffee, Arkansas, on the night of March 23, 1944, Hans Geller, parachutist, twenty-one years old, who had voiced anti-Nazi sentiments, was attacked by Fehme terrorists who leaped at him from behind a building in the compound. He was knocked down and hit several times with a thick piece of lumber about two feet long. Geller's skull was fractured and he died two days later.

At Camp Gordon, Georgia, on the night of April 6, 1944, the Fehme unit murdered Corporal Horst Gunther, age twenty-four, of Westmark, Germany. Gunther had been denounced by the *Fehmgericht* as a traitor and anti-Nazi. The official investigation established that he was lured to a tent some distance from the compound, where he was strangled to death, and then his body was carried elsewhere and tied to a telegraph pole to make it appear that he had hanged himself. . . .

Thus the new Fehme of the Nazi officers' corps claimed its victims even in the United States of America.

CHAPTER FOUR

ARMY OF MURDERERS

"Who is Fritz Mueller? The son of a sergeant and the grandson of a corporal. Before the war he worked as a salesman in KDW (Kaufhaus des Westens) but that was only a sort of furlough. He knew from his childhood he was to be a conqueror of the world. He studied history as though it were a directory of future victories. To him peace was only a period of preparation for war. He had one ideal, and that was to see the German flag flying on top of Mount Blanc, the Andes, Ararat and the Himalayas. Why the German flag should be flying there was something he never thought about. From the time when by the laws of nature children begin to think, Fritz Mueller was weaned from thinking. He was weaned from thought as from his mother's breast. His mind was stuffed with technical knowledge and legalized prejudices. His soul was planed, ground and polished. It was a soul established to the pattern of the vile soul of a robber and assassin."

Ilya Ehrenburg, June 1944

"I have wanted to fight for a long time—at the time of the Abyssinian campaign, during the Spanish war, and when our army invaded Austria and Czechoslovakia. You know I have often regretted it was not my destiny to participate in the World War of 1914-18. Oh, what exaltation I felt when I read German books about war!"

From the diary of Private Wolfgang Frentzell of the German Army, 1942.

THE secret postwar plan of the German General Staff, which is being systematically carried out by the Nazis, goes beyond organization of underground officers' corps and secret terrorist and propaganda units. If the German plan prevails, the Nazi *Wehrmacht* itself—the instrument by which the German General Staff imposed its rule on twenty-three countries and menaced the freedom of the world—will become the means by which the Nazi grip on Germany is perpetuated and all possibility of complete Allied victory and lasting peace frustrated.

All eyewitness reports by American, British and Soviet war correspondents testify to the horrifying success of the Nazi indoctrination techniques in numbing the moral sense and intelligence of the rank-and-file German soldiers. The long years of rule by lies and terrorism, the inculcation of insane brutality and corruption, the incessant repetition of Nazi racist doctrines and glorification of German militarism, have left millions of German soldiers literally incapable of thinking for themselves.

"Mostly you feel you are in a congregation of intellectual zombies," reported Harold Denny, New York *Times* correspondent, on February 18, 1945, after interviewing scores of captured German soldiers on the Western Front. "To almost every question which might evoke an expression of opinion almost every man shrugs it off with: "We could not know about that. Such things are for leaders to 'decide' . . . Or . . . 'Orders must be obeyed or there would be chaos. It is not for us to question our leaders. They know best! . . .' "

Never before in all history had such an army as the Nazi *Wehrmacht* crossed the frontiers of peaceful nations. Led by the officer assassins of the Fehme, the spies, sadists, and anti-Semitic gangsters of the Nazi political underworld, the Nazi *Wehrmacht* was no ordinary army of imperialist aggression. Like a tidal wave of filth and horror, it swept across Europe and into Soviet Russia in 1939-41, and threatened to engulf the entire world.

In the vanguard of the *Wehrmacht,* as it smashed into one country after another, went the graduates of the *Ordensburgen,* the indoctrinated killers and torturers in the uniforms of the Gestapo and the SS, converting the invaded areas into incredible infernos of human suffering and degradation. The blood-curdling deeds formerly perpetrated by these men in German concentration camps and in the Brown Houses of Berlin and Munich were now repeated on a mass scale in Paris, Brussels, Prague, Rotterdam, Warsaw, Kiev and Kharkov.

A special branch of German war production had to be set aside to provide the Gestapo and the SS with the tools of their trade. Factories were set up in Hamburg, Berlin and Dresden for the manufacture of pliers for pulling out nails, thumbscrews, racks, whips, bludgeons, electrical devices for burning men and women alive, apparatuses for scalding people, presses for crushing bones, and a nightmarish variety of other ancient and modern instruments of torture.

In February 1945 the Soviet newspaperman, Boris Polevoi, wrote in *Pravda* after an inspection of the German death camp at Oswiecim in Poland:

> "I saw leather-covered steel rods which had been made wholesale in the Krutz factories at Dresden for beating prisoners. I saw zinc-lined benches with leather straps on which victims were beaten to a pulp.
>
> "I saw heavy oak chairs on which victims were killed after their backs were broken. I saw rubber truncheons with the trademark 'Krutz' for crushing heads and sexual organs."

In Paris alone, during the four years of German occupation, more than 75,000 men and women were tortured and murdered by the Nazis. The German military prisons in the French capital were filled with fiendish implements of torture. There were special baths in which prisoners were held in almost freezing water until they were unconscious; rooms in which men and women were burned with electric currents; pegs in the walls on which they were spread-eagled and beaten.

"When freedom returned to Paris," wrote Sonia Tamara in a dispatch to the New York *Herald Tribune*, "the horror of the German regime of occupation comes into the open and appears greater than anything one could have imagined. I have seen the prisons and the torture rooms in the Rue des Sausaies and the rifle range at Issy-les-Moulineux near the Air Ministry on the Boulevard Victor . . . And there are other places in the Vincennes Castle and at 84 Avenue Foch and in Chatou, a suburb of Paris . . ."

The same story of horror came from liberated Belgium. On January 3, 1945, the British Army published an official 12-page report of tortures committed by the Nazi occupationists upon Belgian men, women and children. The report, which dealt with the German Breendonck concentration camp near Malines, stated that the acts of the Nazis rivaled "the practises associated with the Spanish Inquisition." The British army authorities placed on exhibition thumbscrews, hand-presses, whips, shackles, chain-handcuffs and other instruments of torture, as well as a volume of horrifying photographs taken by the Nazis themselves of people being tortured.

The British Army report listed these as the chief methods of torture used by the Germans at Breendonck:

> blows across the face or body, particularly below the belt, with a truncheon or cat-o'-nine-tails;
> binding the victim across a table and thrashing him;
> hoisting the victim to the ceiling by a pulley and lashing him in mid-air, or releasing him to fall on sharp-pointed wooden blocks;
> burning with cigar ends;
> crushing fingers in a medieval-style screw-press;
> burning with a four-pointed electrical needle instrument.

The terrorism of the Nazi *Wehrmacht* was not confined to Army officers, Gestapo agents and SS men. Every German soldier was involved. The brutality of the *Wehrmacht* was deliberately designed, not only to stamp out opposition and terrorize the population in the invaded countries, but also to create a special kind of "morale" among the German troops. Each German soldier was to be a partner in the crime of the General Staff. By order of the General Staff, the German soldier was to be a looter and a rapist, a torturer and an assassin. The looting and rape, murder and robbery perpetrated by German soldiers throughout the conquered and invaded areas of Europe represented a system of warfare carefully elaborated by the German General Staff as a means of making each individual German soldier an accomplice in its own immense criminal undertaking.

Secret instructions issued by the Nazi Supreme Command to all Propaganda Company Commanders of the *Wehrmacht* on July 17, 1941, stated: "Foster in every officer and soldier of the German Army a sense of personal material interest in the war . . ."

Wherever they went, German officers and soldiers indulged in orgies of pillage. They ransacked homes, smashing and burning what they could not carry away. They stole clothing, footwear, watches, kitchen utensils, baby wear, underwear, furs. They looted shops, driving up to them in army trucks and carting away their entire contents. They stripped civilians in the streets of their shoes, clothing and valuables.

Special transport provisions were arranged by the Nazi Supreme Command so that German soldiers and officers could send their loot home. Railroad freight cars and trucks loaded with stolen goods streamed into Germany. German homes were crammed with stolen furniture and food. German farms overflowed with stolen livestock. German shops were filled with stolen articles bearing the trademarks of manufacturers all over Europe. German women and children walked through the streets of their home towns wearing clothing that had belonged to the women and children of France, Belgium, Poland, Czechoslovakia and Russia.

Pillage and terror went hand in hand in the Nazi *Wehrmacht*.

Here are two excerpts from the diary of a German soldier, Private Kurt Fuchs, Company I, 512 Infantry Regiment:

> "*July 7*. At 2 p.m. we arrived at the town of Motol. Lots of strawberries. In the market-place we shot fifty women and children . . .
>
> "*July 14*. Rokitno. In the evening punishment administered to a seventeen-year-old fellow. Sentence—twenty-five strokes, in the market-place. Everybody looked on. I have been out to arrange matters. Result: sixty eggs and lard.

Here are excerpts from letters written by German soldiers to their friends and relatives in Germany:

> "Dear Greta—In the next parcel I'll send you a bottle of famous Don champagne so you can drink to my health. Then when this hellish Russian campaign is over we will build a wonderful village on the banks of the Don and live here under the southern sun. Just wait a little until we introduce the new order here!"
>
> *Letter addressed to his wife in Breslau from SS Private Paul Meyer, 1942.*

> "Dear Wife—Retreating at night, we burn everything. Whole villages burn, the entire harvest in the field must also burn. We ransack the houses as the residents leave the villages. What do

you think—is it better to drag the goods around or send them to you?"

Letter from Private Johann Hauster, Field Post 11981, 1943

"We annihilate little representatives of a frightful tribe . . ."

From an unsigned letter of a German soldier, 1943.

The robbery and massacre of defenseless prisoners was systematically encouraged in the Nazi *Wehrmacht.*

On December 31, 1944, Allied Supreme Headquarters, confirming front reports of a mass German slaughter of American prisoners, issued an official statement declaring that 115 helpless captured American soldiers had been murdered in cold blood near Malmedy on December 17, shortly after the opening of the German counter-offensive. The statement from Allied Headquarters said that the captured Americans were lined up in ranks six deep in a field and, after being looted of all possessions by German soldiers, were mowed down by machine-gun fire from German tanks. As the Americans fell dead or wounded, "German infantrymen on top of the tanks fired their small arms into the helpless mass."

American correspondents traveling with the Allied armies in France and Belgium discovered more and more proof of Nazi atrocities. They found whole villages gutted by the retreating German armies, and heard one story after another from the local inhabitants of German pillage and slaughter.

On January 11, 1945, John McDermott of the United Press reported the typical case of a village which American troops had taken from the Germans in the Ardennes bulge. Fourteen of the villagers had been shot down in cold blood by the Nazis; and two hundred of the men in the village had been imprisoned without food in an unheated cellar for four days, while the German soldiers made off with their wives and daughters. American soldiers who had been captured by the Germans in the fighting near the village had been stripped of their uniforms in sub-zero weather and mowed down by German machine-gun fire. Some of the American victims of the German mass execution had been "packed in straw and pyramided into a funeral pyre." One such funeral pyre was still intact when the American Army recaptured the territory. "Apparently," wrote John McDermott, "the Germans, retreating in haste before the rapid American advance, had no chance to set it afire."

Wholesale massacres of Jewish men, women and children were carried out by all formations of the *Wehrmacht* as a matter of course, in line with the "race policy" of the Nazi Government.

Obergefreiter Heidenreich, a Nazi soldier who was educated at a Hitler-Jugend school in Germany and then sent to the Eastern Front, kept a diary which he entitled "My Experiences in Russia." Here are some excerpts from the diary of this German top corporal:

> "Arrived in Minsk. The mission of our battalion is to guard prisoners of war and shoot all Jews in the city. During the night we dispatched 500 Jews alone.
>
> "*July 7*—We marched on. Our objective was Krupki. With that as our base, our mission was to clear Kholopenichi, Voluber, Virki, Kurichenko and the adjoining villages. We divided into companies, surrounded the villages and set them on fire.
>
> "*October 5*—In the evening the Lieutenant called for 15 men with strong nerves. I volunteered. Each one of us was asked whether he could stand the sight of blood. We all laughed. We were ordered to take along 300 rounds of ammunition each and to line up in front of company headquarters in our helmets the next morning at five o'clock. We waited for the morning with impatience.
>
> "The Lieutenant explained our mission: there were about 1,000 Jews in Krupki and we were to shoot them that day. All the Jews—men, women and children—reported at an assembly spot. Lists were read and the whole column set out for a nearby marsh. The firing squad of which I was a member marched in front; an escorting squad marched on both sides, keeping watch. It was raining. The Jews had been told they would be sent to work in Germany, but many guessed what their fate was going to be, particularly when we crossed the railway embankment and made for the marsh. Panic ensued and the guards had their hands full keeping the Jews herded.
>
> "When we got to the marsh all the Jews were ordered to sit down, facing the side from which they had just come. About 50 meters away was a deep ditch filled with water. The first 10 Jews

were stood up at the ditch and ordered to take off their clothes; the men remained in their trousers only and the women and children in their skirts. Then they were ordered to step into the ditch. We stood above, on the edge. The Lieutenant and one sergeant were with us. A volley was fired and 10 Jews gave up their ghosts. This went on until all were done for. The children clung to their mothers, the girls to their sweethearts. It was a sight! A few days later about the same number of Jews were shot at Kholopenichi. I was in it, too. There was no marsh there, only a sand pit into which we piled the Jews."

The German officers and soldiers who perpetrated the worst brutalities against war prisoners and civilians in occupied countries were decorated and promoted for having shown "no mercy" to the enemy. The authenticated accounts of their atrocities constitute the most frightful records of bestiality, sadism and depravity.

From the testimony of Soviet war prisoners, as well as of French nationals, who were held at the German Yanovska concentration camp in Lvov, the Soviet Extraordinary State Committee established these dreadful facts:

"The Commandant of the Yanovska Camp, Obersturmfuehrer Wilhaus, partly for sport and partly to amuse his wife and daughter, used regularly to fire with a tommy gun from the balcony of the camp office at war prisoners occupied in the workshops. Then he would pass his tommy gun to his wife, who also shot at them. On one occasion, to please his nine-year-old daughter, Wilhaus made someone toss two four-year-old children into the air, while he fired at them. His daughter applauded and cried: 'Papa, do it again; papa, do it again.' He did so.

"In this camp war prisoners were exterminated without any pretext, often for a bet. Wepke, a Gestapo Kommissar, boasted to other camp executioners that he would cut a boy into two parts with one blow of a hatchet. They did not believe him, so he caught a ten-year-old-boy in the street, forced him to his knees, made him put his palms together and hide his face in them, made a trial stroke, adjusted the boy's head and with a single blow of the hatchet slashed him in two. The Hitlerites congratulated Wepke warmly and shook him by the hand . . ."

Children were used by the Nazis as living targets. Ida Vasseau, an elderly French woman who witnessed instances of this unspeakable barbarism in Lvov, told the Soviet authorities:

"The little children were martyrs. They were given away to the Hitler-Jugend which used them as live targets for shooting practice . . ."

Describing conditions at the Nazi camp at Klooga, Estonia, the escaped prisoner Jeremiah Ratner told the Soviet Extraordinary State Committee: "In February, 1944, two babies were born in the Klooga camp. Both were thrown into the boiler-room furnace and burned alive. I personally saw how they burned children. In May, 1944, a third baby was born in the camp, and Unterschartfuehrer Bar strangled it at once."

No one can tell where the individual atrocities ended and the organized mass atrocities of the German Army began.

Here are excerpts from the diary of Otto Berger, a staff lance corporal of the Second Security Battalion in Soviet Russia:

"Stary Bykhov is completely demolished; 250 Jews were shot . . . We have eaten well . . . The prisoners of war dug their own graves. We lined them up and shot them down, row after row . . . Shot a Communist. We drove him to the forest with a whip and made him dig his own grave . . . In the evening we shot two men. They dug their grave, kissed each other and lay down. They were father and son . . . Our field police shot 50 Ukrainians. Shostka is a pretty little town. Fifty prisoners were brought here and given to us to use for target practice . . . The prisoners of war eat rotten potatoes. They have no strength at all . . . Dead bodies lie in three or four layers . . . All the Jews were shot on New Year's Eve in Smolensk . . . We are at Fishgovo. There are two Russian girls here, 17 and 18, very pretty. We shall have to rape them. We are in Navarovo. Shot 156 guerillas today . . . I wonder where the boundary of power of the German state will be . . ."

The German war prisoner Lance Corporal Johann Gold, of the 574th Infantry Regiment of the 304th Division, told Red Army officers in 1944:

"In the town of Stalino I personally burned down one house and blew up two more buildings. Two houses had been tenanted by civilians and the third was a train store. Before the explosion I did not warn the tenants and did not think it necessary to warn them, as we were ordered not to do any talking, but to blow up and burn down buildings regardless of whether there were people in them. Immediately after the explosion in one house, I heard shrieks and wailing of women and saw the killed and wounded among them crushed by bricks and timbers, but I did not pay any attention to it. I was acting on orders of my superiors."

German officers and soldiers made a regular habit of recording their "war experiences" in diaries and letters. They also took snapshots which they carried around or sent home. These snapshots showed German soldiers standing in grinning groups around hanged men and women, men and women being buried alive, men and women being lashed, girls being raped, and piles of loot and corpses. Thousands of these pictures, taken by the Germans themselves, have been collected by the governments of the countries invaded by the *Wehrmacht*.

But perhaps the most revealing document of all is the diary kept by the German officer, Friedrich Schmidt, Secretary of the Secret Field Police of the 626th Group attached to the First Tank Army of the German armed forces in Soviet Russia. Schmidt began this diary near Mariupol on February 22, 1943. The diary ended on May 5 when Schmidt was captured by the Red Army.

Here are some excerpts from the diary of Friedrich Schmidt:

"*February 25:* I never expected that today would be one of the busiest days of my life. . . . The woman Yekaterina Skoroyedova knew that the Russians were going to attack Budyennovka some days before it actually came off. She criticized the Russians who are working with us. She was shot at 12:00. . . . The old man Saveli Petrovich Stepanenko and his wife from Samsonovka were shot too. . . . The four-year-old child of Goravilin's mistress was also put out of the way. About four o'clock they brought in four 18-year-old girls who had crossed the ice from Yeisk. . . . A touch of the whip made them see sense. They're all four students, peaches. . . . It's awful in the prison cells, they're crammed . . .

"*February 26:* Today's doings break the record. . . . The beauty, Tamara, roused a lot of interest. Then they brought in six fellows and a girl. No persuasions, not even most severe beatings with the lash, did any good. The girl never gritted her teeth. After beating her mercilessly, my arm went on strike. . . . I've come into two bottles of cognac, one from Lieutenant Koch of the staff of Graf von Foerster, the other from the Rumanians. I'm happy again. It's blowing from the south, the thaw is setting in. The first company of field gendarmerie caught five fellows, of about 17, three kilometers north of Budyennovka. They brought them to me. We started to beat them. I broke the handle of the lash into little bits. Two of us beat at a time. . . . However, they wouldn't confess anything. . . . Two Red Army men were brought to me. . . . They were also flogged. I'm 'finishing off' the shoemaker from Budyennovka, who thought he could allow himself some offensive remarks about our army. The muscles of my right arm are aching. It's still thawing. . . .

"*March 1:* Another war Sunday. . . . I got my salary, 105 marks 50 pfennigs. . . . Today I again dined with the Rumanians. I had a splendid dinner. At 4:00 P.M. I was unexpectedly invited to coffee with General von Foerster. . . .

"*March 2:* I'm off my color. I got diarrhea all of a sudden. Have to stay in bed. . . .

"*March 3:* I examined Lieutenant Ponomarenko, about whom I had received a report. Ponomarenko was wounded in the head on March 2, ran away to the Rosa Luxumberg collective farm, changed his clothing and hid. The family that hid him lied at first. It stands to reason I flogged them. . . . In the evening they again brought in five fellows from Yeisk. As is often the case, they're only boys. Applying my simplified method, that has already justified itself, I made them own up; I got the whip to work, as usual. The weather's getting warmer.

"*March 4:* Beautiful sunny weather . . . Corporal Voigt has already shot the shoemaker Alexander Yakubenko. He's been thrown into the common grave. I'm frightfully itchy all the time.

"*March 6:* I gave forty marks to the winter aid fund.

"*March 7:* We still live well. I get butter, eggs, fowl and milk. Every day I have some hors d'oeuvre. . . . At 4:00 P.M. they again brought me four young guerillas. . . .

"*March 8:* Corporal Springwald and Frau Reidman have returned from Mariupol. They have brought the mail and a written order to Groschek about shooting. . . . Today I have already had six shot. . . . They tell me that another 17-year-old, a girl, has arrived from Vessyolyi.

"*March 9:* How jolly the sunshine is, and how the snow glitters. But even the golden sun can't cheer me up. Today has been a hard day. I woke up at 3 A.M. I had an awful dream, that was because today I had to do away with 30 young chaps who had been caught. This morning Maria cooked me a nice tart. At 10:00 they again brought me two girls and six fellows. . . . I had to beat them mercilessly. Then the mass shootings began: yesterday there were six, today 33 miserable wretches gone astray. I can't eat. It'll be all up if they catch me. I no longer feel safe in Budyennovka. They hate me for a certainty. But I had to do as I did. If my folk knew what a hard day I've had. The ditch is almost full of corpses now. And how heroically these boys and girls die. What is it that's got into their blood? Some of them, especially the girls, didn't shed a single tear. I call it real courage! They were made to strip (we have to sell the clothing) . . . It'll be all up with me, if ever they catch me!

"*March 11:* The only way to teach a lower race is by flogging them. Near my flat I had a decent lavatory fixed up and hung up a big notice that civilians are forbidden to use it . . . Opposite my bedroom there is the burgomaster's office where workers engaged on earthworks come in the mornings. In spite of the notice they use the lavatory. I am beating the liver and lights out of them for it. In future I'll have them shot.

"*March 13:* I'm so overworked, it's a long time since I wrote home. To tell the truth, I don't particularly want to write my folk; they don't deserve it anyway. . . . Then I ordered a Russian, aged 57, to be flogged, and his son-in-law, for showing insufficient respect to Germans. Then I visited the Rumanian colonel . . .

"*March 14:* It's frightfully cold again. I've got another attack of diarrhea, and pains around the heart. I order a doctor to be called. . . . He diagnosed upset stomach and nervous heart. . . . Today I gave orders for Lyudmila Chukanova, aged 17, to be shot. It seems as though I have to kill off boys and girls; that's why I have a nervous condition of the heart.

"*March 17:* My first work since morning: I ordered the fifth Russian parachutist to be taken from the hospital on a cart, and right here before the common grave had him shot. . . . After this I spent the day peacefully. After dinner I had a walk. The ground is frozen.

"*March 19:* I stayed in bed. Ordered our military doctor to be called. He listened and said that my heart was all right. He stated that I was suffering from mental depression. He gave me pills for constipation and some ointment for the itching. . . . We've got a good pig. We've ordered sausages.

"*March 21:* Such a frightful day we've never before had in Budyennovka. In the evening a Russian bomber appeared, dropped flares, and then 12 bombs. The windows rattled in their frames. You can imagine my feelings as I lay in bed listening to the drone of the plane and the explosions.

"*March 23:* Today I cross-examined a woman who had robbed my interpreter, Frau Reidman. We gave her a good thrashing on her bare behind. Even Frau Reidman cried when she saw it. Then I went for a walk in the village and dropped in on our butcher, who's preparing me the sausages. . . . Then I examined two fellows who had tried to get away to Rostov over the ice. They were shot as spies. Then they brought me a youngster who came over the ice from Yeisk some days ago. . . . By the way, they're bringing me liver sausage. It's not half bad. There's a girl I wanted to thrash. . . .

"*March 27:* The night passed quietly. . . . I examined two 14-year-old boys found wandering about in the neighborhood. I ordered a woman to be beaten for not registering herself.

"*March 28:* I paid a visit to Colonel Arbeitsfuehrer Weiner. At 6:00 P.M. I ordered a man and a woman to be shot who were trying to get away over the ice. . . .

"*April 1:* I received 108 marks in rubles—a big wad of money. Valya is massaging and bathing me again. . . .

"*April 10:* The sun is baking hot. When Maria opens the window in the morning, bright sunshine floods my bed. Now I've got a swollen nose. Maria hunts lice on me. The ice has disappeared, and now it's only airplanes that threaten us. I again had several girls and fellows thrashed for not getting registered. Among them was the elder's daughter. I get an unpleasant feeling when it begins to get dark; then I think about bombers.

"*April 12:* Every morning I drink hot milk and eat an omelette. . . . There's not so much work now. . . . Now we work only on a local scale. Punishments consist either of flogging or shooting. Usually I have people flogged on their bare buttocks.

"*April 16:* Today's been a quiet day. The only thing I did was to settle a quarrel between the elder and the chief of the militia, and then I thrashed three men and one woman who, in spite of the fact that it's forbidden, came to Budyennovka looking for work. . . . Then I thrashed another female in uniform; she admitted she was a Red Cross worker. . . . I several times got vodka, cigarettes and sugar from the Rumanians. I'm happy again. At last Groschek got to the point of recommending that I should be awarded a cross with swords of the second rank for military service, and I received the award.

"*April 17:* . . . In the evening some reports came in, and I went with the interpreter to investigate on the spot. Women's gossip. I thrashed two girls here in my flat on the bare buttocks. . . .

"*April 18:* A dull, rainy day. I summoned a lot of girls who didn't approve of the Secret Field Police. I thrashed them all."

The most significant thing about this document written by the German officer, Friedrich Schmidt, who was awarded the Cross with Swords of the Second Rank for "military services," and who drank coffee with Graf von Foerster of the General Staff, is that it is not at all unique. It is typical of innumerable other self-portraits left in the diaries, letters and photographs of German officers and soldiers.

Friedrich Schmidt multiplied by millions was the Nazi *Wehrmacht.*

The German General Staff wants speedy demobilization of captured German soldiers and their prompt return to Germany. The German General Staff hopes to make further use of the millions of Germans who have been schooled in the Nazi *Wehrmacht.*

Adolf Hitler, in his speech on the 11th anniversary of the Nazi regime, on January 30, 1944, stated that after the war "millions of [Nazi] soldiers and war prisoners" would be converted into "millions of propagandists" to spread the Nazi doctrines throughout the world.

Ordinary armies can be demobilized. The Nazi *Wehrmacht* cannot be demobilized. It may be temporarily stripped of its guns and uniforms; but millions of Germans will remain the obedient creatures of the German General Staff for the rest of their lives, unless they are forcibly removed from that influence or re-educated after the traditional rulers of that nation have been eliminated once and for all.

PART II

CHAPTER FIVE

THE SECRET HISTORY OF NAZISM

I. *The Ruling Combine*

THE rule of a secret Teutonic Order, or General Staff, of rapacious and ambitious military and economic overlords has prevailed in Germany for centuries. Since the Middle Ages, the German people have sought in vain to shake off this incubus of secret caste rule. The great peasant revolts led by Thomas Muenzer and others in the 16th century were drowned out in oceans of blood by the ruling feudal order. In 1848, the German peasants, workers and burghers again revolted under the leadership of Carl Schurz and others, and were again bloodily suppressed. In 1918, the last German popular revolution led by Karl Liebknecht was betrayed and stamped out in a veritable holocaust of treachery and terrorism by the officer-agents of the General Staff, the modern incarnation of the ancient secret Teutonic ruling order.

The continuity of German aggression and conspiracy in recent years was no accident. During the past forty years Germany has had three entirely different political regimes. Until 1918, Germany was a Monarchy under Kaiser Wilhelm II. Until 1933, Germany was a Republic under Social Democratic ministers. From 1933 on, Germany was a fascist dictatorship under Adolf Hitler. Yet under each regime, the same men ruled in Germany. Behind each political façade, the reins of power were held by a small group of not more than a few thousand military leaders, industrialists, Junkers and scientific experts who constitute the German General Staff.

This General Staff is the real permanent government of Germany, not only controlling Germany's military affairs, but also

German economy, technology, schools, university and politics. The German General Staff exists for a single purpose: war and world conquest.

The continuity of German aggression since 1918 is reflected in the continuity of the General Staff itself. Without exception, the chief members of the Supreme Command of the Nazi *Wehrmacht* took part in the First World War as members of the Kaiser's High Command. The men who created Hitler's *panzer* divisions and tank corps—von Rundstedt, von Brauchitsch, von Kleist, von Bock, von Witzleben—all spring from the same ruling Prussian military caste and all participated as leading officers in the Kaiser's war. The head of the Kaiser's Military Intelligence, Colonel Walther Nicolai, was the secret organizer of the Nazi Military Intelligence. The head of the Kaiser's Naval Intelligence, Admiral Canaris, was the secret organizer of the Nazi Naval Intelligence.

The same continuity is reflected in German industry, the most monopolized and cartelized industry in the world. The names of the most notorious financiers and industrial backers of the Kaiser's bid for world conquest—Krupp, Thyssen, Hugenberg, Stinnes, Kirdorf, Siemens—all recur again in the list of men who financed Hitler, built his war machine and followed in the wake of the conquering Nazi armies to establish their "economic colonies" in one European country after another.

These men, the industrialists with their international connections, the army officers rooted in the feudal Junker-Prussian caste, together with their satellite scientists, university professors and political propagandists, have constituted themselves a self-perpetuating conspiracy behind every German regime, whether monarchist, republican or fascist. The law of this secret German ruling combine, according to the émigré writer, Karl Otten, in his book, *A Combine of Aggression*, is: "that it should never cease to represent itself, to perpetuate itself, and to render itself immortal, through its innermost core, the brain of the bellicose nation's brains: through the Great General Staff which, in anonymity and immunity, resides at unknown places, secluded from the world, controlling politics no less than operations in the field."

It was this General Staff which successfully resurrected German militarism after 1918 and is again plotting to preserve its power in 1945. For several generations, the directing ideology and aim of this ruling combine has been Pan-Germanism.

II. *Pan-Germanism*

The ultimate goal of the secret ruling combine known as the German General Staff is the realization of Pan-German world hegemony. Hitler, like the Kaiser, has been the political instrument of the century-old Pan-German masterplan. In the very first pages of *Mein Kampf,* Hitler reveals how from his earliest days he was a "pupil" of the Pan-Germans in Austria. During his "trial" in Munich in 1924, Hitler declared: "I left Vienna a confirmed anti-Semite, a deadly foe of the whole Marxist philosophy and a Pan-German in my political principles."

The original Pan-German Plan called for the mobilization of millions of German emigrants in every country into a secret instrument of German military aggression and conquest. Nazism was the fascist phase of this Pan-German Plan; its fascist character introduced a new element into the Pan-German conspiracy.

The advent of Hitlerite fascism in Germany meant that the German General Staff was able to draw into its conspiracy as its allies and sympathizers not only German emigrants, but all fascist and pro-fascist elements throughout the world. Nazism meant that Pan-Germanism had developed a new, twentieth-century dynamic of aggression, overriding all national boundaries and limits, and aiming at nothing less than the enslavement of free peoples everywhere.

The Nazi alliance of Pan-Germanism with international fascism explains the sudden rise in every country of the Nazi-fascist Fifth Columns, which sought by treachery, terror and propaganda to impose pro-German fascist regimes on their own peoples. It also explains how it may be possible for the German General Staff to maintain these Fifth Columns, and to preserve its international economic and political reserves, even after the defeat of the German Army and the crushing of the German state in the Second World War. . . .

Nazism, the fascist phase of Pan-Germanism, was initiated in Germany immediately after the Armistice of 1918 by direct instigation of the German General Staff. But almost all the peculiar features of Hitler's regime, its unbridled aggressiveness, its inordinate brutality, its homicidal racial chauvinism, have been characteristic of past political manifestations of the Pan-German secret ruling combine of Junkerism, Prussian militarism and economic feudalism.

The first public proclamation of Pan-Germanism published in Zurich on June 24, 1890, read:

> "We must convince the masses of the German people that German evolution did not come to an end with the years 1870 and 1871.* Only then did Germany take the first decisive step on the road to a position of power in the world."

The proclamation concluded with the words: *"Germany, Awake!"*

These same words are still the official slogan of Adolf Hitler's Nazi Party.

The Pan-German League (*All-Deutscher Verband*) was formally founded in 1894. One of its first members was the industrialist Alfred Hugenberg, then a young millionaire Prussian government official. From 1894 to 1918, Hugenberg helped finance the Kaiser's military machine. From 1923 to 1933, Hugenberg's vast fortune, Hugenberg's newspapers and radio stations were placed at the disposal of Nazism. In February 1945, as Hitler's regime neared collapse, this seventy-nine-year-old Pan-German industrialist still held the position of senior member of Hitler's Reichstag. . . .

Through the efforts of men like Hugenberg, Kirdorf, Krupp and Thyssen, the Pan-German League rapidly became the richest and most powerful organization of its kind in Germany. Its agents penetrated politics, the schools and universities, the press

* In 1870, Prussia invaded and conquered France. In 1871 the Prussian leader Bismarck proclaimed the establishment of the First German Reich in the Hall of Mirrors at Versailles.

and scientific institutions. It had branches and affiliates in countries throughout the world wherever Germans had emigrated. Its agents were particularly active in the United States, South and Central America, the Balkans and Russia.

The Pan-German League announced that it was an organization "above politics." It did not care what political parties governed Germany. Its aim was that of the General Staff: to mobilize all Germans and infuse them with the spirit of German world supremacy.

From the outset, Pan-Germanism envisaged a war of enslavement of whole peoples.

One of the earliest proponents of the Pan-German ideology was Professor Paul A. de Lagarde, a German orientalist. In his book *Deutsche Schriften* (German Writings), Lagarde set forth the original plan for Pan-German colonization in Europe which first the Kaiser and then Hitler were to undertake as a practical military program. Lagarde wrote:

> "We must create a Central Europe which will guarantee the peace of the entire Continent from the moment when it shall have driven the Russians from the Black Sea and the Slavs from the South and shall have conquered large tracts to the east of our frontiers for German colonization. We cannot let loose *ex abrupto* the war which will create this Central Europe. All we can do is to accustom our people to the thought that this war must come."

Another prominent Pan-German ideologist, Gustav Frantz, in his book, *Welt Politik* (World Politics), also written before the First World War, called for a "New Europe." Austria, Holland, Belgium, Flanders, Lorraine, Switzerland, France-Comité, Savoy, the Balkans and large tracts of Russian territory were to be incorporated under German domination.

In 1893, the Pan-German Junker leader General Count von Haeseler announced that the German people must prepare themselves to take by force what they needed. Gottlieb wrote: "Our civilization must build its temples on mountains of corpses, oceans of tears, and innumerable dying men. It cannot be otherwise."

Professor Ernst Hasse of Leipzig, who in 1894 became the

first President of the Pan-German League, declared: "We want territory even if it be inhabited by foreign peoples, so that we may shape their future in accordance with our needs."

These ideas were not the expressions of crackpot German nationalists or isolated individuals. They were the considered statements of the most prominent military, political, scientific and industrial leaders of Germany. These and similar statements were circulated throughout the country, quoted approvingly by lecturers and school-teachers, repeated at industrial banquets and board meetings, printed in the press, in books and pamphlets, as part of the General Staff's ideological preparations for the First World War.

Here are some more statements, drawn from early Pan-German writings, to which Nazism finally gave practical form:

In 1904, the Pan-German professor Friedrich Lange wrote in his book, *A Pure Germany:*

> "What we take, we must also keep. A foreign territory is not incorporated until the day when German property rights are rooted in its soil. A process of expropriation should be inaugurated, by which the Poles, Alsatians and Lorrainers, and so forth, are gradually transported to the interior of the empire while Germans replace them on the frontiers."

In 1905, Joseph Ludwig Reimer, in his book, *Pan-German Germany* wrote:

> "We desire and must desire . . . a world empire of Teutonic stock under the hegemony of the German people."

In 1906, in his book, *War,* the Pan-German politician Klaus Wagner wrote:

> "Let us bravely organize great forced migrations of the inferior peoples of Europe. Posterity will be grateful to us. Coercion will be necessary. They must be driven into reserves where we shall keep them segregated so that we may obtain the space necessary for our expansion."

In 1911, the Pan-German Otto Richard Tannenberg in his book, *Greater Germany, The Work of the Twentieth Century,* wrote:

> "The German nation is fighting for world Empire."

In 1913, twenty years before Hitler became Chancellor of the Reich, Heinrich Class, who succeeded Hesse as President of the Pan-German League, wrote in his Pan-German classic, *If I Were Kaiser:*

> "We must close our hearts to compassion. The Jewish race is the source of all dangers. The Jew and the German are like fire and water. The bearers of the prevailing materialism are the Jews, and those who call themselves democrats are nothing but the instruments of Jewry. . . .
>
> ". . . little countries like Holland and Belgium have lost their right to exist, because only such states as can protect their independence by force of arms deserve to have it. . . .
>
> "We must pursue an aggressive policy. . . . France must be crushed once and for all. . . . Let war be sacred to us. Let it be welcome, as the physician of our soul. . . .
>
> "We await the Fuehrer! Patience, patience, he will come. Persevere, work, and unite!"

In 1913, the famous Pan-German, General von Bernhardi of the Kaiser's High Command, wrote in his book, *Our Future:*

> "For us there are two alternatives and no third—world dominion or ruin."

In 1914, twenty-five years before Hitler invaded Poland and openly launched the Second World War, the official slogans of the Pan-German League on the outbreak of the First World War read:

> "Heil the Kaiser! Heil the Army! . . . We must gather all men of German tongues into one Reich and one people. An everlasting master race will then direct the progress of mankind!"

In 1917, in the midst of the First World War, the Pan-German M. Scheler prophesied in his book, *Der Genius des Krieges und der deutsche Krieg* (The Genius of War and the German War), that eventually all Europe would come under German military domination; Europe would be purged of the "foreign poisons" of "Anglo-American capitalism" and "Calvinist-Puritan Christianity." Once Europe was German-dominated, Germany would turn East, conquer Russia and strike for World Empire.

In January 1918, Krupp-Director Haux publicly stated

that it was Germany's destiny to rule Belgium, Poland and the Baltic provinces of Russia. Krupp-Director Haux added:

> "We Germans are a nation of almost one hundred million people and occupy an extremely difficult position in the center of Europe. We can reasonably and rightly demand that the lesser races on our frontiers recognize our situation. Such demand is both proper and justifiable and the rights of the lesser peoples must give way to those of the greater, for reasons that are morally undisputable."

After the First World War, Pan-Germanism was discredited. Its policies were known and the whole world was on guard against Pan-German propaganda and Pan-German conspiracy. Along with the German General Staff, Pan-Germanism went underground. When it came to the surface again, it was called National Socialism. . . .

In the spring of 1919, a so-called Reichswehr "instructor," or spy, stationed as a corporal at the depot of the 16th Regiment in Munich, received orders from his superiors to go into an organization called the German Workers Party and to help other Reichswehr agents reorganize it as an instrument of General Staff propaganda for the postwar period. The officer who gave these orders was Captain Ernst Roehm, founder of the Freikorps *Reichsflagge* and in charge of Reichswehr political intrigue in the Munich area. The name of the spy who received these orders was Adolf Schickelgruber, a former Pan-German propagandist from Vienna, who had adopted the alias of Adolf Hitler, and who was currently being trained as a mass agitator by the Political Department of the District Army Command under General von Lossow.

The German Workers Party had originally been set up by the Pan-German League in collaboration with the "Kaiser's Socialists," the Social Democratic ministers in the German Cabinet, to win popular support for the Kaiser's war aims. After the Armistice, the organization had collapsed. On instructions from the Reichswehr Political Department, the Pan-German agent Gottfried Feder was trying to revive the German Workers Party as an anti-Semitic and anti-Communist mass propaganda organization. Hitler was one of several Pan-German propagandists, spies and agents sent by the Reichswehr Political Department to assist Feder in this work.

In the first pages of *Mein Kampf,* Hitler writes:

> "I joined a regiment, then in garrison at Munich, as instructing officer. . . . One day I was ordered by my superiors to look into an apparently political organization that, under the name of the 'German Workers Party,' was soon to hold a meeting at which Gottfried Feder was to speak."

Hitler joined the German Workers Party as Member Number Seven. Other members included Captain Ernst Roehm; the Reichswehr agents and Pan-German propagandists, Gottfried Feder, Anton Drexler and Dietrich Eckhart; and the Freikorps leader, General von Epp. These men reorganized the party and renamed it the German Workers National Socialist Party. Among the first recruits were the Egyptian-born international adventurer and ex-officer, Rudolph Hess, and the Baltic White Guard and anti-Semitic propagandist from Czarist Russia, Alfred Rosenberg.

Out of this underworld political alliance of Pan-German propagandists, Reichswehr spies, Freikorps leaders and international adventurers, the Nazi Party was born.

III. Psychological Mobilization

For the fulfillment of its plan after the First World War, Pan-Germanism required a new mass movement, an ideological mobilization of the whole German people. The Freikorps organizations, based solely on the staff officers and Junkers, were useful in preserving the cadres of the army officer corps and for terrorizing the insurgent population. But Pan-Germanism after 1918 needed more than this; it needed a mass Army. To this task, the whole apparatus of the secret General Staff in German military, political, academic and industrial life was devoted. In the terminology of the General Staff this was styled Psychological Rearmament.

The authoritative study, *German Psychological Warfare,* published by the U. S. Committee for National Morale in 1941, states:

> ". . . the Germans concluded that Germany must undergo a long process of physical and mental reconstruction for a second world war. . . . The critique of military psychology led to the advocacy of the morale-mobilization of the whole nation and to the use of psychology as an instrument of politics, diplomacy and military strategy. . . . The Germans began psychological re-armament immediately after the war."

The General Staff was able to throw its full weight behind the Psychological Rearmament Plan because, among other reasons, the Allies had as yet no real understanding of the German use of psychology as a weapon of war. Secondly, the General Staff masked its psychological rearmament as "anti-Bolshevik" and "nationalist" indoctrination. Colonel Walther Nicolai in his book *Secret Powers,* published in Germany in 1924, revealed that immediately after the Armistice the General Staff began planning the war morale-mobilization of the German masses through the use of special propaganda agencies such as the Pan-German League, the Fatherland Party and the German Workers National Socialist Party. Nicolai wrote that "propaganda replaced military considerations and became a political weapon."

Ludendorff, Nicolai and other Pan-German army leaders of the General Staff clamored for a "supreme commander," who would seize the imagination of the masses and, as an instrument of the General Staff, solve the problem of a "unified military and political leadership" in the next world war. With the aid of their scientific assistants they actually began to consider how best to create a German Fuehrer who would carry out the secret war plans of the General Staff. Other General Staff theorists analyzed problems of Leadership, Symbols and Superstition. Others examined how the press, radio, motion pictures and other information or popular entertainment vehicles could be utilized for the war morale-mobilization of the German people. Others studied the problems of influencing foreign nations, the reorganization of the old Pan-German leagues abroad, the creation of espionage and sabotage centers, the bribing and corrupting of foreign statesmen and officials. All of this "psychological" work was undertaken by the German General Staff immediately after the Armistice and twenty years before the open proclamation of Nazi power.

By 1925, when *Mein Kampf* was published, literally hundreds of books and scientific treatises had been written by the Pan-German theorists under the direction of the General Staff as part of the Psychological Rearmament Plan and in preparation for the Second World War. Several hundred of such books and treatises are listed by the U. S. Committee for National Morale in *German Psychological Warfare.*

Among them were:

1920: Preussentum und Sozialismus (Prussianism and Socialism) by O. Spengler.

The author claims that Prussianism and "genuine Socialism"—not of Marx, but of Friedrich Wilhelm I, which was "authoritarian, anti-democratic and anti-revolutionary"—are consolidated in the old Prussian spirit and are equal to each other because both mean power. This thesis was taken up by the Nazis.

1921: Propaganda als politisches Instrument (Propaganda as a Political Instrument) by E. Stern-Rubarth.

The author offers Pan-Germanism as the most effective political goal towards mobilizing the sympathies of Germany for a new war.

1922: Der zweite Weltkrieg (The Second World War) by W. Grassegger.

A militant presentation of Germany as the arsenal of the Second World War which will finally settle all the problems which the First World War proved incapable of solving. One of the hundreds of books published in Germany after the last war to preserve and heighten militaristic spirit for Der Tag.

1922: Der Feldherr Psychologos; Ein Suchen nach dem Fuehrer der deutschen Zukunft (War Lord Psychologos; A Search for the Leader of the German Future) by K. Hesse.

A first lieutenant in the last war, Hesse joined the fascist-minded officers' clique after the Versailles Treaty limited Germany's army to 100,000 men. Hesse later became a war economist, and at the outbreak of war joined the Nazi propaganda regiment, with the rank of colonel.

1922: Deutsche Propaganda. Die Lehre von Propaganda als praktische Gesellschaftslehre. (German Propaganda; the Science of Propaganda as a Practical Social Science) by J. Plenge.

The author, director of the first German Propaganda Research

Institute of the University of Muenster, advocates (already in 1922) the establishment of a new national system of upbringing and education. There, he predicts, lies the secret of German power in the future. Plenge's ideas became the basis for Nazi education methods.

1924: Die Kunst der Massenbeeinflussung in den Vereinigten Staaten von Amerika (The Art of Influencing the Masses in the United States of America) by F. Schoenemann.

The author is recognized as the Nazis' foremost expert on the United States.

1925: Die Wirtschaftlichen und politischen Aufgaben des Auslanddeutschtums (Economic and Political Tasks of Germandom Abroad) by W. von Hauff.

The problem of "Germandom abroad" was in the center of German imperialist interests long before Hitler came to power. The Nazis merely took over and reorganized the international Pan-German cells.

The official program of the Nazi Party which the world believes was worked out by Adolf Hitler and the other Nazi demagogues, was in fact fully elaborated by the Pan-German General Staff before the Nazi Party was organized. Hitler's job was to sell it to the German people.

On November 15, 1918, only a few days after the Armistice, the Pan-German League published a proclamation of its aims which were later to become the official aims of Hitler. The proclamation stated:

> "We demand Anschluss with Austria and the immediate re-establishment of our connections with all the Germans living abroad."

In February 1919, a second proclamation of the League announced what was later to become the official propaganda line of the Nazi Party. This second proclamation stated:

> "Neither the Supreme Army Command nor our national-minded citizens, but certain unscrupulous traitors are responsible for Germany's collapse. Germany did not want the war, although France, England and Russia systematically planned the destruction of Germany. We owe all our gratitude to Hindenburg and Ludendorff."

Hindenburg and Ludendorff! In the Munich Nazi *putsch* in

1920, the man who marched beside Adolf Hitler was: Erich Ludendorff. In January 1933, the man who formally handed state power to Adolf Hitler was: Paul von Hindenburg.

In March 1919, William Kube, leading Pan-German politician in Berlin, outlined the future Nazi policy for the Second World War. Kube stated:

> "We Germans cannot long remain satisfied with a passive role. The happiest era in the history of the world was that which saw triumphant Germandom led by great, iron personalities advancing across the fields of the earth. . . . We openly proclaim that we are the party of revenge! We demand immediate *Anschluss* with Austria and the Baltic countries, and the return of all our colonies. And to begin with, we shall settle our accounts with the Czechs and the Poles."

In 1923, Kube joined the Nazi Party. In 1933, Kube became Gauleiter of Brandenburg. In 1941, Hitler made him Governor of White Russia.

IV. *The Birth of Nazi Germany*

At 6:30 a.m., on the morning of March 13, 1920, the first major political *putsch* of the underground German General Staff after the First World War went into operation in Berlin. It was premature, as the leaders immediately recognized; but it was significant for the future. Already, at this early date, Pan-Germanism revealed its alliance with international fascism.

The men who led the *putsch* were typical Pan-German and fascist adventurers of the kind that were later to strut in Warsaw, Rotterdam, Brussels, Paris and Kharkov as the Gauleiters of the New Order. . . .

Dr. Wolfgang Kapp, the leader of the *putsch,* was a fanatical Pan-German who had been born in Brooklyn, U. S. A.; General von Lüttwitz, his second-in-command, had been the Kaiser's military governor of Brussels and was Commander of the Reichswehr and the husband of a rich American woman; Major Pabst, another General Staff luminary, had commanded the officers who murdered Karl Liebknecht and Rosa Luxumberg;

and as Press Censor for the Kapp regime there was Ignatz Trebitsch Lincoln, international fascist adventurer and former German spy in Britain and the United States.

Dr. Kapp and General von Lüttwitz began their *putsch* with the announcement:

> "We consider it urgent to take this action for the protection of Europe against the danger of the East. Nothing is being done by the Allies to stay the advance of Bolshevism!"

The Kapp New Order ruled Berlin for four days. Hitler was dispatched from Munich by special military plane to contact the Kapp putschists and aid their propaganda. But the elements of German democracy were still alive. A general strike and the immediate mobilization of German workers and anti-militarists threatened to sweep away the whole General Staff conspiracy. Hastily, Kapp proclaimed the *putsch* adjourned—until a more favorable time. General von Lüttwitz handed over his command of the Reichswehr to the "democratic" General Hans von Seeckt, who promptly mobilized the German Army to "put down Bolshevism in Germany" and shot German workers in Berlin and Essen who had taken up arms to defend the German Republic against the Kapp fascist *putsch*.

After the Kapp *putsch*, the Allied Governments demanded that the German Government take steps to disband the armed fascist officers' groups in Berlin currently operating under such names as *Orgesch* and *Einwohnerwehr* organizations ("national defense" organizations and "home police.") The German authorities replied that these fascist organizations were necessary in Germany as a protection against "Bolshevism." Lord D'Abernon, the British Ambassador in Berlin at the time, recorded in his famous diplomatic diary, a few months after the Kapp *putsch:*

> *"Berlin, October 22, 1920.* A long conversation with Dr. Simons at the Foreign Office. Regarding Disarmament. Dr. Simons said that the demands of the Entente for the dismemberment of various Einwohnerwehr and Orgesch organizations were equivalent

to delivering up the orderly sections of the population to their greatest foes. Without organization the bourgeois element cannot resist the Reds, who are a real danger."

Three years later, the German General Staff staged its second major political move in postwar Germany, again under the slogan of "anti-Bolshevism." This time the *putsch* was led by the General Staff's trained agitator, Adolf Hitler.

The New York *Times* of January 28, 1923, reported that Adolf Hitler was "marching on the Bavarian capital with his Fascisti." Three thousand armed and steel-helmeted Storm Troopers, carrying banners with the old Pan-German Imperial colors, red with a black swastika in a circular field of white, followed Hitler into Munich.

The German General Staff was already introducing Hitler to pro-fascist circles in the United States. A few months before, the Pan-German Count Hugo Lerchenfeld, who had married an American heiress, told American newspapermen:

> "In Bavaria a new prophet has arisen and preached a faith which has filled thousands with enthusiasm and new hope. Who is this man Adolf Hitler? . . . Lack of higher schooling prevented his rising above the rank of non-commissioned officer. At the close of the war Hitler settled in Munich and founded the National Socialist Labor Party. . . . The first and most important dogma in Hitler's creed from the very beginning has been anti-Semitism. . . . Like Mussolini he has unfolded the banner of nationalism. The spirit of the trenches, the spirit of unswerving fidelity to the Fatherland, must be revived in order to strengthen and unite the German people. Hitler looks upon Socialism and Internationalism as purely Jewish inventions. . . ."

On February 8, 1923, the New York *Times* carried another Hitler item of interest to America. The *Times* reported that "two of Herr Hitler's lieutenants on whom French francs and American dollars were found" had recently been arrested in Germany, and that, in commenting on the arrests, Vice-President Auer of the Bavarian Diet had stated:

"The Bavarian Diet has long had information that the Hitler movement was partly financed by an American anti-Semitic chief, who is Henry Ford. Mr. Ford's interest in the Bavarian anti-Jewish movement began a year ago when one of Mr. Ford's agents came in contact with Dietrich Eckhart, the notorious Pan-German. Shortly after, Herr Eckhart asked Mr. Ford's agent for financial aid. The agent returned to America and immediately Mr. Ford's money began coming to Munich. Herr Hitler openly boasts of Mr. Ford's support and praises Mr. Ford not as a great individualist but as a great anti-Semite."*

On the evening of November 8, 1923, Hitler occupied the Buergerbraeu (Beerhall) in Munich with three hundred of his armed followers, most of them officers or cadets from the Reichswehr Munich Infantry Training School. Hitler rushed into the Buergerbraeu with a revolver in each hand, interrupting a nationalist meeting which was in session, leaped on a table, fired three shots into the ceiling, and announced the Pan-German fascist seizure of power.

Hitler was acting in collaboration with General Erich von Ludendorff, the fanatical former Quarter Master-General of the Imperial Army and second-in-command to Hindenburg, who had lost patience with the protracted but systematic methods of the underground General Staff's conspiracy. Together with Captain Roehm and Colonel Hermann Kriebl, formerly of the German Armistice Commission in Munich, Ludendorff had ordered Hitler and his National Socialist Party into action.

But the chiefs of the General Staff were not yet ready for open military seizure of power. In London, a committee of international financial experts was meeting to consider a plan to sustain German postwar economy. It was called the Dawes Plan after the name of the chairman of the committee. Its authors were the American banker, Owen D. Young, and the British banker, Sir Josiah Stamp. As a result of the Dawes Plan, Ger-

* Other international financial backers of Nazism in its early years included Sir Henri Deterding, Anglo-Dutch chairman of the oil trust Royal Dutch Shell; Otto Kreuger, the Swedish match king and international swindler; and the French directors of the munitions trust, Schneider-Creusot, which controlled the great Skoda works in Czechoslovakia.

many was to get an international loan of eight hundred million gold marks to sustain her currency and promote her trade. The loan was used by Germany to finance her secret preparations for another war. Clearly, the time chosen by the hotheaded General Ludendorff and Corporal Hitler for their Munich *putsch* was not propitious. . . .

Once again, as in 1920, the Reichswehr commander, General Hans von Seeckt was asked to straighten matters out. Seeckt became a Nazi himself a few years later; but in 1923 he used the Reichswehr to put down the premature Nazi insurrection. One of the fourteen casualties was Hitler's friend, the former Freikorps leader from Czarist Russia, Schneuber-Richter, who got a bullet in his head. Ludendorff and Hitler were arrested. The German Government, under pressure from the labor unions, put them on trial for treason.

The trial began in February 1924. Hitler said: "I did what I did because Bolshevism was brewing in Germany!" Hitler and his associates turned the court into a forum for their fascist, anti-Semitic and Pan-German propaganda. No attempt was made by the judge to restrain the Nazi defendants. Ludendorff was acquitted. Hitler, an alien who had just headed a violent armed attempt to overthrow the German Republic, was formally sentenced to five years' imprisonment, of which he actually served eight and a half months in comfortable confinement in a military fortress at Landsberg-am-Lech.*

* One of the first persons to visit Hitler at Landsberg was the Pan-German professor of geography at the University of Munich, Dr. Karl Haushofer, one of the chief scientific experts of the underground German General Staff. Haushofer was the inventor of the Nazi "science" of geopolitics. In 1908, the Bavarian General Staff had sent Haushofer, then Major Haushofer, on a two-year mission to Japan. His task was to contact Japanese militarists and to sound them out on a possible future military alliance between Germany and Japan. One of the outcomes of Haushofer's mission was a book, published by him in 1913, entitled *Dai-Nippon*. In this book, Haushofer stated that war between Japan and the United States was inevitable and that a Japanese campaign against China had been decided on by the Japanese General Staff. Haushofer regarded German collaboration with Japan as a natural necessity. "Among nations educated in the military tradition," wrote Haushofer, "there are no racial differences." After the Nazis took power in Germany, Haushofer was appointed head of a "geopolitical institute" in Berlin staffed with 1,000 scientists and technicians who worked under Haushofer's direction on geopolitical problems of world conquest.

At Landsberg, Hitler began writing *Mein Kampf,* a popularly written hodge-podge of all the Pan-German, fascist and anti-Semitic propaganda and theoretical works which the scientific agents of the General Staff had been pouring out since 1918. *Mein Kampf* was to be the basic propaganda document of the Nazi Party.

V. *The Triumph of Treason*

In May 1920, a surprise visit by officers of the Inter-Allied Control Commission revealed that the giant Krupp munitions works at Essen had resumed the manufacture of two-inch field guns prohibited by the Versailles Treaty. By 1923, with a careful eye to future military use, the Krupp former armor-plate rolling plant was turning out the thickest plates in the world; Krupp trucks being delivered to the German Government and to local authorities had chassis readily adaptable for artillery purposes; Krupp tractors were modifications of light tanks.

On April 16, 1943, a Stockholm dispatch to the New York *Times* revealed that the secret rearmament of Germany was fully under way as far back as 1921. The *Times* dispatch read:

> "Dr. Waninger, draftroom chief of the Rheinmetal-Borsig, in a lecture today, boasted cynically that the Germans began experimenting with secret arms construction as early as 1921. At that time, when the republic had barely been born, heavy industry managed to devote much time to producing new gun types, he declared. This work was carried on in the Borsig drafting room, right under the noses of Allied control commissions, without their suspecting a thing. . . . To achieve this degree of secrecy the office had to be kept moving back and forth between various factories. It was in Berlin first, but later removed to an isolated spot on the Leunerberger-Heide, outside the capital."*

* Dr. Karl Waninger's speech was quoted in detail by the official Nazi Party organ, *Voelkischer Beobachter,* on April 15, 1943. Dr. Waninger, addressing Nazi technicians on the subject of the Rheinmetal-Borsig's contribution to German secret rearmament, declared: "The prohibition of development of any

By 1924, three years after the Versailles Treaty that was supposed to have disarmed Germany forever, Colonel William Taylor, European agent of the American DuPont Corporation, was writing in a confidential memorandum to his company headquarters at Delaware:

> "The European monopoly in military material [is] passing slowly into German hands."

In 1925, a report of investigators of the Inter-Allied Control Commission definitely accused Germany of secret rearmament for a Second World War.

In Berlin, in January 1925, the German Foreign Minister Gustav Stresemann assured representatives of foreign newspapers that "Germany is fully disarmed in accordance with the Versailles Treaty. All statements to the contrary are fairy tales!" Stresemann insisted that Germany had no secret military plans and, even if some German generals still dreamed of revenge for 1918, "what could Seeckt do with 100,000 men! Germany cannot even fight a defensive war today!" The Foreign Minister accused the former allies of seeking to destroy Germany.

In the United States, the German-American press and Pan-German propaganda organs immediately rushed to the defense of the "persecuted" fatherland. Editors, lecturers and writers started a violent agitation against continued occupation of Cologne and the Rhineland by Allied forces.

On January 10, 1925, the *Literary Digest* recorded some typical current German-American propaganda on behalf of German militarism. The St. Louis *Westliche Post* declared: "The American people have suffered too much by propaganda to be deceived by the attempt to pass off some pile of junk as

---

new guns in Germany led to a cautious and far-sighted measure when in July, 1921, at the demand of the Reich Naval Command, the firm opened a construction branch on the Friedrichstrasse in Berlin disguised as a transfer office. Because of an anonymous denunciation, the Inter-Allied Military Commission attempted to locate the artillery construction office. This naturally met with no success."

parts of Germany's alleged secret rearmament." The Pittsburgh *Volksblatt* denounced the Inter-Allied Control Commissions in Germany as "parasites living on the fat of the land, at the expense of the enslaved population." The Omaha *Tribune* demanded immediate withdrawal of the Allied Commission from Germany and held out the prospect that "Germany might in the future become sufficiently strong to resist uninterrupted exploitation." The Milwaukee *Herald* stated, "Everybody in the world knows that the German people are disarmed in regard to all practical war purposes." The New York *Staats Zeitung* vociferously charged "bad faith" by the Allies and a "conspiracy against Germany."

Inside Germany, the officers' Fehme, the Nazi Gestapo and other General Staff terrorist agencies took steps to silence any Germans who dared to voice opposition to the secret military plans or to betray the underground preparations for war. Those who were not murdered by the terrorists were silenced by the German Government.

The British correspondent, Robert Dell, reported from Berlin in January 1925:

> "Dr. Zeigner, formerly Prime Minister of Saxony, is awaiting his trial for high treason for having revealed to 'enemy powers' the connection of the illegal armed organizations with the Reichswehr in a speech in the Saxon Landtag. The truth of his statements is not denied. On the contrary, his prosecution is based on the assumption that they are true, for otherwise no charge of treason could by German law be made against him."

On December 11, 1925, the pacifist German chemist Walter Bullerjahn was put on trial before a Berlin court for "treason." His accuser was Paul von Gontard, general director of the Berlin-Karlsruhe Industriewerke. Gontard had been establishing secret arsenals for the Black Reichswehr. Bullerjahn had discovered the existence of these arsenals and was going to reveal his information to the Allies. The German Court sentenced Bullerjahn to 15 years in prison for "treason."

Soon after this, Carl von Ossietzky, world famous editor of the anti-militarist *Weltbuenne,* and subsequent Nobel Peace

Prize winner, was convicted by a German court of "treason." He had published facts in his journal which might have led to disclosure of Germany's secret war plans. When Hitler came to power, Ossietzky was thrown into concentration camp and murdered there.

In an article in the *Nation,* on March 11, 1925, entitled *Treason in the German Republic,* the American correspondent Edgar Ansell Mowrer wrote:

> "Kapp of the Kapp putsch, Captain Erhardt, Erich Ludendorff are not traitors—just as the assassins of Liebknecht and Walther Rathenau and Erzberger are not murderers. It depends on the motive. A traitor is not a traitor when he seeks to restore the monarchy or institute a military dictatorship. . . . A venerable German pacifist, like Professor Ludwig Quidde, who publishes a letter calling attention to the clandestine activity of the Reichswehr and the German Government in connection with the training of youths and the organization of secret patriotic and super-patriotic organizations, is a traitor!"

And so by *putsches* and secret preparations, treachery, terror and propaganda, the underground German General Staff systematically eliminated the elements of German democracy and opened the way for its agent, Hitler, to come to power.

In the fall of 1930, three years before Hitler became dictator of the Reich, the Pan-German League celebrated its fortieth anniversary in Berlin. Heinz Pol, an editor of the Berlin daily *Vossiche Zeitung,* the oldest democratic newspaper in Berlin, attended the Pan-German celebration. Subsequently, in his book *The Hidden Enemy,* Pol described the event. Here is his description of the fortieth anniversary of the Pan-German League in Berlin, 1930:

> "The speakers' platform was occupied by the leaders of the League. To their right and left the honorary guests were assembled. There were the leaders of the big Rightist parties and reactionary associations; present, sitting close together, were three Hohenzollern princes—Eitel, Oscar and August Wilhelm—the last-named in a splendidly tailored Storm Trooper uniform. There were four delegates of the Reichswehr Ministry, dignified officers

who saluted solemnly when Colonel von Hindenburg, the son of the President of the Reich, entered. Close to Hindenburg sat Hjalmar Schacht, whose political career had also begun in the Pan-German League . . . behind Schacht sat the representatives of German industry—only a few men, but they represent billions of marks: Albert Voegler, chairman of the board of the Rheinish-Westphalian Coal Syndicate; old Emil Kirdorf, founder of the Electro-Montan concern, who forty years earlier had become one of the most active members of the Pan-German League; and Herr Blohm, co-owner of the Hamburg shipyards Blohm and Voss. Around another small table sat the representatives of the German Nobility Association, and Count Kalckreuth, one of the political leaders of the Prussian Junkers. In the foreground, near the audience, flanked by a dozen young men in Storm Trooper and Elite Guard uniforms, sat the delegates of the Nazi Party: Hermann Goering, in civilian clothes, for though he was already one of the big shots of the party, his official position was that of a Reichstag deputy, and, beside him, looking sombrely at the audience, Rudolph Hess, the 'personal envoy of Adolf Hitler.'"

Among others at the celebration, reports Pol, were prominent men from the fields of politics, science and economy. Many of the delegates had come from abroad, from Pan-German branches in New York, San Francisco, Haifa, Hong Kong, Melbourne, Montreal, Buenos Aires, China, Sumatra and Japan.

Alfred Hugenberg presided. Dry, wizened, his foxy eyes behind old-fashioned spectacles, old Hugenberg cried to the audience: "I am happy to know that Hitler's party, which symbolizes the coming Germany, has won such a brilliant electoral victory! . . . It was the Pan-Germans who took up the fight for German honor and power—for a power which was not to limit itself to the small German territory in Europe, but would extend to the entire world! During these forty years, we, the Pan-Germans, have influenced the thinking and acting of innumerable people, we have created a mass movement, called new parties into being and breathed new life into the old parties . . . Now we are close to our goal: it will not be long before Germany awakens . . . Long live Pan-Germany!"

Everywhere in the hall, reports Pol, people jumped from their seats, shouted and gesticulated, and waved swastika flags.

The delegates from the Reichswehr stood at attention. Goering, Hess and their followers raised their hands in the Hitler salute. The audience roared: *"Hoch!"* and *"Heil!"*

In January 1933, the General Staff representative and President of the German Republic, Paul von Hindenburg, handed over the German State to Adolf Hitler.

Germany was ready for the Second World War.

CHAPTER SIX

POLICY OF GENOCIDE

"I could scarcely believe that such things could occur in a twentieth-century civilization."

President Franklin D. Roosevelt, commenting on the Nazi pogrom against the Jews in Berlin in November 1938.

"We know that there is no war in all our history where such ruthless and deliberate steps have been taken for the disintegration of civilian life and the suffering and the death of civilian populations."

Hugh R. Jackson, Special Assistant to the Director of Foreign Relief and Rehabilitation Operations, U. S. Department of State, 1943.

I. *Slavery*

WITH an instrument such as the Nazi *Wehrmacht* at its command, the German General Staff was able to put into practise the century-old plans of its Pan-German race theorists, industrialists and military experts. The dreams of Lagarde, Hasse, Haux, Hugenberg, Krupp and Ludendorff were now to be realized in Europe.

The Pan-German planners had called for "mountains of corpses"—now they were to get them.

The Pan-German planners had called for "colonization" of Europe by "pure-blooded Germans"—and now, in the wake of the murderous *Wehrmacht,* the German "colonists" moved in on the occupied regions like a horde of locusts.

By the millions, civilian Poles, Letts, Estonians, Czechs, Frenchmen, Ukrainians and Russians were herded into cattle-cars and transported across the frontiers into Germany to become slave-laborers working for the German war-machine.

German "colonists" took possession of their farms, their factories, their livestock, their household goods and their homes. Week after week the slick magazines printed in Berlin and Hamburg published photographs of German couples in their "new apartments" in occupied Poland, of German farmers cultivating their "new estates" in the occupied Ukraine. The magazines urged more German families to move to the east and settle on the "free land."

"A new aristocracy of German masters [*Herrenvolk*] will be created," announced R. Walther Darre, Reich Minister of Agriculture, in a speech which was reprinted in *Life* magazine on December 9, 1940. "This aristocracy will have slaves assigned to it, these slaves to be their property and to consist of landless, non-German nationals."

In 1942, according to an official statement by Gauleiter Fritz Sauckel, Reich Commissioner for the Utilization of Labor-Power, some 2,000,000 men and women were dispatched to Germany from occupied regions in eastern Europe. Another 2,000,000 persons were transported to Germany from France. By 1943, there were some 12,000,000 foreign slaves working in Germany for German masters.

Those slaves not destined for direct utilization by the Nazi state in war industries and vast military construction projects were sold at regular slave auctions throughout Germany to small businessmen, farmers and housewives. Girl slaves were in particular demand.

On April 20, 1942, Gauleiter Sauckel stated in an official government document entitled *Program of the Chief Commissioner for the Utilization of Labor Power:* ". . . the Fuehrer charged me with the task of delivering to Germany 400,000 to 500,000 picked sound and strong girls from the Eastern regions."

The slaves were kept in the most wretched conditions of misery and squalor. They died of starvation and disease by the tens of thousands; but there were always more of them coming in on the cattlecars from the occupied regions. On the special auction days, German housewives, businessmen and farmers gathered in chattering throngs around the barbed-wire slave pens to inspect the new arrivals. The slaves were brought out by Nazi guards armed with guns and whips and led to the auction blocks. Prospective buyers felt the muscles of the men and women on sale, thumped their chests, examined their teeth. By government order, the price per slave, male or female, was from 10 to 15 Reichsmarks.

As with its soldiers, the German General Staff sought to involve the German civilian population in its crimes. "By compelling even the hesitant to become accomplices in acts of violence," Hitler declared, "you automatically make them your slaves."

The extent to which the German General Staff succeeded in debasing the German population is indicated by countless letters written by German women to soldiers at the front telling of the slaves they had bought and the treatment they accorded them.

Here are a few typical excerpts from these letters of German women:

> "Recently the Russians arrived here in Pufenhausen. Our life will be an interesting one: a dictionary in one pocket and a revolver in the other."
>
> *Letter from Lotta Meller of Pufenhausen to Private Elin Schilling, August 10, 1942.*

> "I do not have that Ukrainian any longer. . . . He refused to obey and was terribly lazy. . . . I informed the labor bureau of that by telephone. But they could not tell me when a fresh transport arrives."
>
> *Letter from Ruth Knappe in Anhalt to Senior Corporal Franz Knappe, Field Post No. 08999, 1942.*

> "On Wednesday two more Russians were buried here. Now five of them lie buried in our cemetery and two of them are dying. And why should they live, they all ought to be killed. . . ."
>
> *Letter from Frieda Putz to Private Otto Tesk, August 30, 1942.*

> "I did not write you about the receipt of 100 marks you sent. I gave them at once to your mother so that she could buy war prisoners. Now this is not so expensive."
>
> *Letter from Maria Wickert of Franweiler to non-com Joseph Wickert, Field Post No. 261873, 1943.*

> "We now have a Ukrainian wench of 19 working for us. Don't

you worry—she will work. On Sunday 20 more Russians will come to the village. I will take several.

Letter from Lorenz Spear to Private Joseph Spear, 1943.

"I'm told they mean to take away my Russian maid. It will be terrible. You cannot imagine what it means to have a good servant in the house. Before the war only the rich could afford that luxury, so the war has done some good. I don't even feel the absence of you and Martha, as this Russian woman does the work of three, so that I can lie in bed and think of you, my dear hubby."

Letter from Gertrude Schwalbach of Frankenthal to Private Schwalbach, July 19, 1944.

German businessmen, state officials and farmers wrote similar letters about their slaves. Here are characteristic excerpts from their letters:

"In Leiden there is a camp for the Russians, where one may see them. They are not afraid of guns but we talk to them by means of a stout whip."

Letter received by Corporal Heinrich Zimlich from his brother, Mattias.

"The plant took the Frenchmen away from us. I selected six Russians from the Minsk district. They are far more hardy than the French. Only one of them has died; the rest continue to work in the field and on the farm. It does not cost us anything to keep them. . . . Yesterday I subjected two of the Russian beasts to a light flogging when they were caught gobbling the skimmed milk intended for the sows."

Letter to Lieutenant Otto von Schirach from Manager Reinhart.

"We now have Russian prisoners here. These fellows devour earthworms on the airfield grounds, they attack the slop-bucket. I saw them eat weeds. To think that they are human beings."

Letter to Lieutenant Helmuth Weisgand from Otto Essman.

But the enslavement of millions of men, women and children was only one aspect of the Pan-German plan which the German General Staff methodically followed in its European conquests. The General Staff employed a wide variety of measures aimed at the ultimate subjugation of some 500,000,000 people in Europe and Soviet Russia by some 80,000,000 German rulers.

As the secret memorandum of General von Stuelpnagel which fell into Allied hands in North Africa stated:

> "The conquest of the world will require numerous stages, but the essential is that the end of each stage brings us to an economic and industrial potential greater than that of our enemies."

II. *Biological Superiority*

What the Nazis have done to reduce the economic and industrial potential of Europe has to be seen to be believed. Eyewitnesses report scenes of unprecedented and unimaginable havoc, waste and desolation. Twenty-three countries lie shattered after German occupation. In Florence, Paris, Brussels, Rotterdam, Warsaw, Kiev, wherever the Nazi plague descended, the labor of centuries has been undone. Many liberated regions are great areas of ashes; cities are rubble; all transport is smashed; farms, factories and commercial enterprises are reduced to a shambles. Tens of millions of human beings are starving and homeless.*

All of this chaos and destruction was part of a deliberate program. The German General Staff ravaged according to plan. Further proof of this came into Allied possession in the form of a captured copy of a special address delivered by Marshal von Runstedt before the Reich Military Academy in Berlin in 1943.

* A typical example of the manner in which towns and cities were methodically torn apart and gutted by the *Wehrmacht* is the Soviet industrial center of Stalino. Here is what the German Army did to that city: demolished 113 schools, 62 kindergartens, the Summer and Winter Theatres, the Art Gallery and the finest buildings in the town; burned down the Children's Hospital, which had 2,000 beds, the Voroshilov Clinical Hospital with 1,000 beds, twelve medical institutions, with a total of 2,000 beds, and five polyclinics; destroyed the Medical Institute, which had an enrollment of 2,000 students; leveled to the ground all the buildings of the Industrial Institute, which had an enrollment of 15,000 students, and burned 530,000 volumes of scientific literature and fiction; carried out wholesale destruction of factories, shops, apartment buildings and private homes.

What happened in Stalino was duplicated in Warsaw, Rotterdam, Kharkov, Kiev, Tallinn, Riga, Kaunas, Cracow, Minsk, Vitebsk and scores of other cities occupied by the Nazis.

"The destruction of neighboring people and their riches," von Runstedt instructed the Reich Military Academy, "is indispensable to our victory. One of the great mistakes of 1918 was to spare the civil life of the enemy countries, for it is necessary for the Germans to be always at least double the number of the peoples of the contiguous countries. We are therefore obliged to destroy at least a third of their inhabitants . . ."

Even if Germany lost the military phase of operations of the Second World War, Germany was to emerge stronger in economic, industrial and manpower potential than any of her neighbors. That, in essence, has been the underlying German strategy since the defeat of the German Army at Stalingrad.

The maintenance of German "biological superiority" over all other countries in Europe has always been a basic aim of Pan-Germanism. The first task was to ensure the superiority of German manpower.

During the First World War, the German General Staff organized mass illegitimate breeding in Germany so that it would have sufficient cannonfodder at its disposal twenty years later. A special German Army program of so-called "lateral" or "secondary" marriages was initiated by the General Staff. A pamphlet was distributed among all German troops in 1917 which stated:

> "*The Empty Cradles of Germany Must be Filled:* The Fatherland needs healthy children. . . . You married men and your wives should put jealousy from your mind and consider whether you have not also a duty to the Fatherland. You should consider whether you may not honorably contract an alliance with one of the million of bachelor women. See if your wife will not sanction the relation. Remember, all of you, the empty cradles of Germany must be filled."

In 1943, the Nazi Supreme Command issued a special booklet entitled *Merkblatt für den Compagnie-Unterricht* (Memorandum for Company Education). The Nazi booklet stated: "Every new born healthy boy is one strong soldier in twenty years."

As part of the Nazi manpower program, thousands of captive women from specially chosen areas of Nazi-conquered

Europe were forcibly prostituted to German youths of the Hitler-Jugend. Children born to these women were taken from the mothers and placed in German institutions. Various other methods were used by the Nazis to ensure the future manpower of the German Army. Human breeding-factories were erected throughout the Reich. Extensive experimentation was carried on in connection with the artificial impregnation of women. Carefully selected foreign workers were mobilized to mate with German women in regions where there was an unusually small number of German men.

"The Germans have destroyed all the fixed notions on which Christendom has lived in war and peace through more than a thousand years . . . ," wrote the famous French commentator on international affairs, Pertinax, in an article in the New York *Times* on January 25, 1945. "It is said that the German authorities are taking unbelievable steps to make sure that, with a much reduced male population, their birth rate will not decline in forthcoming years. No limit can be set in advance to what German fanaticism will be ready to do."

In order to secure the long-range biological inferiority of its enemies, the German General Staff instituted a policy such as had never been known or conceived of in the entire history of warfare and crime. To describe this policy—for which there was no word in the English language—the noted Polish scholar and attorney, Raphael Lemkin, in his authoritative work, *Axis Rule in Occupied Europe,* has coined a new word: *genocide.* The word is derived from the Greek *genos,* meaning race or tribe, and the Latin *cide,* meaning killing. Genocide is the policy of exterminating whole races, tribes and nations of people. Here is how Dr. Lemkin describes the German General Staff's policy of genocide:

> "The enemy nation within the control of Germany must be destroyed, disintegrated, or weakened in different degrees for decades to come. Thus the German people in the post-war period will be in a position to deal with other European peoples from the vantage point of biological superiority. Because the imposition of this policy of genocide is more destructive for a people

than injuries suffered in actual fighting, the German people will be stronger than the subjugated peoples after the war even if the German army is defeated. In this respect genocide is a new technique of occupation aimed at winning the peace even though the war itself be lost."

By the systematic application of this policy of genocide in the course of the Second World War, the German General Staff has sought to permanently cripple all neighboring nations.

III. *The Science of Depopulation*

In the 1920's, the former Nazi Hermann Rauschning records in his book, *Voice of Destruction,* Hitler had already determined on a Pan-German policy of systematic "depopulation" of certain European areas. But at that time Hitler was still looking for an adequate "technique of depopulation." He told Rauschning:

"We shall have to develop a technique of depopulation. If you ask me what I mean by depopulation, I mean the removal of entire racial units. And that is what I intend to carry out—that, roughly, is my task. Nature is cruel, therefore, we, too, may be cruel. If I can send the flower of the German nation into the hell of war without the smallest pity for the spilling of precious German blood, then surely I have the right to remove millions of an inferior human race that breeds like vermin! And by 'remove' I don't necessarily mean destroy; I shall simply take systematic measures to dam their great natural fertility. For example, I shall keep their men and women separated for years. Do you remember the falling birthrate of the world war? Why should we not do quite consciously and through a number of years what was at that time merely the inevitable consequence of the long war? There are many ways . . . of causing undesirable races to die out."

Throughout the 1920's and 1930's the German General Staff conducted a series of scientific studies of the various techniques by which enemy nations might be completely destroyed or permanently crippled. Under the supervision of the General Staff, military experts and specialists in the fields of medicine, psychology, economy and sociology drew up detailed programs for systematically undermining the physical, cultural, economic and political life of enemy nations.

"The enemy nation's originally solid, powerful and well-knit fabric must be gradually disintegrated, broken down, rotted, so that it falls apart like a fungus treated upon in a forest," wrote the Berlin professor of military science, Dr. Ewald Banse, in *Raum und Volk im Weltkrieg* (Space and People in World War), which was published in Germany in 1931. Later, Dr. Banse became widely known as one of the outstanding Nazi strategists of terror.

The ultimate product of the extensive research carried on by the scientists of the German General Staff was the policy of genocide.

These were some of the results achieved by the German General Staff's application of the policy of genocide in occupied territory:

Poland: 5,000,000 civilians killed; 2,000,000 deported.

France: 250,000 civilians killed during and after hostilities; 2,000,000 deported; 1,000,000 war prisoners held in Germany; 700,000 children dead of malnutrition.

Belgium: 15,000 to 20,000 murdered; 600,000 deported.

Netherlands: 125,000 dead; 565,000 deported.

Greece: 85,000 murdered; 325,000 deported; 600,000 dead of malnutrition; 80% of all children undernourished or diseased.

Yugoslavia: 1,500,000 murdered; 350,000 deported.

Czechoslovakia: 60,000 murdered; 300,000 in concentration camps; 750,000 deported.*

The first victims of the policy of genocide were the Jews of Germany. Immediately after Hitler came to power, the Nazi Government launched a systematic campaign aimed at the ultimate extermination of the Jewish population of the Third Reich. The Nazis initiated their campaign by methodically

* The figures in this list are only approximate and are all on the conservative side. It will be years before the full consequences of German rule can be accurately estimated.

driving the Jews out of the political, economic and social life of Germany. The Jews were deprived of their basic rights of citizenship and at the same time of their means of subsistence. This was the period of the so-called "cold pogrom." Later, Jewish men, women and children were rounded up by the tens of thousands, herded in concentration camps, subjected to wholesale sterilization and butchered in mass executions and bloody pogroms.

When the Nazi plague swept through Europe, the Jewish people in the occupied countries were ruthlessly wiped out by the hundreds of thousands. On December 17, 1942, the Joint Declaration by the United Nations, issued simultaneously in Washington and London, declared:

> "From all the occupied countries Jews are being transported in conditions of appalling horror and brutality to Eastern Europe. In Poland, which has been made the principal Nazi slaughter-house, the ghettos established by the German invader are being systematically emptied of all Jews except a few highly skilled workers required for war industries. None of those taken away are ever heard of again. The able-bodied are slowly worked to death in labor camps. The infirm are left to die of exposure and starvation or are deliberately massacred in mass executions. The number of victims of these bloody cruelties is reckoned in many hundreds of thousands of entirely innocent men, women and children."

The extermination of the Jews in Nazi-occupied territory was so ruthless and systematic that in many regions the Allied armies later found less than one per cent of the original Jewish population still alive. The few who had not been killed had in most cases saved their lives by joining guerilla bands or by somehow managing to hide from the Germans.

According to an official Soviet report to the World Jewish Congress, which was made public by Dr. Stephen Wise on February 18, 1945, the total Jewish population in thirty-eight Russian and Polish cities and towns liberated by the Red Army was found to have been reduced by the Nazis from 400,000 to 3,122.

The report which had been prepared by the Jewish Anti-

Fascist Committee of Moscow, included these statistics on the extermination of Jews in Nazi-occupied cities:

City	*Jewish population in 1939*	*Jewish population in 1944*
Riga	100,000	158
Lublin	83,000	685
Vilna	55,000	506
Bialystok	40,000	113
Kovno	25,000	574

In some towns, such as Dvinsk, not a single Jew was found alive by the returning Red Army.

By 1945 the Nazis had exterminated between 5,000,000 and 6,000,000 Jews in Europe and Soviet Russia.*

This methodical extermination of helpless men, women and children was not limited to the Jewish people. The Nazis applied their policy of genocide to all conquered peoples in accordance with the program outlined by the "national experts" of the German General Staff. Conquered peoples were systematically impoverished and their standard of living drastically reduced. Food was rationed by "racial principle." Only citizens of the Third Reich and persons of German origin were properly fed. "The German people," declared Reich Minister Goering in October 1942, "come before all other peoples for food." For countless thousands the Nazi system of food rationing meant slow starvation.

As was intended by the German General Staff, the health of whole populations swiftly declined. In Warsaw by 1942 anemia had risen 113 per cent among Poles and 435 per cent among Jews. Epidemics and disease spread throughout Nazi-occupied Europe. Death rates soared. In July 1941 the Polish mortality in Warsaw amounted to 1,316; in August to 1,739; in September

* The Nazi policy of genocide as applied to the Jewish people differed from the policy adopted toward other peoples in that the Nazis aimed at the complete and final extermination of the Jews, whereas with other peoples the Nazis planned to retain certain drastically reduced sections of their populations to serve as slaves of the German empire.

to 2,160. The death rate per thousand in 1941 in the Netherlands amounted to 10 per cent; in Belgium to 14.5 per cent; in Bohemia and Moravia to 13.4.*

Special measures were taken to deprive "undesirable national groups" of the elemental necessities for preserving health and life. In winter, firewood and medicines were withheld from the people. Warm clothing and blankets were requisitioned during the bitterly cold months. Here, for example, is Order No. 1422-41 issued by the German Northern Army Group on November 6, 1941, over the signature of Lieutenant Beyer:

> "All felt boots in the possession of the Russian civilian population, including children's boots, are subject to immediate requisition. To own felt boots is forbidden and is punishable as the unauthorized carrying of arms."

According to the German instructions, violators of this regulation were to be shot.

Still other techniques were used to carry out Hitler's promise of "depopulation." A series of special measures were taken with the object of decreasing birthrates. Thousands of men and women were sterilized. Marriages among Poles were forbidden without the express permission of the *Reichsstatthalter* (Governor of the District).†

Millions of men in conquered regions were separated from the women of their countries by such means as deporting them for forced labor. By 1944, some 3,000,000 Frenchmen alone were being held in Germany. Approximately a million of these were

* While food prices in general soared, the Germans deliberately kept down the price of alcohol. Drinking was systematically encouraged. Peasants, for instance, were compelled to accept alcohol in payment for their agricultural produce. This was part of a systematic program aimed at debasing the conquered peoples and lowering their moral standards, their national consciousness and their will to resist. As part of this program, the Germans distributed pornographic publications and moving pictures in occupied territory.

† The manner in which German officials arranged marriages is indicated in this excerpt from a letter found on the body of Sergeant Major Robert Grade of the German Army on the Eastern Front. "Old Otto is doing splendidly. He is now a commandant. And you know what? He arranges marriages, and even makes gifts of vodka and matches for the wedding. But in return for this he has the right of the first night . . ."

prisoners of war. The balance had been brought in for forced labor or as political deportees.*

In France, as in other occupied countries, deliberate undernourishment of the population caused a drastic increase in tuberculosis and anemia. Accordingly, the number of stillbirths and the mortality rate of children rose to unprecedented heights. *L'Avenir Medical,* the French medical journal, reported that as a result of the "scientific" German methods, the postwar population of France may drop to 29,000,000 from its prewar population of 45,000,000.

IV. *Death Ditches and Gaswagen*

It was against the Slav peoples, the traditional enemy of Pan-Germanism, that the policy of genocide was most extensively applied. "It will be one of the chief tasks of German statesmanship," Hitler had told Hermann Rauschning, "for all time to prevent, by every means in our power, the further increase of the Slav races." Hitler continued: "Natural instincts bid all living beings not merely conquer their enemies, but also destroy them. In former days, it was the victor's prerogative to destroy entire tribes, entire peoples."

Immediately after the invasion of the Soviet Union, the German High Command arranged in their military schools and

* The Germans not only cut down the French birthrate by keeping these Frenchmen in the Reich. They also took measures to undermine the health of the French prisoners, in case they should ever return to France. By 1944 French prisoners of war in Germany were suffering so dreadfully from undernourishment that they began eating rats and mice and boiling flower bulbs to make soup. Some letters describing their plight evaded the German censors and reached their relatives in France. These are excerpts from the letters:

"We tried to cook some dahlia bulbs that had been damaged by the first frosts. They appear to be edible . . ."

"I hope the cold will make the parasites disappear (fleas and lice) but as for the rats and mice they are amusing animals—and very good to eat, according to those who have tried it."

"A complete cessation of individual or collective food parcels (sent through the International Red Cross) worries us justifiably, for our health has been rendered fragile by four years of captivity and undernourishment. We don't want to return handicapped to the rest of our days by too great physical deficiencies."

institutions special courses of lectures emphasizing the necessity of exterminating masses of the Russian people. Among those who attended these courses was Senior Corporal Reinhard Retzlaff, official of the German Secret Field Police who was subsequently captured by the Red Army, placed on trial and executed for his part in the atrocities committed by the German Army in Kharkov. During the preliminary investigation conducted by the Soviet authorities, Retzlaff gave this testimony regarding his training in the Altenburg Special Battalion:

> "At the courses, several special lectures were even arranged, and delivered by leading officials of the GFP (German Field Police), who definitely stated that the peoples of the U.S.S.R., and those of Russian nationality in particular, were inferior, that the vast number of them should be exterminated, while a small section should be utilized by the big German landowners in the capacity of slaves.
>
> "These instructions followed logically from the policy pursued by the German government towards the peoples in occupied territories, and it must be admitted that all those serving in the German Army, including myself, have undeviatingly carried them out in their practical work."

As the Nazi *Wehrmacht* drove toward Moscow in the summer and autumn of 1941, it conducted ferocious massacres of tens of thousands of Soviet men, women and children. These mass executions, unprecedented for scale and savagery, were not a matter of military expediency. They were part of the Pan-German program of wiping out the Slav peoples and preparing the land for colonization by German settlers.

In village after village, town after town, Soviet citizens were rounded up, loaded onto German trucks and driven to the outskirts. There they were mowed down by machine-gun fire and buried in great ditches, which often they themselves had been forced to dig, or in large pits and ravines. Counter-attacking Red Army forces discovered scores of these mass graves and exhumed hundreds of thousands of corpses from them. At the ghastly Babar Yar ravine near Kiev, the corpses of approximately 80,000 Soviet civilians and 25,000 war prisoners were found. In a ditch on the outskirts of Mineralnye Vody, the bodies of 6,300 Russian men, women and children were found. About 80,000

Russian war prisoners were executed and buried near the village of Glinischen. In thirty-four grave pits in the Blagovschina Forest near Minsk, the Nazis buried 150,000 people; 10,000 in a ditch near Drozdy; 254 children in a ditch near Kerch . . .

When the bodies were exhumed from these mass graves, Soviet medical experts established that many of the victims had been buried alive. Large numbers of the bodies were dreadfully mutilated and bore evidence of fearful tortures inflicted by the Nazis. Frequently, the bodies of fathers and mothers were found with their dead children and infants still clutched in their arms.*

Scenes of unspeakable horror took place during the mass executions of Soviet men, women and children. Here is how Alexander Bespalov, a Soviet citizen, described to the Soviet authorities the ghastly episode he witnessed in a forest near Kharkov in June 1943:

> "At the end of June, last year, I myself saw as many as 300 girls and women brought to the woods in ten or twelve motor trucks.
>
> "These poor people ran hither and thither weeping, tearing their hair and clothes, many of them dropping in a swoon, but the German fascists paid no attention to this. They punched them and beat them with their rifle butts and clubs to make them get up; if they did not get up the butchers tore their clothes off and threw them into the pit. Several girls and children tried to run away, but were killed.
>
> "After a round was fired from automatic rifles I saw several women stagger and throw their arms helplessly and, uttering heartrending shrieks, run towards the Germans standing about. The Germans shot them down with pistols . . . mothers, driven out of their minds by fear and grief, ran shrieking about the glade, pressing their babies to their breasts, seeking safety.
>
> "The Gestapo men tore the children out of their mothers' arms and, swinging them by their legs or arms, threw them

* The famous Soviet novelist and journalist, Ilya Ehrenburg, wrote: "The word 'ravine' used to be a good word—it spoke of grass, rivulet, sand and the big-eyed daisies which children used to pull apart murmuring, 'He loves me, he loves me not.' But the word ravine has become a terrible word. One feels that at any moment the dead will come stalking out of a ravine. And not only out of the ravine in Tripolye—for there is a ravine in Kiev, too . . . Every Ukrainian town has its ravine. And everywhere it is the same story: patches of under-linen, rigid corpses, children's toys sprinkled with blood."

alive into the pit. As the mothers ran after them, they were shot down."

In 1942 the Nazi leaders decided that the extermination of Soviet citizens was not proceeding at a sufficiently rapid rate. At a conference between Adolf Hitler, Heinrich Himmler and Ernst Kalterbrunner, the chief of the *Sicherheitdienst* (Security Service, or special operations division, of the SS), it was agreed that the use of poison gas should be introduced as the most effective and speedy means of killing people in large numbers. . . .

The former official of the German Secret Field Police, Senior Corporal Reinhard Retzlaff, told Soviet authorities after his capture:

> "Wholesale execution by hanging and shooting appeared to the German Command to be too bothersome and slow a means of fulfilling the tasks set the punitive organizations, and it was therefore deemed necessary to devise simpler means of exterminating the population; and it must be said that these means were found."

Retzlaff went on to relate how in 1942 he had seen a large, gray, strange-looking automobile, standing near the entrance to one of the Gestapo prisons in Kharkov and surrounded by a group of German policemen. His curiosity aroused, Retzlaff asked a police official he knew, named Kaminsky, what sort of an automobile it was. "Kaminsky," related Retzlaff, "told me that it was a 'gas van,' and that it was used for putting people to death."

Retzlaff added:

> "Later, I had numerous opportunities of seeing this automobile at work, and on several occasions, I took a direct part in loading it with prisoners confined in the Kharkov prison. On these occasions I was able to convince myself that the gas van fully answered its purpose."

The *Gaswagen,* or "gas vans," which were brought into the Soviet Union in 1942 to speed up the process of exterminating Soviet citizens, were large, covered automobiles, painted a dark gray and furnished with Diesel engines. The interior of these automobiles was lined with zinc-plated sheet iron. In the rear they had double doors, which could be hermetically sealed. The floor had a grating, beneath which there was a pipe connected with the exhaust pipe of the engine. When the motors were running, the waste gas from the Diesel engine poured through the grating in the floor. The waste gas contained a high concentration of carbon monoxide and caused the rapid poisoning and death from asphyxiation of persons locked in the rear compartment.

Thousands of Russian men, women and children were to die in these Nazi death vans.

Obersturmbannfuehrer Georg Heinisch, the former Deputy Chief of Rudolf Hess's staff and a member of the Nazi Party since 1923, who held the post of Regional Commissar of the city of Meltipol (a rank equal to that of Major-General), made this extraordinary statement to the Soviet authorities in the fall of 1943 after he had been captured by Red Army soldiers:

> "In the middle of August 1943, in a village near the town of Rovno, a conference was held of 28 Regional Commissars of the Ukraine.
>
> "The proceedings of this conference were directed by Reichskommissar of the Ukraine, Koch.
>
> "From the reports of the Regional Commissars it was evident that the population was resisting their forcible mobilization for work in Germany.
>
> "In this connection Koch stated that it was necessary to intensify the measures against the population, and that we must not hesitate to exterminate an extra several thousand people."

Obersturmbannfuehrer Heinisch went on:

> "In particular, he [Koch] said he had decided to send to work in Germany the largest possible number of able-bodied inhabitants of the districts of the Northern Ukraine and to exterminate all the rest of the inhabitants of these districts. . . .
>
> "The extermination of the bulk of the citizens of Soviet Russia could only be to the advantage of Germany, as it would enfeeble Russia.
>
> "These last words of Koch's expressed the policy of Hitler and his General Staff."

But even these mass shootings and gassings were not sufficient to carry out the plan of the German General Staff. For the systematic extermination of millions of people an even more highly organized and efficient technique than ravine massacres and mobile gas vans was necessary. The German General Staff provided it.

By order of the General Staff, the Death Camps were built.

CHAPTER SEVEN

FACTORIES OF DEATH

FOLLOWING the liberation of Lublin in the summer of 1944, a group of some thirty foreign correspondents visited the Maidenak Death Camp. Among the correspondents was the American newspaperman, W. H. Lawrence. On August 27, 1944, Lawrence sent a dispatch to the New York *Times* which opened with these words:

> "I have just seen the most terrible place on the face of the earth—the German concentration camp at Maidenak, which was a veritable River Rouge for the production of death, in which it is estimated that nearly 1,500,000 persons from nearly every country in Europe were killed in the last three years. . . . This is a place that must be seen to be believed. . . ."

Another American correspondent, Ralph Parker, cabled to the New York newspaper *PM:*

> "Perhaps I would not have believed it, had I not seen Maidenak for myself. . . ."

The Soviet war correspondent, Konstantin Simonov, wrote:

> "What I am now about to relate is too enormous and too gruesome to be fully conceived. There can be no doubt that jurists, physicians, historians and politicians will devote long studies to these terrible facts. And some time in the future, after a thorough and painstaking inquiry, the full immensity of this crime committed by the Germans against humanity will come to light. I myself am in possession of only a fraction of the facts; I have spoken with perhaps only 100 witnesses and maybe have seen only one-tenth of the traces of the crime. But a man who has seen what I have seen cannot hold his peace and cannot wait to speak. . . ."

The construction of Camp Maidenak was started by order of the German Government and military Supreme Command late in 1940 in an enormous field about a mile and a quarter from Lublin, near the highway running between Chelm and Cracow. Polish war prisoners and Jews, working under the supervision of SS troops, built the camp. When finished it contained 144 barracks. Each of the barracks housed 300 persons or more, and the camp as a whole could accommodate approximately 45,000 prisoners. In addition to the barracks, there were a number of other buildings, such as storehouses, workshops and quarters for the Nazi guards. The whole area of the camp was studded with tall towers for sentries with machine-guns. At one end were kennels for 200 large, savage dogs specially trained for tracking down escaped prisoners. The camp covered a total area of 675 acres.

From the Chelm highway, the Maidenak Camp looked like a small well-kept city. Its hundreds of trim, low gray-roofed buildings gave a neat, orderly appearance. "You turn off the road," wrote Konstantin Simonov in his article describing the camp, "and drive through a gateway in a barbed-wire fence, past rows of neat huts with trim front gardens in which stand rustic armchairs and benches. These were the quarters of the SS Guards and officers. There too is the *Soldatenheim,* a smallish hut which served as a brothel for the guards. Women were selected exclusively from the prisoners and as soon as any one of them became pregnant she was sent to be annihilated . . ."

The original Gestapo plans for Maidenak bore the title "Camp Dachau No. 2." Later, this name was changed, and official documents from Berlin referred to the camp as the "Lublin concentration camp of the SS troops." By the summer of 1942 unofficial documents and letters were referring to the camp as the "*Vernichtungslager*" or "Extermination Camp."

"The main purpose of the camp," stated Heinz Stalbe, a German ex-convict and one of the SS guards at Maidenak, who was captured by the Red Army, "was to exterminate the greatest possible number of people, and for this reason it was named the *Vernichtungslager* or 'Extermination Camp.' "

Murder on the gigantic scale contemplated by the German General Staff at Maidenak and other death camps required as much organization and elaborate machinery as the mass production of tanks, planes and guns. Complex problems were involved in the extermination of millions of human beings, the disposal of their bodies and the accumulation and distribution of their possessions. To solve these problems the Nazi leaders called upon various experts. Among them was Friedrich Wilhelm Kreuger, Secretary of State for Public Security of the Government General of Poland.

A former member of the terrorist Luetzow Freikorps and one-time Social Democrat, Friedrich Kreuger had joined the Nazi Party in 1929. He rose rapidly in the movement, and by 1934 was appointed *SS Obergruppenfuehrer* (Superior Group Leader of the SS) and "Inspector of the Frontier Units" *(Grenzeinheiten)*. In this capacity Kreuger organized the murder of a number of well-known anti-Nazis who had fled across the German border after Hitler came to power. One of the most famous men murdered by Kreuger's agents was the famous pacifist philosopher, Professor Theodor Lessing. But it was not only Kreuger's record as a Party member and terrorist which fitted him for the job of helping plan the Nazi campaign of mass murder. Kreuger had other important qualifications. In addition to being a Nazi terrorist, Kreuger was also a successful businessman. In 1924 he had been appointed the director of the corporation which handled the disposal of refuse and garbage in Berlin. As such, he had entirely reorganized the collection of refuse and devised a special system for its incineration.

Here is an extract from an article in the German *Brockhaus* dictionary describing the Kreuger method of burning refuse:

> "The burning takes mostly place in chamber or shaft stoves on solid or movable iron where a temperature of 700 to 1,400 degrees can be reached."

And here is an extract from a report by the Soviet newspaperman, Konstantin Simonov, describing the furnaces in which the bodies of executed prisoners were burned at the Maidenak Death Camp at Lublin:

> "The crematorium consists of five big chamber stoves, one next to the other, the iron doors of which are firmly closed. . . . Experts who examined the remnants of the stoves established the temperature at 1,500."

Mass executions at Maidenak began in the winter of 1941. At first, shooting was the usual method of execution. Out of a party of 2,000 Soviet war prisoners brought to the camp, only eighty remained alive after a few days; the remainder had been shot. Early in 1942, 6,000 men, women and children were shot within the course of two days. On another occasion, in a single day, eighty-eight truckloads of civilian prisoners were driven to the Krempek Forest which stood near the camp; they were shot, and their bodies were thrown into huge pits.

The greatest of the mass executions by shooting occurred on November 3, 1943. On that single day 18,400 prisoners from all over Europe were shot on the prison grounds and their bodies buried in tremendous ditches that had been previously prepared. Ten thousand of those executed were civilians brought in from the town of Lublin; the other 8,400 were inmates of the Maidenak Camp.

"Besides people brought from the town, 8,400 persons were taken on that day from Lublin and shot," the captured SS guard, Herman Vogel, told Soviet authorities. "I know this figure exactly because next day an official report on the extermination of 8,400 persons was presented to the clothing store where I worked, as we had to write off their clothing."

The shooting began early in the morning of November 3, 1943, and ended late at night. To drown out the shrieks of the victims and the sound of the shots, the Germans installed powerful loudspeakers throughout the camp and played loud music over them all day long. According to the subsequent findings of the Polish-Soviet Atrocities Commission:

> "SS troopers brought out the people—stripped naked—in groups of 50 to 100 to the pits, laid them on the bottom of the pits face

downwards and shot them from tommy guns. Another group of live people was then laid upon the dead bodies and shot in the same manner, and so on until the pits were filled. Then the bodies were covered with a thin layer of earth and two or three days later removed and buried in the crematorium or on the bonfires.'

On the night of November 3rd the German officials at Maidenak dispatched a report to Berlin, which read in part:

> "The difference between the number of prisoners in the camp in the morning and in the evening is the result of a special annihilation of 18,000 persons."

Shooting was by no means the only form of execution at Maidenak. Thousands of prisoners died as a result of slow starvation. The standard ration was coffee made of burned turnips once a day, soup of grass twice a day, and a tiny portion of bread made half of sawdust or chestnut flour. Other thousands died of artificially stimulated diseases. New arrivals at the camp, who were not immediately executed, were quarantined in the camp hospital for twenty-one days before going to the general barracks. There they were confined in close quarters with prisoners suffering from severe cases of tuberculosis. As was intended, large numbers of the new arrivals would contract the disease. According to the records kept by the Nazis, 70 to 80 per cent of the so-called natural deaths in the camp resulted from tuberculosis . . .

Simonov later wrote:

> "Here there were thousands of war prisoners . . . who died at a terrible rate from hunger and disease. Here there were fields where thousands and tens of thousands of persons were burned on funeral pyres . . . Here there were types of 'murder vans,' as well as solidly built casements where victims were asphyxiated by 'cyclone' gas. Here bodies were burned in the most primitive method of ancient India; a row of logs and a row of corpses, then another row of logs and another row of corpses, but also in simply constructed furnaces like giant cauldrons, as well as in perfected furnaces for blitz cremation. Here people were shot in ditches or killed with a blow of an iron rod which broke their necks. Here people were drowned in artificial ponds or hanged on gallows of different types, from a simple gibbet with a crossbar to an up-to-date portable scaffold furnished with pulleys and a flywheel. This was a regular death factory where the size of the

daily slaughterings were regulated by two factors; by the number of people entering the camp and by the amount of labor needed for the never-ending construction work."

In 1942, shortly after the conference in Berlin between Hitler, Himmler and Kaltenbrunner at which the decision was reached to use gas for mass killings, special arrangements were made at the Maidenak Camp for large-scale executions by gas. Six concrete cells were constructed with heavy steel doors that could be hermetically sealed. In the walls of each cell were small apertures from which pipes led to the outside. In each cell there was also a little window of thick glass, barred on the inside by a stout steel grid. A total of approximately 2,000 people could be packed into the six cells at one time.

Adjoining the six cells were small rooms for specially trained SS men. The pipes from the cells reached into these rooms. In each of the rooms were stacks of hermetically sealed cylindrical tins on which was inscribed "Cyclone B-2—for special use in Eastern Germany."

Here, in Simonov's words, is how the poison cells worked:

> "The people were stripped naked before they were pushed into the cell and they were packed so tight they occupied little space . . . The steel door was closed upon them and its edges sealed with clay. Then specially trained operators wearing gas masks poured the 'cyclone' out of the cylindrical tins into the chamber. The small bluish innocent-looking crystals, on contact with the oxygen of the air, immediately began to generate poisonous gases which simultaneously affect all centers of the human organism.
>
> "An SS man of the commanding squad turned on a switch in the next room illuminating the poison chamber and through the spy hole watched all stages of the asphyxiation, which according to witnesses lasted from two to ten minutes. He could safely watch the action of the gases and the faces of the dying. The spy hole was set into the wall at roughly the height of a human face. He had no need to look down, for the people were packed so close they did not fall as they died, but continued in an upright position."

The selection of people for asphyxiation was systematically arranged by the German army doctors. The prisoners to be killed were ordinarily divided into groups. In one group would be typhus cases, in another those unfit for manual labor, in a third prisoners who had been exhausted by starvation and unendurable work, and so on. Women and children were usually killed together. A former Polish prisoner at the camp, Jan Wolski, later described to the Polish-Soviet Atrocities Commission some of the executions he had witnessed:

> "In October, 1942, a great number of women and children were brought to the camp. Those in good health were picked out for work, while the exhausted and sick women as well as children were asphyxiated in a gas cell. In March, 1943, 250 more women and children were murdered with gas in the same cell . . . On May 16 or 17, 1943, 158 children of two to ten years were brought to the camp in trucks. These children were murdered in a gas cell. . . ."

Oberscharfuehrer Adolf Terners, an SS man at Maidenak who was captured by Red Army soldiers, told the Polish-Soviet Atrocities Commission, "On the evening of October 21, 1943, Camp Doctor SS Untersturmfuehrer Rindfleisch told me that on that very day 300 children of three to ten years of age had been asphyxiated with the cyclone preparation in a gas cell."

Day after day black smoke poured from the chimneys of the crematorium at Maidenak and hung in great clouds over the town of Lublin. The townspeople frequently walked through the streets with handkerchiefs held over their noses. "The stench of the corpses often penetrated the town, at least in its eastern part," Lieutenant General Hilmar Moser, the former German military commander of Lublin, told Red Army officers after his capture. "It was clear, even to less well-informed persons, what was going on in that horrible place."*

* General Moser, who belatedly discovered that he had a conscience when he was captured by the Red Army in 1944, also said: "I have no reason to keep silent on Hitler's crimes or to cover them up, and I consider it my duty to tell the whole truth about the so-called extermination Camp set up by the Hitlerites near the town of Lublin along the Chelm highway . . . In the winter of 1943-44 a great number of those were exterminated, including, to my indignation, women and children. The number of murdered people ran into the hundreds of thousands . . . I was told many times that in the Extermination Camp the doomed people were forced to perform extremely hard work beyond their strength and were forced on by brutal beatings. I learned that prisoners in the

The crematorium presented a ghastly sight to those who examined it after Lublin was liberated by Red Army forces. "Built of brick," wrote the American correspondent, W. H. Lawrence, "it looked and was operated not unlike a small blast furnace for a steel mill, operating with coal as fuel, fanned by an electrically operated blower." On each side of the crematorium were five large furnace doors. Bodies on steel frames were loaded into one side, and the other side the ashes were removed. The daily capacity of the furnace was almost 2,000 bodies.

Simonov wrote:

> "The round doors are open now. The deep fireboxes are half filled with decomposing vertebrae and with ashes. On platforms in front of each firebox lie half-burned skeletons that had been prepared for cremation when the Germans set fire to the building [before fleeing from Maidenak]. In front of three of the fire boxes are the large skeletons of either men or women, and in front of the other two are the skeletons—judging by their size—of children between the ages of 10 and 12. There are five or six skeletons at each firebox, which held six bodies at once. If the sixth body did not fit in easily, the furnacemen would lop off the part of the body which did not fit—an arm, leg or the head—and then slam the door to."

Sometimes living prisoners were thrown into the furnaces. Lawrence, reported:

> ". . . There is a story as it came from the lips of a German who had been made a prisoner in Maidenak and was left behind by the retreating Germans. He is Hans Staub, a 31-year-old, tall, husky man with close-cropped hair who had been imprisoned for engaging in black-market meat operations in Germany.
>
> "Despite German orders that prisoners were to keep out of the crematorium area, he managed to slip inside the brick fence one day and secrete himself about the time a truck loaded with a dozen persons drove up. Among them was a Polish woman he estimated to have been 28 or 29 years old. The prisoners were guarded by tommy-gunners, who ordered them to alight from the truck and undress. The woman refused and this enraged

---

camp were also tortured before they were killed . . . Himmler himself visited the camp when he arrived in Lublin in the summer of 1943 . . ."

Mussfeld who beat her. She screamed and Mussfeld lost his temper, shouting, 'I'll burn you alive.'

"According to Staub, Mussfeld then directed two attendants to grab the woman and bind her arms and legs. They then threw her on an iron stretcher, still clothed, and pushed her body into the oven.

" 'I heard one loud scream, saw her hair aflame, and then she disappeared into the furnace,' Staub said."

To relieve the monotony of the daily mass executions, the Nazi guards amused themselves by inflicting horrible tortures and "jokes" upon the prisoners. One of the favorite "jokes" was this. An SS guard would tell a prisoner that he was to be shot for some infringement of the camp regulations, and stand him against a wall with a pistol to his head. Usually, in anticipation of the shot the victim instinctively closed his eyes. The SS guard would then fire into the air, while another struck the prisoner heavily over the head with a board. When the prisoner recovered consciousness, he would find a group of SS men standing over him. "You see," they would mock at him, "you're in the other world. There are Germans here too and you can't get away from them." In most cases the prisoner was unable to rise, and the "joke" ended with his being shot as he lay on the ground.

Another "joke" was practised at a big pool in the camp. The victim would be stripped and pushed into the pool. SS men standing on the edge of the pool would kick the prisoner back in when he tried to climb out. If he was able to avoid their blows and clamber out of the pool, the victim was given three seconds in which to dress himself. Failing to accomplish this, he was then thrown back into the pool. This "joke" was kept up until the victim drowned.

Simonov describes another method by which the SS men amused themselves:

"Before a prisoner guilty of some misdemeanor was killed he would be led over to a large, sparkling white wringer used by the camp laundry and made to place his fingers between the heavy rubber rollers. Then an SS man—or perhaps another prisoner forced into their service—would turn the handle. The victim's arms would be literally mangled up to the shoulder. The agonizing screams of the tortured victim would afford great entertainment to his tormentors. . . ."

The women prisoners, of whom there were sometimes as many as 10,000 in the camp, were subjected to tortures no less fiendish than those of the men. They were guarded by SS women, notorious for their brutality and sadism. Simonov describes one of these women guards:

> "She never appeared without her whip, consisting of a piece of thick wire two meters long wound round with rubber and covered with leather. A gaunt, ugly creature, she was noted for her sadism, the result of some sexual abnormality. She was half insane. At morning or evening roll call she would inspect the rows of thin, wretched women, and, selecting one who had retained some faint semblance of beauty, would raise her whip and strike the woman on the breast. When her victim dropped to the ground she would deal her a blow between the legs and finish up with a savage kick in the same place with her hobnailed boot. After the same thing happened once or twice the woman would be crippled and would die. . . ."

A former prisoner named Atrokov told the Polish-Soviet Atrocities Commission: "They took away a baby from its mother's breast and killed it before her eyes by smashing it against the barracks wall."

"I, myself," said Edward Baran, another witness, "saw how babies were taken from their mothers and killed before their eyes; they would take a baby by one foot and step on the other, and so tear the baby apart."

With the exception of human lives, nothing at Camp Maidenak was wasted.

Near the crematorium there stood a concrete table. The Germans placed all corpses on this table before cremation, carefully inspected the mouths of the dead, and knocked out any gold teeth or fillings. These were accumulated for shipping to the Third Reich. No body was accepted for cremation unless there was a stamp on the chest certifying it had been searched for gold teeth.

A large number of earthenware urns were kept close to the

furnaces. The ashes of the victims were placed in these and were sold to their families for prices ranging up to 2,500 marks.

The Germans systematically accumulated the clothing and possessions of the men, women and children who had been killed, and stored the articles in enormous warehouses. In dozens of various-sized rooms, the possessions of the dead were carefully sorted out, neatly stacked and packed, and made ready for periodic shipments to Germany. In one room were tens of thousands of women's dresses; in another, great piles of trousers; in a third, stacks of children's clothing; in a fourth, huge mounds of underwear. Other rooms were filled with children's toys, bathrobes, shaving brushes, women's belts, men's ties, nipples for babies' feeding bottles, pajamas, and tons of other articles taken from the dead.

"I was assistant chief of the clothing store at Maidenak Camp," Rotenfuehrer SS trooper Herman Vogel told the Polish-Soviet Atrocities Commission. "The clothing and footwear of exterminated prisoners were sorted there, and the best articles were sent to Germany. I myself in 1944 dispatched over 18 carloads of clothing and footwear to Germany . . . What I dispatched was only part of what was sent to Germany. Everything was sent to the address: Platzenses—Berlin, Straf-Anstalt."

Sometimes, in spite of the careful organization, errors occurred. In July 1942 these special instructions from Germany reached the Maidenak officials:

> *"SS—Central Commissary Administration. Chief of Administration D-concentration camps. D—1 AC:14 DZ. Oranienburg, July 11, 1942.*
>
> "To all commandants of concentration camps. According to a statement of the Central Administration of State Security, packages of clothing were sent from concentration camps chiefly to the Gestapo Administration in Bruenn, and on several occasions these articles had bullet holes in them or were stained with blood. Some of these packages were damaged, and thus outsiders were able to learn what the packages contained. Insofar as the Central Administration of State Security will shortly issue regulations concerning the disposal of articles left after the death of prisoners, immediately discontinue sending of articles pending final clarification of the question of the disposal of articles left after

the execution of prisoners. (Signed) Glicks, SS Brigade Commander and Major General of SS troops."

When Red Army troops entered the Maidenak Camp in 1944, they found 820,000 pairs of different types of footwear in one of the camp's warehouses. The shoes and boots had trademarks of firms in Paris, Vienna, Brussels, Warsaw, Trieste, Prague, Riga, Antwerp, Amsterdam, Kiev, Cracow, Lublin, Lvov and other cities in Russia and Western Europe.

"I have been in a wooden warehouse at the camp . . ." wrote the American correspondent, W. H. Lawrence, "in which I walked across literally tens of thousands of shoes spread across the floor like grain in a half-filled elevator."

Here is how Simonov described this warehouse:

> "It is hard to say exactly how many pairs of shoes there are here . . . There are so many that they overflow through the windows and the doors. In one place their weight has broken the wall and part of the wall has fallen out together with a mountain of shoes. There is footwear of all shades and descriptions: torn Russian soldiers' boots, Polish army boots, men's shoes, women's slippers, rubber overshoes, and most terrible of all, tens of thousands of children's shoes; sandals, boots and shoes worn by children of ten, eight, six, and even the booties of one-year-old infants. It is hard to imagine a more horrifying spectacle than this mute witness to the death of hundreds of thousands of men, women and children."

No one will ever know exactly how many human beings perished between 1941 and 1944 at the Maidenak Camp at Lublin. The statement of the Polish-Soviet Extraordinary Commission listed these as incomplete figures of the dead:

600,000 bodies burned in the crematorium furnaces
300,000 bodies burned on great bonfires in the Krempek forest
400,000 bodies burned by various means in the camp (not in the furnaces)
80,000 bodies burned in two old furnaces.

And Camp Maidenak was not the only, or even the largest, extermination center built by the Nazis . . .

On November 25, 1944, the United States War Refugee Board made public a detailed report on an extermination camp which the Nazis had built at Oswiecim in southwest Poland. The report of the War Refugee Board stated:

> "It is a fact beyond denial that the Germans have deliberately and systematically murdered millions of innocent civilians—Jews and Christians alike—all over Europe.
>
> "This campaign of terror and brutality, which is unprecedented in all history and which even now continues unabated, is part of the German plan to subjugate the free peoples of the world.
>
> "So revolting and diabolical are the German atrocities that the minds of civilized people find it difficult to believe that they have actually taken place. But the Governments of the United States and of other countries have evidence which clearly substantiates the facts."

From the evidence in its possession, the War Refugee Board gave the following figures on the nationalities of persons executed at the Nazi camp at Oswiecim:

Poland (transported by truck)	300,000
Poland (transported by train)	600,000
Holland	100,000
France	150,000
Germany	60,000
Belgium	50,000
Yugoslavia, Italy and Norway	50,000
Lithuania	50,000
Greece	45,000
Bohemia, Moravia and Austria	30,000
Slovakia	30,000
Camps for foreign Jews in Poland	300,000
Total	1,765,000

At the Sobibur concentration camp in Poland, eight to ten trainloads of victims arrived daily. Well over a million men, women and children were murdered at Sobibur between 1942 and 1944. . . .

The Death Camp in Tremblinka, Poland, specialized in the extermination of Jews. Here over a million Jews from Germany, Bulgaria, Armenia, Czechoslovakia, Russia and Poland were exterminated by shooting, gassing and other forms of execution. The American correspondent, Ralph Parker, reported on November 12, 1944, that at Tremblinka, "There was an experimental department with a staff of German doctors and psychologists working on 'problems arising from a mixture of Aryan and Jewish blood.' Here were sent Jewish women made pregnant by Germans."

Other factories for the wholesale extermination of human beings were constructed by the Germans in other parts of Soviet Russia and Poland, in Czechoslovakia and in France.*

This mass murder was not only a preparation for future wars; it was also big business for the German conquerors. Throughout 1942, 1943 and 1944 heavy freight trains rumbled toward the Death Camps, carrying human cargo jammed tightly into sealed cars. Returning from the camps the freight trains carried goods for delivery to Germany and other points; barrels filled with human fat for making soap; sacks of women's hair for the stuffing of mattresses; boxes of gold extracted from the teeth of the victims; cases filled with human ashes for sale to relatives of the dead; carloads of clothing, shoes, children's toys and similar articles for distribution and sale in Germany.

As the massive Soviet counter-offensives drove the *Wehrmacht* back from the territory it had occupied, the Nazi High Command made every effort to obliterate evidence of the colossal butchery of war prisoners and civilians. Battalions of slave

* When the Allied armies liberated France in 1944, they discovered a number of German factories of death. One of them was at Struthof, Alsace. On December 31, 1944, the documents section of the United States Seventh Army in France completed a study of records seized at the Struthof camp. These records showed that approximately 60,000 men and women had been herded into the camp between April 1941 and November 1944, and that at least 15,000 of these prisoners had been slaughtered.

Most of these victims were murdered in a gas chamber similar to those in other Nazi death camps. "The German custodians of the camp," stated Milton Bracker in a dispatch to the New York *Times,* "who were well protected from the stains and accidents of their work by an ample array of washbasins and fire extinguishers, officially labeled the chamber with the gas outlet as 'fumigation.'"

According to testimony given by three witnesses to officers of the American Seventh Army, this was one instance of the operation of the Struthof gas chamber:

> "At 9:30 on the night of August 10, 1943, the screams of eighty women, including sixteen-year-old girls, terrified all within hearing of the 'fumigation unit' . . . two German specialists had come to witness this mass killing as a test of new gases and the bodies were examined to chart their effects."

laborers were organized to dig up the buried bodies of their victims. The corpses were then systematically destroyed in great bonfires that burned for days on end. The remaining bones were crushed in machines specially constructed for this purpose, and the powdered bones and ashes were scattered across the fields.

In June 1943, for example, on the instructions of Gestapo chief Heinrich Himmler and Major General of SS Police Katzmann, special measures were taken to exhume and burn the bodies of civilians and war prisoners who had been tortured to death and shot in the Lvov Region. A special *Sonderkommando,* No. 1,005, consisting of 125 men, headed by Hauptsturmbannfuehrer Scherlak, was organized to carry out this work. Under the supervision of this *Sonderkommando,* the murdered civilians and war prisoners were extracted from the pits in which they had been buried; their corpses were then laid on platforms holding 1,200 to 1,600 bodies; tar and gasoline were poured on the bodies, which were then set ablaze. The ashes and remnants of bones were sifted in order to collect gold articles, such as gold teeth or rings and watches that the executioners had overlooked. According to the eyewitness testimony of several slave laborers, who later escaped, 110 kilograms of gold were sifted out of the ashes of the burned bodies for shipment to Germany. "The ashes were scattered on the fields or buried," records the Soviet Extraordinary State Committee; "large bones were collected separately and crushed in a bone-crusher which was specially designed to speed up the 'work.' "

The Germans fled from the Lvov Region in such haste that they failed to take with them or destroy their bone-crushing machine, and it fell into the hands of the Red Army.

According to the statement of the Extraordinary State Committee of the Soviet Union issued in December 1944:

> "To spread their experience in methods of exterminating people, burning bodies and covering up crimes, the Germans created in the Yanovska Camp, Lvov, a special school for 'skilled cadres.' To this school came camp commandants from Lublin, Warsaw, Cracow, and other towns. Right on the spot the Chief of Sonderkommando No. 1,005, Scherlak, taught commandants how to exhume bodies from the earth, how to stack them up, burn

them, sift the ashes, crush the bones, fill the pits and camouflage them by planting trees and shrubbery."

When advance Red Army units reached a German labor concentration camp of the Todt organization near Klooga, Estonia, in the fall of 1944 the troops were sickened by a smell of burning flesh which came from the surrounding forest. The Red Army men discovered in the forest four huge funeral pyres which were still smouldering. The pyres contained the bodies of some 3,000 men, women and children who had been butchered a short time before. Many of the victims, as an investigation subsequently established, had been intellectuals from Vilna, Riga and Tallinn. A number of them were Soviet prisoners of war.

According to the testimony of a Vilna attorney who had been among a small group of prisoners that managed to escape from the concentration camp, the Germans had ordered all prisoners from their barracks at 5 A.M. on September 19. Although the camp ordinarily produced concrete, the prisoners were told that morning to obtain a supply of wood. Each prisoner was ordered to bring one or more pine logs to a forest glade near the camp.

The Lithuanian attorney who escaped described to officers of the Red Army the scene that then took place:

"The Germans gave orders to place the logs on the grass in a row. After this was done the Germans counted a group of people corresponding to the number of logs and told them to lie down with their faces turned to the ground as close to one another as possible. After this, SS men shot these people with tommy-guns. The noise of the shooting could not muffle the screams of the people. One of them tried to run away, but a tommy-gunner shot him and brought him back to the logs.

"Then the Germans compelled a second group of people to place on dead bodies another row of logs and to lie down on these logs. Again they were shot by tommy-gunners. Thus it continued until there were four or five rows of corpses.

"Finishing with the first group, the SS men took a second one. By noon there already were four hills of dead bodies. Another supply of logs had been prepared, but the Germans were in a hurry. They poured gasoline on the corpses, set them afire and hurried to the barracks.

"The SS men drove those who still remained alive, including women and children, into the barracks, forced them to lie down on the floor and shot them. Then the barracks also were set afire. Several wounded men and women jumped out of the windows, but were immediately killed. Their bodies, in half-burned clothes, are still there in front of the barracks."

An English correspondent visited the terrible site of the pyre, accompanied by Jeremiah Ratner, a former Lithuanian prisoner in the Klooga Camp. With tears streaming down his face, Ratner pointed to three of the bodies. "Look, that's the body of my fifteen-year-old boy, Matthias," he said. "There's my wife and my sixteen-year-old daughter."

Then Jeremiah Ratner said to the English correspondent:

"Will people believe what you write of the things you've seen here? I know that the Russians will show no mercy to the criminals who burned my fifteen-year-old boy, but can we count on the people in Britain and America to show the same determination?"

CHAPTER EIGHT

PUNISHMENT FOR CRIME

> "If we are not tough and hard toward war criminals, we will encourage other tyrants to try the same thing—to murder, persecute and loot . . . Conviction and punishment of war criminals is not just a matter of revenge. It is justice."
>
> *Herbert Pell, former United States Minister to Hungary and Portugal, and American representative of the United Nations' War Crimes Commission.*

> "We are marching to Berlin, not for revenge, but for justice!"
>
> *Ilya Ehrenburg.*

I. *Anonymous Obstruction*

THE policy of the United Nations with regard to the punishment of war criminals is clear and unequivocal. The Moscow Declaration, issued jointly by Roosevelt, Churchill and Stalin on November 1, 1943, categorically states that all "German officers and men and members of the Nazi Party" responsible for the commission of "atrocities, massacres and executions" are to be apprehended, judged and punished by the United Nations. Subsequently, the historic Crimea Declaration reaffirmed this basic policy of United Nations' justice.

In January 1945, Under-Secretary of State Joseph E. Grew reiterated this policy on behalf of the United States Government:

> "Our position has been repeatedly stated by President Roosevelt, Secretary of State Stettinius and others. It is unchanged today. It is the policy of this Government that the Axis leaders and their henchmen who are guilty of war crimes shall be brought to the bar of justice. We in the Government have a definite program which, I can assure you, is comprehensive and forthright."

Under-Secretary Grew spoke forcibly. A forcible re-statement of the policy of punishment for war criminals was necessary in January 1945 because, ever since the Moscow Declaration, an insidious campaign had been afoot in Britain and the United States to obstruct this United Nations' policy and to save the chief war criminals of the Nazi and fascist states from paying the full penalty of their crimes. German agents and pro-Nazi elements in Europe and the Americas were spreading propaganda to the effect that "Bolshevik Russia, thirsting for bloody vengeance" was inciting the United Nations to the "un-Christian" policy of punishing war criminals. This propaganda was being echoed by certain appeasement and pacifist circles and promoted by a few highly-placed individuals who had special, personal reasons for opposing the trial and punishment of war criminals. Arguments against punishing the war criminals were widely circulated throughout Britain and the United States by newspapers which formerly had advocated the appeasement of Nazi Germany.

Moreover, certain European government officials became entangled in legal red tape and endless disputes about procedure when it came to trying and punishing the war criminals. All sorts of "problems" and pseudo-juridical "difficulties" were discovered. General Marcel de Baer, Belgian representative to the United Nations Commission for the Investigation of War Crimes in London, told foreign correspondents on January 3, 1944, that "while he was strongly in favor of the general principle of punishment for the guilty," nevertheless he could not see, for example, "how Rudolph Hess, once Hitler's righthand man and now a prisoner of the British, could possibly be brought to trial before the United Nations had made available the Berlin records which might prove his complicity in the crimes committed by the Nazis."

The first chairman of the London War Crimes Commission, Sir Cecil Hurst, resigned abruptly in January 1945, having struggled with legal hairsplitting for two years and having accomplished nothing. The official British explanation for his retirement was "ill health." Sir Cecil was more explicit. In his letter of resignation he stated that he was forced to resign because he had been unable to obtain any "satisfaction" from the British Foreign Office. He had offered numerous practical proposals for the trying and punishing of the leading war criminals, and all of them had been ignored or rejected.

In London, the man chiefly responsible for Sir Cecil's dilemma was the British Lord Chancellor John Simon, who was advising the Foreign Office on questions of war crimes procedure. Before the war, Lord Simon, then Sir John Simon, had been a prominent member of the notorious British appeasement circle, the so-called Cliveden Set.

A New York *Times* dispatch from London on January 11, 1945, reported that several members of the London War Crimes Commission believed "that Lord Simon, when asked to add Adolf Hitler, Benito Mussolini and other heads of States to the list of war criminals could not help being influenced by a desire to make his present consistent with his past as an appeaser of these men."

On January 15, 1945, another *Times* dispatch from London stated that "conservative politicians" feared trials of war criminals apparently because "in a regular trial their own past praise of fascism or endorsement of the Nazi leaders might be quoted."

Herbert Pell, the distinguished American representative to the London War Crimes Commission, who had consistently fought for the fulfillment of the Moscow Declaration and for the punishment of all war criminals regardless of rank, was abruptly withdrawn from the Commission on January 26, 1945. The reason given was that the United States Congress had "failed to appropriate the necessary funds for the continuation of Pell's services in London." The total amount involved to cover salaries and expenses of Pell's staff was only $30,000. Pell offered to carry on without any salary for himself. He was told that this would be "illegal." . . .

"Obviously," Pell told American newspapermen at a press conference in Washington a few days later, "the $30,000 is not a large sum and obviously my work on the Commission was not satisfactory to someone. . . ."

Pell added, "They know where I stand. I stand for hard, tough treatment of every war criminal. They know that I favor that Nazis be brought to trial for atrocities against their own Jewish citizens as well as for the atrocities against peoples in other countries."*

Both American and British official policy on punishment of war criminals remained clear and forthright. The war criminals were to be apprehended, tried and punished according to their deserts. But behind the scenes in both countries anonymous forces were seeking to obstruct this policy, to protect the leading war criminals and to so confuse and befuddle the issues that the tragic farce of Leipzig would again be perpetrated at the expense of the peoples of the world.

II. *Farce at Leipzig*

In 1914-1918, the German General Staff also employed mass terrorism as a weapon of war. At the outbreak of hostilities, Kaiser Wilhelm II wrote in a confidential letter to his ally, Emperor Franz Josef of Austro-Hungary:

> "My soul is torn; it is necessary to put everything to fire and blood; to slaughter men and women, the children and the aged; not to leave standing a tree or a house. By means of these measures of terrorism, the only ones capable of striking a people so degenerate as the French, we may finish the war before two months. If I respect humanitarian considerations, the war may be prolonged for several years. . . ."

The First World War was a "rehearsal" for the German General Staff. The Pan-German plan was tried out and the Pan-German policy of systematic devastation and frightfulness was tested in action by the Kaiser's Army. In 1911, the Pan-German Professor Otto Tannenberg demanded that the enemies of Germany should be left "nothing but their eyes to weep with." In 1918, as the Kaiser's Army withdrew from northern France and Belgium, all fruit trees were methodically sawed within a meter of the ground by the retreating German troops; coal mines were blown up and filled with water; entire factories

* As this book goes to press, it was reported that Herbert Pell was being reinstated in his post on the War Crimes Commission.

and thousands of heads of cattle were transported to Germany or ruthlessly destroyed. Officers of the Kaiser's Army, soon to become killers of the Freikorps, the Fehme and the Gestapo, massacred and tortured Allied prisoners, and committed innumerable acts of rapine, pillage and murder. These ruthless acts were not haphazard. They were according to plan. The German General Staff was methodically enfeebling and demoralizing French and Belgian manpower in preparation for the next war.

After the First World War, on January 25, 1919, the Allied Preliminary Peace Conference at Paris set up a Commission of Fifteen to investigate and report on German violations of international law during the period of hostilities.

The Commission's report might have been written today. Here is what the Commission had to say regarding the methods of warfare employed by the German General Staff in 1914-1918:

> "It is impossible to imagine a list of cases so diverse and so painful. Violations of the rights of combatants, of the rights of civilians, and of the rights of both, are multiplied in this list of the most cruel practices which primitive barbarism, aided by all the resources of modern science, could devise for the execution of a system of terrorism carefully planned and carried out to the end. Not even prisoners, or wounded, or women, or children have been respected by belligerents who deliberately sought to strike terror into every heart for the purpose of repressing all resistance.
>
> "Murders and massacres, tortures, shields formed of living human beings, collective penalties, the arrest and execution of hostages, the requisition of services for military purposes, the arbitrary destruction of public and private property, the aerial bombardment of open towns without there being any regular siege, the destruction of merchant ships without previous visit, and without any precaution for the safety of passengers and crew, the massacre of prisoners, attacks on hospital ships, the poisoning of springs and wells, outrages and profanations without regard for religion or the honor of human beings . . . the methodical and deliberate destruction of industries with no other object than to promote German economic supremacy after the war, constitute the most striking list of crimes that has ever been drawn up to the eternal shame of those who committed them."

At the Peace Conference in Paris in 1919 the Allied statesmen agreed on a Special Clause which was to be affixed to the final peace treaty with Germany. The clause called for the public indictment and arrest of Kaiser Wilhelm II as the supreme author of the war crimes of the German Army.

The first paragraph of this Special Clause read:

> "Wilhelm II is publicly arraigned for a supreme offense against international morality and the sanctity of Treaties. He will be tried by a special tribunal consisting or five judges, appointed by the Principal Allied and Associated Powers.
>
> "A request for his extradition will be addressed to the Netherland Government."

But the Kaiser was never extradited, never tried and never punished. He continued to live as a "romantic exile" on a private estate at Doorn in Holland, maintaining his secret connections with the German General Staff and aiding and financing Germany's secret rearmament. A few years later, the German Government made the exiled Kaiser a multi-millionaire by paying him enormous sums of money allegedly to "indemnify" him for the "loss of properties" which he had incurred as a result of his flight to Holland. By the early 1930's, the Kaiser was already in direct communication with Hitler and other Nazi leaders. When Hitler came to power, the Kaiser telegraphed his congratulations to the man who had "resurrected the German soul." . . .

The second paragraph of the Special Clause on the punishment of German war criminals which was agreed on at Paris in 1919 stated:

> "Persons accused of acts in violation of the laws and customs of war shall be brought before the military tribunals of the Allied and Associated Powers.
>
> "Germany undertakes to hand over the persons accused . . .
>
> "Germany undertakes to furnish all necessary documents and information."

A year later, early in 1920, a partial list of accused German war criminals was submitted by the Allies to the German Government. The list contained 896 names. Among the accused were Generals Hindenburg, Ludendorff, von Mackensen, von

Stuelpnagel, Prince Rupprecht of Bavaria, Duke Albrecht of Württemberg, ex-Chancellor von Bethman-Hollweg, and a number of German admirals, including Admiral von Tirpitz.

Not one of these leading German war criminals was ever brought to trial by the Allied Governments.

Instead of being made to answer for their crimes in the First World War, these men were permitted to go free and to carry on their secret preparations for a Second World War. . . .

In 1919, the new "democratic" German Government was "horrified" at the thought of being asked to hand over these leading members of the German General Staff to Allied justice.

"No German official would lend a hand in the arrest of a German in order to deliver him to the justice of the Entente," Baron von Lersner, the President of the German Peace Delegation, told Allied diplomats in Paris. "The mere proposal of an order of this kind would create such a storm of indignation that the entire peace structure would be gravely threatened."

The Baron waved the Bolshevik bogey under Allied noses. If the Allies insisted on the surrender of German war criminals, said the Baron, they might easily provoke "political and economic revolution" in Germany. . . .

Later, the Baron revealed in an article published in Germany in 1929 that one of his chief tasks as head of the German Peace Delegation had been "to initiate diplomatic steps which would prevent the surrender of our 'war criminals.' "

While Baron von Lersner initiated his "diplomatic steps" the German General Staff went to work on the homefront. Mass demonstrations were organized throughout Germany protesting against the surrender of German war criminals to the Allies. Militarists and clergymen, cabinet members and Freikorps leaders, professors and industrialists, Pan-German leaders, Social Democrats and Junkers joined voices in the indignant outcry.

Outside of Germany, German agents and other persons spread propaganda to the effect that the principle of punishment for war crimes, as stated by Wilson and the other Allied leaders in Paris in 1919, was "undemocratic" and "un-Christian."

Germany's Chancellor Scheidemann proposed a "compromise" to the Allied Governments. The German authorities would try the accused German war criminals in a German court.

"To this end," stated the German Government, "Germany would make all conceivable guarantees for the impartial and firm execution of the proceedings, especially through the assistance of official representatives of interested opposition states."

The German Government declared "its earnest will to punish Germans guilty of a war crime or misdemeanor."

Chancellor Scheidemann's ruse succeeded. The Allies agreed to submit the names of German war criminals for trial in German courts. Later, Baron von Lersner wrote:

> "This first great demand which the Entente Government imposed upon us by virtue of the *Diktat von Versailles* was shattered, like glass upon a stone, against the unity of the German people."

The Allies submitted a "test list" of 45 war criminals to be tried by the Germans. By various subterfuges, the German Government kept whittling the list down. One of the accused, Admiral von Kapelle, had fled to Switzerland. Another, Lieutenant-Commander Werner, had disappeared. It was "impossible to locate" other important culprits—among them U-boat Commander Patzig, who had ordered the sinking of the British hospital ship, *Llandovery Castle,* and the shelling of its lifeboats, which resulted in the killing of 234 of the wounded passengers. Further "difficulties" arose in obtaining certain vital evidence. With every week new "problems" developed.

When the trial of German war criminals finally opened two years after the war, on May 23, 1921, before the Criminal Senate of the Imperial Court of Justice of Germany, the "test list" of forty-five names submitted by the Allies had been reduced to twelve. With one exception, these twelve were insignificant underlings, about whose fate even the German General Staff was not particularly concerned. Yet even these criminals were not to pay the full penalty for their crimes. . . .

From the first day of the trials, the German War Crimes Court at Leipzig was converted by the German Government into an agency of anti-Allied and militarist propaganda for the German General Staff. The courtroom and the streets outside were packed with crowds of "nationalist" German army officers and civilian agitators. Feeling against the Allies ran so high that the British and French Mission had to be guarded by special police units against possible assault. As the trials proceeded, the German defense counsels made every effort to stimulate the audience's anti-Allied hatred and prejudices. When the court was forced to find any of the accused guilty of the crimes charged against them, members of the audience ran up to the convicted criminals to express their sympathies and indignation. When any of the accused were acquitted, loud cheers rang through the courtroom and echoed in the streets outside.

The first of the accused to be tried was Sergeant Karl Heyen. Overwhelming evidence showed that Sergeant Heyen had been guilty of the most atrocious acts of cruelty against Allied war prisoners who had been doing forced labor under his supervision at the Friedrich der Grosse coal mines in Herne, Westphalia.

On behalf of the German General Staff, General von Fransecky testified in defense of Sergeant Heyen's conduct. Elderly and urbane, the German General justified Heyen's conduct on the grounds that his brutal actions had been carried out "in the line of duty."

The court sentenced Heyen to ten months' imprisonment. Throughout Germany, Heyen was hailed as a "martyr" and a "national hero" persecuted by Allied vindictiveness. He served a few months of his sentence, and was then set free.

The next defendant was Captain Emil Mueller, a sadistic and mentally warped six-foot former German lawyer who had been responsible for incredible acts of wanton brutality while in charge of a German prison camp at Flavy-le-Martel. Under Mueller's vicious rule, hundreds of Allied prisoners had died in this camp from undernourishment and maltreatment. While the evidence against Captain Mueller was being read into the record, the defendant hid his face in his hands and burst into tears. Even the German Court declared of Mueller's conduct:

> "There has been an accumulation of offenses which show an almost habitually harsh and contemptuous, and even a frankly

brutal, treatment of prisoners entrusted to his care. His conduct has sometimes been unworthy of a human being."

Once again the German General Staff interceded on behalf of its underling. General von Fransecky and General von Kuhe informed the court that Captain Mueller's acts had been a matter of "military expediency." The court thereupon concluded that, although Mueller was unquestionably guilty of the atrocities with which he was charged, there were extenuating circumstances. The court stated:

> "It must be emphasized that the accused has not acted dishonorably; that is to say, his honor both as a citizen and as an officer remains untarnished. . . . He was over-excited. His excesses were only due to that military enthusiasm which worked him up to an exaggerated conception of military necessity and discipline."

For the sixteen offenses of which he was found guilty Captain Mueller was sentenced to a total of six months' imprisonment. . . .

The farce of Leipzig proceeded. The third defendant to take the stand was Private Robert Neumann. Conclusive evidence and testimony were introduced to show that Neumann had repeatedly beaten and tortured Allied prisoners at the German prison camp where he was stationed during the war.

As soon as account of Neumann's brutal habits had been read into the record, General von Fransecky addressed the court. The General declared that he regarded Private Neumann as "a pattern of what a German soldier should be." He expressed regret that due to the demands of the front, German guards at prison camps had usually been most inadequate. "In this sad picture," said General von Fransecky, "Neumann is the one redeeming feature."

Private Robert Neumann was sentenced to six months' imprisonment.*

Through June and July, 1921, the farce at Leipzig dragged on. Day by day the German Judges solemnly pored over piles of incriminating documentary evidence, attentively listened to

* As in the other cases, this sentence was inclusive of the time the prisoner had already spent in custody. Since Neumann, for example, had been under arrest for four months, he had only two more months to serve.

the damning testimony of eyewitnesses and the admissions of the accused, and then proceeded to compose verbose records exonerating the accused whenever possible, and, when there was no denying their guilt, to hand down ludicrously lenient sentences.

In the case of the U-boat officer, Lieutenant-Captain Karl Neumann, who admitted sinking the British hospital ship *Dover Castle* but said he was "acting under orders," the court reached this conclusion:

> "The accused . . . sank the *Dover Castle* in obedience to a service order of his highest superiors, an order which he considered to be binding. He cannot, therefore, be punished for his conduct."

The most sensational case at Leipzig involved Lieutenant-General Karl Stenger and his former aide, Major Benno Crusius. As Commander of the 58th Infantry Brigade, General Stenger had issued the following orders to members of his staff on August 26, 1914:

> "Beginning with today, no more prisoners will be taken. All prisoners, whether wounded or not, are to be killed;
>
> "All prisoners will be massacred; the wounded whether armed or not, are to be massacred; even men captured in large or organized units are to be massacred. No enemy must remain alive behind us."

General Stenger told the court that he could not remember issuing the massacre order. His aide, Major Crusius, testified that he had passed on Stenger's order to his company. As a result, large numbers of Allied prisoners and wounded had been massacred.

The Leipzig court, after lengthy deliberations, found Major Crusius guilty of "homicide caused by negligence." The court stated that Major Crusius had not been "conscious of the illegality of such an order and therefore considered that he might pass on the order to his company, and indeed must do so." The court also declared that, at the time of the massacre, Major Crusius was "intensely excited and suffering from nervous complaints."

Major Crusius was sentenced to two years' imprisonment. After a period of detention under German "military supervision," Major Crusius was released.

General Stenger, the author of the massacre order, was found to have committed no offense by the Leipzig court and was acquitted.

The results of the Leipzig War Crimes Trials were as follows:

Number of accused in original Allied list	896
Number in "test list"	45
Number tried by Germans	12
Total number convicted	6

There were no more trials of the German war criminals of the First World War.

III. *Justice at Kharkov*

The leaders and peoples of the United Nations are determined that there shall be no repetition of the tragic farce of Leipzig. In spite of the flood of Nazi and appeasement propaganda against punishment of the war criminals, the whole free world applauded the action of punishment of German war criminals by the Soviet Government at Kharkov. Not being party to the protracted legal disputations and evasions obstructing the work of the London War Crimes Commission, the Soviet Government, which had previously set up its own war crimes commission, was free to act according to the spirit and letter of the Moscow Declaration.

An official Soviet pronouncement stated:

> "All mankind already is aware of the names and sanguinary crimes of the ringleaders of the criminal Hitlerite gang . . . The Soviet Government considers itself, as well as the governments of all states . . . obliged to regard severe punishment of these already unmasked ringleaders of the criminal Hitlerite gang as its urgent duty to innumerable widows and orphans, relatives and kin of those innocent people who have been brutally tortured to death and murdered on instructions of the criminals."

On December 15, 1943, shortly after the Red Army liberated Kharkov, three German army officers and one Russian traitor went on trial before the Military Tribunal of the Red Army. It was a history-making occasion. With this trial, the Soviet Government initiated the first prosecution of the war criminals of the Second World War to be undertaken by any of the United Nations.

The accused at the Kharkov Trial were:

Captain Wilhelm Langheld, officer of the German Military Intelligence Service;

Untersturmfuehrer Hans Ritz, Deputy Commander of an SS company;

Senior Corporal Reinhard Retzlaff, official of the German Secret Field Police;

Mikhail Petrovitch Bulanov, a Russian traitor employed by the German Army during the occupation of Kharkov.

The Soviet Justice Major General A. N. Myasnikov presided over the court.

The three German officers and the Russian traitor were charged with having directly participated in the atrocities, executions and tortures by which 30,000 citizens of Kharkov, including aged women and children, had been exterminated by the Nazi German occupationists.

Without exception, each of the accused, while admitting participation in atrocities, pleaded that he had been acting "under orders" and was therefore not responsible for what he had done. This same plea had been the chief argument of the German war criminals at Leipzig . . .

At the Kharkov Trial, the first to take the stand was the German Intelligence officer, Captain Wilhelm Langheld. The Captain was fifty-two years old. He had a long, gaunt, clean-shaven face, thin lips, reddish hair and small eyes that blinked nervously at the crowded courtroom. He had fought in the German Army during the First World War, had joined the Nazi Party in 1933 and, before returning to army service, had held a post of prominence in the civil administration of Frankfort-on-the-Main. During the Second World War he had received three awards from the German High Command for exemplary conduct.

Captain Langheld's cold haughty demeanor belied the nervous twitching of his eyes. Under the questioning of the Soviet State Prosecutor, Colonel N. K. Dunayev, Langheld testified that on one occasion, he had been criticized by his superior officer, a Major Lulai, because there were too few executions of Russian soldiers in the prison camp at Kharkov where he was stationed. "I apologized," Langheld told the court, "and said that I had not been in the camp long and had not yet had an opportunity to show what I could do."

"*State Prosecutor:* But did you not attempt to prove to the Major that the prisoners of war had not committed any crime?

Langheld: I knew that no crimes had been committed and that there were no cases, but I took the Major's remarks as an order to manufacture them; if there were no cases then I was to invent them. I ordered one of the most exhausted prisoners of war to be brought to me, thinking that I would easily succeed in receiving the necessary evidence from him.

State Prosecutor: That is, fictitious evidence?

Langheld: Yes, of course, fictitious evidence, obtained by fraud. When the prisoner was brought to me I asked him whether he knew who it was among the prisoners that was plotting to escape, and there and then I promised to provide him with better food. The prisoner firmly refused to mention any names, saying that he did not know of anybody plotting to escape. But since I was obliged to carry out the Major's orders, I ordered the prisoner to be thrown on the floor and I beat him with a stick until he was unconscious. Then I drew up a statement and punching the half-unconscious prisoner, I pulled him to his feet and tried to compel him to sign. Again he refused.

State Prosecutor: Who, in the end, signed the affidavit?

Langheld: The interpreter.

State Prosecutor: In that case, the affidavit was a forgery?

Langheld: Yes.

State Prosecutor: What was written in it?

Langheld: We wrote that twenty prisoners of war were plotting to escape. We chose the names quite arbitrarily. I simply took them from the camp list. Next day the affidavit was submitted to the Major, and he ordered all the men mentioned in it to be shot. This order was carried out."

In a dispassionate monotone, Captain Langheld then went

on to describe how, on another occasion, when six Ukrainian peasant women came to visit the prisoners, he arrested them and accused them of trying to establish communications between the prisoners and the partisans. One of the women had a five-year-old child with her. In an effort to obtain "confessions" from these six women, said Langheld, he had them stripped, thrown across a bench and beaten with sticks and ramrods. Despite the torture, the women refused to utter a word. They were beaten until they were unconscious.

"How did the woman with the child behave?" asked the State Prosecutor. "And how did the child behave?"

"At first," Langheld replied, "the child clung to its mother and cried but later it crept into a corner and cowered there in a terrible fright."

Five of the women were turned over to the Commandant by Langheld to be shot.

"But there were six women," the State Prosecutor said. "What happened to the sixth?"

Captain Langheld told the court that there had been no reason to mention the sixth woman in his report as she had died as a result of the beating. This woman was the one with the five-year-old child.

When the State Prosecutor asked what happened to the child, Langheld answered: "It clung to its dead mother, crying loudly. The Corporal who came to drag the mother's body out of the room got fed up with this and shot the child."

"Tell me, Langheld," said the Soviet prosecutor, "how many Soviet citizens did you kill yourself?"

The courtroom was silent as Langheld lifted his eyes to the ceiling and concentrated for a few moments. "I can't tell you the exact number," he said, "but I think it was not less than a hundred."

Finally, Langheld was asked how he explained the fact that he committed the crimes of which he admitted he was guilty. His answer was the same as that given by the German war criminals at the Leipzig Court:

"I carried out the orders of my superior," said Captain

Langheld. "Had I not done so I would have been court-martialed" . . .

Untersturmfuehrer Hans Ritz was the second of the accused to be examined. He had been Deputy Commander of an SS company in the Kharkov Region. Twenty-four years old, with a weak chinless face and cunning eyes, Ritz was a professor's son and a graduate of the University of Koenigsberg, where he studied law and music. He had joined the Hitler Youth in 1933, had held the post of President of the Court of Honor of the Hitler Youth in Posen, and in 1937 had become a member of the Nazi Party. Following his graduation from the university, he had practised law for two years in Posen before being called up for service in the German Army and dispatched to the Eastern Front.

Calmly and deliberately, with an impassive face, young Ritz told the court about his participation in mass executions of Russian men, women and children. He described how the Nazis had shot 3,000 citizens of Kharkov for enthusiastically welcoming the Red Army when the Russians had briefly recaptured the city the previous winter. During this wholesale execution, Ritz related, a Major Hanebitter had said to him, "Well, show me what you can do." Ritz told the court: "I, being a soldier and an officer, unable to refuse, borrowed a tommy-gun from one of the SS men and fired a round into the prisoners."

The Soviet prosecutor asked Ritz whether there had been women and children in the group. Ritz answered that there had been. He remembered one woman who tried to save her child's life by covering its body with hers. She failed, added Ritz, because the bullets "penetrated her body and the child's."

Throughout his testimony, Untersturmfuehrer Ritz stood erect, as if at attention.

"Now, you, Ritz," said the State Prosecutor, "are a man of higher legal education and evidently regard yourself as a man of culture, how could you not only look on but even take an active part in beating up and shooting absolutely innocent people; and not because you were compelled to, but of your own free will?"

Ritz's reply was automatic. "I had to carry out orders, because if I failed to carry out orders I would have been court-martialed and would certainly have been sentenced to death."

The third Nazi to be examined was Senior Corporal Reinhard Retzlaff, an official of the German Secret Field Police. Thirty-five years old, diminutive, and sullen-faced, Retzlaff had been the chief of the mailing department of a newspaper in Frankfort-on-the-Main before the war.

Under questioning, Retzlaff testified how, while participating in the executions at Kharkov, he had torn children from their mothers' arms and thrown them in the *gaswagen*. He told how he tortured Ukrainian peasants by jabbing them with needles and tearing out the hairs of their beards.

The President of the Court asked Retzlaff, "Do you admit that you systematically engaged in exterminating Soviet people?"

"Yes, I admit it," said Retzlaff, "although I did all this by order of my immediate superior."

The last of the accused to take the stand was Mikhail Petrovich Bulanov, the twenty-six-year-old Russian traitor who had served as a chauffeur for the Gestapo in Kharkov. Bulanov told the court how, in addition to driving the Nazi secret police about the city, he had also driven truckloads of Russian women and children to places where they were shot.

"What remuneration did you receive from the Germans for your treasonable activities?" asked the State Prosecutor.

"From the Germans," testified Bulanov, "I received a wage of 90 marks, or 900 rubles, also a soldier's ration. In addition, I got the leavings of the things the Germans took from the Soviet citizens who were shot, after sharing the best things among themselves."

"The Germans sent the best things to Germany, is that it?" asked the State Prosecutor.

"The Germans," said Bulanov, "sent the good things to Germany."

On the morning of December 18, Colonel N. K. Dunayev, the State Prosecutor, made his summing-up speech to the court. Colonel Dunayev concluded his address with these words:

"I appeal to you, citizen judges, and demand that you sternly punish these three despicable representatives of fascist Berlin and their despicable accomplice . . .

"Today they are answering for their crimes before a Soviet court, before our people and before the whole world, for crimes and atrocities whose magnitude and baseness far exceed anything inscribed in the blackest pages of human history, exceed the horrors of medievalism and barbarism.

"Tomorrow their superiors, the chiefs of the brigands who invaded our peaceful, happy land on which our people worked, reared their children and brought up their free state, will answer for their crimes. . . .

"In the name of law and justice, in the name of tens of thousands of tortured and martyred people, in the name of our entire people, I, as the State Prosecutor, ask you, citizen judges, to sentence all four despicable criminals to death by hanging."

After the State Prosecutor's speech, William Langheld, Hans Ritz, Reinhard Retzlaff and Mikhail Bulanov made their final pleas to the court. Each of them admitted his guilt but begged that his life be spared on the grounds that he had been only acting "under orders."

Captain Langheld said:

"I have nothing to add to my evidence. I ask you to take into consideration the fact that I am not the only one. The entire German Army is like that. I am not the only one who committed atrocities. I do not wish to minimize my guilt. I merely wish to point out that the profound cause of all the atrocities and crimes the Germans have committed in Russia must be traced to the German Government. . . . To question these [German] instructions or to fail to carry them out, meant signing one's own death warrant. I, too, was a victim of these orders and instructions. I ask you to take this into consideration. I also ask you to take into consideration my advanced age, and also the fact that during the preliminary investigation and at this trial I told the whole truth."

Untersturmfuehrer Ritz said:

"I do not wish you to gain the impression that I committed murder and atrocities because it gave me any pleasure or satisfaction. . . . The fact is I carried out orders. . . . I ask the Court to take into consideration the ancient principle of Roman Law—the commission of crime under duress. . . . I ask you also to take into consideration my upbringing. When the Hitler system came into force I was still a child; I was only thirteen years old. From that time onwards I was subjected to the continuous and systematic influence of the Hitler system, reared in the spirit of the myth of the supremacy of the Aryan race. . . . My character was systematically moulded by teachers like Hitler, Rosenberg and Himmler. . . ."

Senior Corporal Retzlaff said:

> "I want to emphasize that in every single case I acted on the orders of my immediate superiors. Had I failed to carry out these orders I would have been obliged to take the place of my victims. . . . Summing up all that I have said I ask that I be pardoned. . . ."

The Russian traitor Bulanov also pleaded he had acted under orders. He explained it was "under the threat of German arms" that his crimes were committed. "But citizen judges, one thing I beg of you," said Bulanov, "and that is that when passing sentence to spare my life, so that I may, in future, atone for my guilt towards my country!"

But the "under orders" trick, which had worked at Leipzig, did not work at Kharkov. The three German officers and the Russian traitor were found guilty of their crimes and sentenced to death by hanging.

The sentence was carried out on the morning of December 19, 1943, in Kharkov's great market square. It was the first public execution in Russia under the Soviet regime. Fifty thousand citizens of Kharkov packed the snow-covered cobbled square, which was surrounded by the ruined, windowless and gutted buildings of the desolate city.

At eleven o'clock a truck carrying the condemned men drove through the crowded square and stopped before the gallows. Shaken and pale, the four men had to be helped by Red Army guards onto the platforms on four trucks standing under the gallows. Bulanov almost collapsed as the noose was placed around his neck. The motors of the four trucks were started.

Major General Myasnikov, the President of the Military Tribunal, mounted a stand near the gallows and slowly and solemnly read the sentence of the court into a microphone. A loudspeaking system carried the General's voice throughout the square. The General commanded: "Lieutenant Colonel, carry out the sentence."

The four trucks sprang forward leaving the condemned men hanging.

A Red Army lieutenant standing in the square turned to Richard Lauterbach, the correspondent of *Life* magazine, and said: "Their names are Langheld, Ritz, and Retzlaff. But in our hearts it is Hitler, Himmler and Goering who are hanging there today."

Before Lauterbach could answer, an old Russian woman who had overheard the remark mumbled, walking away:

"Skoro Budyet"—"Soon, soon!"

PART III

CHAPTER NINE

GERMANY IN AMERICA

I. *The German Aim*

FOR generations, Germany's rulers have dreamed of the eventual Pan-German conquest of the United States. In 1904, Ernst Hasse, the president of the Pan-German League in Berlin, eagerly anticipated the day when "North America will be conquered by the German *Geist,* and the German Emperor will perhaps transfer his residence to New York."

The German General Staff has never imagined that it could conquer the United States by direct military attack as it has sought to do three times in France and twice in Russia since 1870. The military invasion of America was to be the culminating point and not the start of the German world strategy. The Pan-German plan for America called for gradual domination by slow stages and by generations of conspiracy, infiltration and propaganda, not only in the United States, but throughout the Western Hemisphere.

Colin Ross, the Pan-German "lecturer" who operated in the United States from 1912 until his exposure as a Nazi agent and subsequent flight in 1939, wrote in his book *Unser Amerika* (Our America): "I believe in America's German Hour . . . The great historical developments of the world usually prepare themselves below the surface until they suddenly break forth as apparent surprises."

Every activity calculated to increase German influence in America, weaken the United States Government and arouse antagonisms which would demoralize and disintegrate the unity of the American people has been systematically financed and encouraged by the German General Staff.

In 1914, the Pan-German professor Eduard Meyer, the Kaiser's adviser on American affairs, wrote in an official report to the German Government:

"Jealousy, envy and hatred prevail among Americans. This state of affairs can and must be utilized."

In 1933, this same professor Eduard Meyer became Nazi Rector of Berlin University and a leading official of the Nazi Propaganda Ministry's "American Bureau."

The first phase of German conspiracy in America involved the mobilization of millions of German and pro-German elements in the United States into a secret army under the direct supervision of the German General Staff. As far back as 1893, the Pan-German League in Berlin began recruiting German elements in America. A secret German terrorist society called the *Schlarrafia,* similar to the Fehme, was transplanted to American soil for the purpose of terrorizing German-Americans and making them subservient to the Pan-German purpose. Another secret German organization set up in America before the turn of the century was the Sons of Herman. Still another was the *Kriegerbund.* These societies, dedicated to maintaining obedience to Prussian militarism and fanatical loyalty to Germany's rulers, operated within the powerful German-American Alliance which by 1914 had a membership of nearly 2,000,000 and no less than 1,200 local *vereins* and *verbaende* throughout the United States.*

By means of systematic infiltration, Pan-German agents held positions of extraordinary influence in American business, politics, press and even government by the time the German General Staff was ready to make its first bid for Pan-German world hegemony. Woodrow Wilson revealed some of the facts concerning this Pan-German conspiracy in America in his War Message to Congress on April 2, 1917.

President Wilson informed Congress:

* It should be pointed out the majority of German-Americans are patriotic American citizens, and have resisted the efforts of Pan-German and Nazi agents to penetrate and dominate the German-American community.

"One of the things that have served to convince us that the Prussian autocracy was not and could never be our friend, is that from the very outset of the present war it has filled our unsuspecting communities and even our offices of Government with spies and set criminal intrigues everywhere afoot against our national unity and counsel, our peace within and without, our industries and our commerce.

"Indeed, it is now evident that its spies were here even before the war began; and it is unhappily not a matter of conjecture, but a fact proved in our courts of justice, that the intrigues which have come more than once perilously near to disturbing the peace and dislocating the industries of the country have been carried on at the instigation, with the support, and even under the personal direction of official agents of the Imperial Government. . . ."

During the First World War, the Pan-German network in America was directly utilized by the German General Staff for purposes of anti-Allied propaganda and military espionage and sabotage. The Kaiser's Government spent at least $40,000,000 on financing its special wartime espionage-sabotage rings in America. German agents under Captain von Rintelen of the Kaiser's Naval Intelligence blew up American factories, destroyed docks and sank ships. The German Military Intelligence agent Anton Dilger organized a sabotage band which roamed the Middle West, spreading disease germs and poisons among American cattle and crops. German economic agents under Dr. Heinrich Albert organized dummy corporations, bribed German-American businessmen and bought up vast quantities of essential raw materials in order to hamstring American war production. The German propaganda agent George Sylvester Viereck financed a syndicate of pro-German and anti-Allied newspapers, formed "peace societies," spread alarmist rumors and lies, and directed a nationwide agitation designed to keep America isolated while Germany conquered Europe.

Instead of ceasing with the end of the war, this secret German war on America flared into new intensity immediately after the Armistice. Krupp, Thyssen, Stinnes, Hugenberg and the other Pan-German industrialists converted their American branches and offices into centers of new German espionage and propaganda.

II. *Preparing for World War II*

The first Ambassador from the "new" Germany to the United States after the First World War was Dr. Otto Wiedfeldt, a Krupp agent. Before the war, Wiedfeldt had been commercial manager of the Krupp munitions works at Essen. At Krupp's request he was appointed Advisor to the Ministry of Transport at Tokyo. During the war years, Wiedfeldt served as Krupp's agent on the German General Staff and headed the German Ukraine Delegation which planned the Pan-German "colonization" of the Ukraine. In 1922, Wiedfeldt came to the United States as German Ambassador at Washington, and stayed until 1925. During this period, Krupp succeeded in negotiating two important American loans, which went towards financing the secret rearmament of the German General Staff. By 1926, Wiedfeldt was back at his old job as director of the firm of Krupp.

The second Ambassador from the "new" Germany to the United States was Baron Ago von Maltzan, the Pan-German Junker son of the owner of a feudal estate in Mecklenburg. . .

Under the diplomatic auspices of Wiedfeldt and von Maltzan, German postwar economic and political intrigue thrived in the United States. Cartels were formed and important Americans drawn into the German conspiracy. Already preparing for the Second World War, German statesmen, aristocrats and high army officers flocked to America to form "contacts," arouse sympathy for "poor Germany" and to promote anti-Soviet and anti-British sentiment in influential American circles.

On another level, the German conspiracy was being carried on by former spies and saboteurs of the Kaiser's underground army in America.

As early as 1923, the first official Nazi Party cells were formed in New York, Detroit, Chicago, Los Angeles and other American cities. The Swastika was introduced to American towns, and the racist anti-Semitic propaganda of Nazism began to be spread throughout the United States. Former Freikorps officers and other special agents of the German General Staff were sent from Germany to help organize the Nazi movement in America.

Here is a list of some of these German agents, who were sent into the United States in the years following the First World War when Germany, supposedly disarmed forever, was "at peace" with America:

Peter and Fritz Gissibl, two German brothers, veterans of World War I, who had taken part in Hitler's Munich *putsch,* came to the United States at the end of 1923. Directly after their arrival they founded in Chicago the National Socialist Society of Teutonia, the first American branch of the Nazi Party. In 1933 the name of this organization was changed to the Friends of New Germany, and in 1936 it became German-American Bund. In 1934, Fritz Gissibl, who was then head of the Friends of New Germany, returned to the Third Reich, where he became an important official in the Nazi Government. Peter Gissibl remained in the United States, became an American citizen and a national officer of the German-American Bund.

Dr. Friedrich Auhagen came to the United States in 1923. A veteran of the German Army and a graduate of the University of Goettingen and the Mining Academy at Clausthal, Auhagen obtained academic positions at a number of well-known American colleges. At the same time, Auhagen was secretly employed as an agent of the German Military Intelligence. After 1933 Auhagen made yearly visits to the Third Reich and carried out important espionage and propaganda assignments for the Nazis in the United States. In 1939 he founded the American Fellowship Forum, which propagandized against U. S. defense preparations. In 1941 he was sentenced to serve eight months to two years' imprisonment for failure to register as a paid agent of the German Government.

William Luedtke came to the United States in 1923, and became an American citizen in 1930. A skillful Nazi propagandist, he became Secretary of the German-American Bund and of the Nazi-directed German-American Business League. In 1942 he was sentenced to five years' imprisonment for having conspired to obstruct the Selective Service Act.

Fritz Streuer came to the United States in 1923. During the First World War, he served five years in the German Army. In 1931 he became an American citizen. He was a leading member of the German-American Bund and an organizer of its affiliate, the *Stahlhelm.* In 1942 he was sentenced to five years' imprisonment for conspiring to obstruct the Selective Service Act.

Dr. T. Ignatz Griebl came to the United States in 1924. During the First World War, Griebl was a First Lieutenant in the German artillery, and subsequently a member of a Freikorps operating in Pomerania. In America, Griebl obtained a degree at the Long Island Medical College and applied for American citizenship. He became a reserve officer on the rolls of the Medical Corps, United States Army, and established himself as a physician in the Yorkville section of New York. Griebl's Yorkville office was actually a center of German Military Intelligence activity. Spanknoebel, Rumrich and other German agents received their instructions and money from Griebl. In 1935, Griebl organized an espionage ring which operated in American aircraft plants, stealing blueprints and other confidential data and transmitting them to Germany. Griebl fled from the United States, on May 10, 1935, aboard the German liner *Bremen* after members of his espionage ring had been arrested by the FBI. American authorities tried to take Griebl off the ship at Cherbourg, but the proper papers were lacking and the captain of the *Bremen* refused to surrender the German spy. Griebl returned to Germany and was subsequently rewarded by the Nazi Government with a profitable medical practise in a fashionable section of Vienna shortly after Austria was invaded by Germany.

Dr. Otto Willumeit came to the United States in 1924. A German veteran of World War I, he played a leading role in the Nazi movement in the United States. After the formation of the German-American Bund, he became the head of its Chicago branch. In August 1942, Willumeit pleaded guilty to the charge of furnishing Germany and Japan with military information before Pearl Harbor and was sentenced to five years' imprisonment.

Fritz Kuhn came to the United States in 1927. During the First World War he had served with the German Army for four years. In 1919 he became a member of the terrorist *Epp Freikorps,* and later was active in the *Oberland Freikorps.* In 1921 he was convicted of theft in Munich and served a short jail sentence. In 1923, Kuhn, who was already working with the Nazi Party, left Germany and went to Mexico. Kuhn worked in Mexico as an "industrial chemist" from 1923 until 1927, when he came to the United States and went to work for the Ford Motor Company. In 1933 Kuhn became an American citizen. From the time of his arrival in the United States, Kuhn worked closely with Fritz Gissibl and the other Nazi leaders in America. In December 1935 Kuhn became head of the Friends of New Germany and, in

March 1936, Bundesfuehrer of the newly-formed German-American Bund. As one of the key organizers of German espionage, sabotage and propaganda activities in the United States, Kuhn frequently visited the Third Reich, where he conferred with top Nazi leaders, including Hitler. In December 1939 Kuhn was tried in a New York court on charges of stealing Bund funds, found guilty and sentenced to serve a four-year term in the penitentiary, and subsequently interned as a dangerous enemy alien.

Alfons Hambacher came to the United States in 1929. A German World War I veteran, he became head of the Bund storm-troop unit, the *Ordnungs Dienst.* In 1942 he was arrested and denaturalized by the Department of Justice.

Dr. Otto Heinrich Friedrich Vollbehr came to the United States in 1930, bringing with him a copy of the Gutenberg Bible and other incunabula, which he sold to the Library of Congress for a total of $1,500,000. (The collection became known at the Library as the Vollbehr Collection.) In 1931 Dr. Vollbehr, who had established temporary residence in Washington, D. C., began spending large sums of money on the distribution of Nazi propaganda in the United States. One of Dr. Vollbehr's propaganda projects was a pro-Nazi bulletin entitled *Memorandum* which he himself edited and sent to hundreds of prominent American politicians, businessmen and educators. Dr. Vollbehr worked closely with Colonel Edwin Emerson, Ignatz T. Griebl and other Nazi propaganda agents or spies in America. After Hitler's coming to power, Dr. Vollbehr made frequent trips to Germany. In 1939 Dr. Vollbehr made his final departure from the United States when he fled to Germany as FBI agents sought him in connection with a Nazi espionage case.

Walter H. Schellenberg came to the United States in 1932 as American representative of Ernst Bohle, chief of the Nazi *Auslands Organization.* A German army officer during the First World War, Schellenberg joined the von Brandis Freikorps which operated in Latvia in 1919. Subsequently he headed a Fehme unit of the Black Reichswehr which had its hideout in Prussia on the Junker estate of Baron von Dangen-Steinkeller. Schellenberg participated in the 1920 Kapp *putsch,* became a paid organizer of the Nazi S.A. and was later trained as an English-speaking agent of the Gestapo. His mission in America in 1932 was to organize German espionage and Nazi propaganda activities. Together with Dr. Albert Degener, secretary of the Board of Trade for German-American Commerce, which had its headquarters in New York, Schellenberg was one of the chief financial sources of Nazi and American fascist Fifth Column organizations in the United States between 1933 and 1941. Schellenberg made frequent trips during this period back to Germany for consultations with Bohle, Hess, Himmler and other Nazi leaders. In July 1941, a warrant for his arrest was sworn out by the United States immigration authorities; but Schellenberg evaded arrest by fleeing on July 15 aboard the liner *West Point* bound for Lisbon. Schellenberg's last public appearance in the United States was on March 22, 1941, in New York City. Reporters noted that Schellenberg was sitting on the platform in Madison Square Garden at a mass rally of the America First Committee. Schellenberg was seen applauding the speeches and waving a small American flag. In February 1945 the Soviet newspaper *Pravda* revealed that Schellenberg had been secretly appointed as one of the leaders of the underground apparatus the Nazis were setting up to operate after the war.

But these were only a few of the German agents who flocked into the United States after the First World War. There were others . . .

In August 1942, eight key German saboteurs who had been secretly landed on the American coast by submarines were tried before a special American military court. Six of them were sentenced to death; the other two received long prison terms. Investigation revealed that they had been sent into the United States equipped with quantities of high explosives, fire-pencils and other sabotage devices, as well as $174,000 in United States currency for paying off American accomplices, to organize widespread wrecking in war production centers throughout the country. All of them spoke fluent English and had previously lived in the United States. Their records showed that, with one exception, these agents of the German Military Intelligence had been originally sent for training in America long before Hitler came to power. Here are their records:

George John Dasch, alias Davis, originally arrived in the United States from Germany in 1922; married an American citizen; was recalled to Germany in 1941.

Herbert Haupt originally arrived in the United States in 1922; became an American citizen; worked in an optical plant in Chicago; was recalled to Germany in 1941.

Werner Thiel, alias John Thomas, originally arrived in the

United States in 1924; worked in Detroit automobile plants; was recalled to Germany in 1939.

Robert Quirin, alias Richard Quintas, originally arrived in the United States in 1927; worked as a mechanic in various parts of the country; was recalled to Germany in 1939.

Ernest Peter Burger, alias Peter Burger, originally arrived in the United States in 1927; became an American citizen; worked as a machinist in Milwaukee and Detroit; joined the Michigan National Guard; was recalled to Germany to supervise training of German sabotage and espionage agents for work in America just after Hitler seized power in 1933.

Edward John Kerling, alias Edward Kelly, originally arrived in the United States in 1929; secured a position with a New Jersey oil company; posed as an Irishman and supervised Nazi activities among Irish-American circles in New York and New Jersey; was recalled to Germany in 1936.

Herman Neubauer, alias Herman Nicholas, originally arrived in the United States in 1931; worked in Hartford and Chicago hotels; married an American citizen; was recalled to Germany in 1940.

Heinrich Harm Heinck, alias Henry Kanor, entered the United states illegally in 1936 as an agent of the German Military Intelligence; worked as a waiter in New York City; was recalled to Germany in 1939.

American authorities in 1945 were still tracking down contacts and accomplices of these eight saboteurs who might still be at large in various parts of the United States.

III. *The German-American Bund*

German agents operated in the United States before and after the outbreak of the Second World War with incredible impunity. The most notorious case was the German-American Bund. The American public is still largely unaware of the real significance of this organization, the purpose for which it was formed by the German Government, and the menace it constitutes to the future peace and security of the United States . . .

The German-American Bund was the American branch of the Nazi Party. Officially founded as an "American, Christian and anti-Communist" organization in 1936, the Bund had in fact been operating in the United States since 1923 under various different names, such as Friends of the Hitler Movement, Teutonia Society and Friends of New Germany. In the winter of 1935, the Nazi Government ordered its branch in the United States to adopt an "American" name and appearance and, on direct orders from Hitler's assistant, Rudolph Hess, it became the German-American Bund.

By 1939, when the Second World War began in Europe, seventy-one branches of the Bund were operating in New York, Chicago, Baltimore, Buffalo, Detroit, Pittsburgh, Milwaukee, Los Angeles, San Francisco and other important American cities. The Bund issued four newspapers in New York, Chicago, Philadelphia and Los Angeles. Each had the same title *Deutscher Weckruf und Beobachter* which was subsequently changed to *The Free American.* Government investigation established that the Bund's yearly expenses for its public activities amounted to not less than $1,000,000. The Bund membership and that of its affiliates at its peak was estimated at 200,000. At least 25,000 active, trained Nazis who had become naturalized Americans constituted the chief permanent Bund cadres.

These men held jobs in American defense plants, on railroads and steamship lines, in hotels, newspaper offices and banks. Each Bund member had to pledge unequivocal allegiance to Adolf Hitler and Nazi Germany. The leaders were taken back to Germany and received by German Intelligence officers and Nazi Party officials. The West Coast Bund leader Hermann Schwinn was summoned to Berlin to get special training at Dr. Goebbels' Propaganda Ministry. Other Bundists went to Germany to take courses at the SS and Military Intelligence espionage-sabotage schools in Berlin, Dresden and Hamburg.

Finances and instructions were passed to the Bund through the official German consulates in the United States. The Bund in Boston was financed by the German Consul Dr. Herbert Scholz, who was chief representative of Heinrich Himmler's SS Intelligence Division in America. The Bund in the New

York area was directly supervised by the German Vice-Consul Dr. Friedhelm Draeger who signed his orders to Bund leaders: *"Draeger: National Leader of the Nazi Party in America."* The Bund in New Orleans was financed by the German Consul Baron Edgard von Spiegel, former U-boat commander, Black Reichswehr leader and officer of the German Naval Intelligence. In San Francisco, the Bund got its orders and money from Baron Manfred von Killinger, the former Freikorps leader and Nazi terrorist who was German Consul General on the West Coast. Later, von Killinger was replaced by another former Freikorps leader, Captain Fritz Wiedemann. According to a report in the New York *Times* on February 20, 1941, Wiedemann was the chief paymaster for Bundist activities in the United States and paid out more than $5,000,000 to these German spies and propagandists.

From the outset, the Bund served as a recruiting agency for the German Military Intelligence. The Bund enlisted and trained hundreds of Nazi spies and saboteurs. In recent years, almost every major spy trial in the United States has involved members of the Bund. Besides recruiting and training Nazi spies in America, the Bund was also used as a means of smuggling important Nazi agents into the country after the war began, and enabling them to hide out and operate under false identities. Figures issued by the Federal Bureau of Investigation revealed that during the year 1940-41 the Bund was responsible for smuggling into the United States and protecting "at least 200 key Nazi agents."

The Bund also operated as a terrorist unit within the German-American community, beating, intimidating and silencing American citizens of German extraction who sought to halt the Nazi infiltration of German-American clubs and societies.

The old Pan-German ideology was not neglected by the Bund. The dream of eventual German domination of America was persistently fostered and furthered by expert Bund propagandists operating under directions of Ernst Bohle, chief of the *Auslands-Buro,* the new controlling agency which the Nazis set up in Stuttgart to supervise Pan-German activities throughout the world.

Here is a typical specimen of Bohle's Pan-German propaganda, first published in the official Nazi organ, *Stuttgarter NS Kurier,* on August 12, 1937, and subsequently distributed in German-American circles in the United States by the Bund propagandists:

> "We want to bring the Germans in the United States, who in part have become alienated from the German fatherland and from the German nation, back to the great community of blood and fate of all Germans. To this end the spiritual regeneration of the Germans after the model of the homeland is necessary. . . .
>
> "German-Americans, thus prepared, economically rejuvenated and politically active, shall then be used under our leadership in the coming struggle with Communism and Jewry *in the reconstruction of America!*"

The official 1937 *Yearbook* of the German-American Bund, circulated among thousands of Bund members in the United States, commented on the organization of German-American Bund "youth groups" as follows:

> ". . . the future of Germandom in America can no longer depend on new recruits from across the sea. It must find its own German future in its own land, and construct it out of its own youth. . . . Within the next few years the entire unified strength of Germandom will be necessary to check the shrinkage of the German population through the Americanization of its youth."

Bundesfuehrer Fritz Kuhn, in a speech published in the Bund organ *Deutscher Weckruf* in 1938, told his followers:

> "We must impel German politics with a pure German feeling. . . . Our task is the consolidation of all German racial groups and second, the acquisition of influence for a subsequent show of power in American politics. This second part is most important. . . . Our battlefield is right here, and here is where we must fight it out."

From 1923 until 1942, the German-American Bund was permitted to operate in the United States almost without any interference whatsoever from the American authorities. Thousands of goosestepping, brown-shirted Bund Storm Troops, complete with swastika armbands, pistols, knuckledusters and rubber truncheons, staged public Nazi demonstrations in American cities, openly *heiling* Hitler and assailing American democracy and the Government of the United States.

Even more fantastic is the fact that this trained army of Nazi spies and propagandists continued functioning on American soil *for seven months after Nazi Germany had formally declared war on the United States!*

It was not until July 1942 that U. S. authorities finally got around to arresting twenty-nine of the top Bund leaders and began rounding up others on charges of conspiring to obstruct the Selective Service Act and concealing their Bund affiliations on Alien Registration forms. Several hundred of the many thousands of active Bundists were arrested and imprisoned or interned for the duration of the war.

"We intend to put the Bund out of business," announced United States Attorney Matthias Correa on July 7, 1942.

The Bund as an organization went underground; but not out of business.

In November 1944, Harry Wohl, a staff writer of the St. Louis *Star Times* interviewed a former Bundsman in Chicago named Homer Maerz, who was currently active in a number of subversive organizations and was spreading violent Nazi racist propaganda throughout the midwestern states.

Formerly, Maerz had served as a liaison between the German-American Bund and the Silver Shirts, an American fascist organization founded by William Dudley Pelley who subsequently was imprisoned in the Federal penitentiary for his subversive activities. In 1939, Maerz came to Chicago to organize branches of the Silver Shirts and the *Deutsch-Amerikanische Einheitsfront,* an important Bund propaganda affiliate. At one of his mass Nazi rallies in Chicago, Maerz promised that America would be converted into such "a living hell for the Jews" that "Hitler will look like a cream puff." In October 1939, Maerz was arrested in Chicago, along with four of his followers. In line with the typical Nazi "propaganda by terror" strategy, Maerz had organized gangs to paint swastikas on Jewish stores, smash windows and stage similar Nazi anti-Semitic terrorist demonstrations. William Wernecke, the Nazi agent and Bund leader in Chicago, paid Maerz's bail. Maerz was found guilty of malicious mischief and sentenced on December 29, 1939, to serve one to ten years in the penitentiary. He was released from jail late in 1940, and immediately founded a new Nazi propaganda agency in Chicago called the Pioneer News Agency. In the fall of 1941, in a raid on Maerz' residence, congressional investigators found more than half a ton of "anti-Semitic, pro-fascist, pro-German and pro-Japanese literature," quantities of stickers reading "Gentile America" and "Long Live Lindbergh," and numerous pictures of Adolf Hitler.

Nevertheless, Maerz remained free.

In 1944, Maerz told the *Star Times* reporter who interviewed him in Chicago, that "the movement" had gone underground to some extent during the war, but it would break out again with "shocking force" the moment hostilities ceased.

"We may be under cover," said Maerz, "but we're never stopped. We're lining up now . . . You won't be able to call us Fascists or Nazis after the war. When the time comes, the big boys will show themselves as leaders. Some are big businessmen and industrialists."

In the spring of 1945, Homer Maerz, expert Nazi propagandist, former Bundsman, Silver Shirt organizer and ex-convict, was still at large and carrying on his work of undermining the foundations of American postwar security and peace.

There were many other Maerzes in America . . .

IV. *American Fascism*

In the years 1933-1941, German agents constructed in America an intricate, nationwide network of American fascist organizations, pro-Axis publications, anti-Semitic, anti-British, anti-Soviet and anti-Administration propaganda centers, military espionage and Nazi racist terrorist cells, which ramified through every level of American life.

The aim of the German agents was to build a mass "native American" Nazi-fascist movement which, as the Silver Shirt leader William Dudley Pelley wrote in 1933 in a letter to a

Nazi agent then active in New York, would be "American in character and personnel, and that shall work shoulder to shoulder with German aims and purposes."

By 1939, when Germany was ready to launch war in Europe, more than seven hundred and fifty American Nazi-fascist organizations had been organized in the United States under various patriotic and nationalist names. All of them cooperated with the German-American Bund or worked, in most cases, directly under the supervision of the Nazi espionage and propaganda leaders in Germany.

Here are a few of these American Nazi-fascist organizations:

American Christian Defenders
American Destiny Party
American Fascist Party
American Federation Against Communism
American Gentile Protective Association
American Nationalist Confederation
American White Guards
Christian Front
Christian Mobilizers
Christian Party
Crusaders for Americanism
Crusader White Shirts
Gentile Workers Party
Knights of the White Camellia
Militant Christian Patriots
National Gentile League
National Liberty Party
National Socialist Party of America
National Unity Party
National Workers League
Patriotic Research Bureau
The Phalanx
Protestant War Veterans
Silver Battalion
Silver Shirts
Social Republic Society of America
Yankee Freemen

These organizations had the finances to publish and regularly distribute hundreds of pro-Axis, anti-Semitic, anti-labor and anti-Administration newspapers, magazines, newsletters and books. They printed and circulated hundreds of millions of copies of Nazi leaflets inciting racial violence, advocating the overthrow of the United States Government and calling for the establishment of American fascism. At mass meetings and in secret conferences, on the radio and through the mails, in cities and throughout the rural areas, in factories, farms, schools and army training centers, they carried on a systematic, multiform, incessant campaign to divide and weaken the American people, to undermine their confidence in their Government, to sabotage their defense preparations, to isolate them from their allies abroad and to lay the groundwork, according to the plans of the German General Staff, for Nazi-fascist control of the United States.*

The American Nazi-fascist leaders enlisted supporters in business and political circles, and sought to gain a foothold in the United States Army. "We are following the pre-Hitler German pattern," wrote George E. Deatherage, head of the Nazi-fascist American Nationalist Confederation, in a private letter to one of his associates in 1938. ". . . Army officers are openly talking of the inevitable purge to come and the seed that has been planted in past years certainly is growing into a nation-wide crop."

Leaders of the organizations, or individual American pro-Nazi propagandists, were invited over to Germany to meet high officials of the German Government. The former Bund leader, Peter Gissibl, testified before a Washington Federal court in May 1944 that American anti-Semitic propagandists were in direct contact with Julius Streicher, the notorious Nazi anti-Semitic chief of Nuremberg. Gissibl named the two leading anti-Semitic propagandists in New York, Robert Edward Edmundson and Edward James Smythe, as having been in direct communication with Streicher.

* In addition to the "native American" fifth column organizations the Nazis set up dozens of similar fascist groups among Ukrainian, Spanish, Irish, Polish, Lithuanian, Armenian, Hungarian, Rumanian and other national minorities in the United States.

Donald Shea, leader of the pro-Nazi National Gentile League of Washington, D. C., regularly received from Germany packages of Nazi propaganda material and instructions for distribution in the United States.

Gerald B. Winrod, publisher of the pro-Nazi propaganda organ, *The Defender,* of Wichita, Kansas; Elizabeth Dilling, publisher of the pro-Nazi *Patriotic Research Bulletin* of Chicago, Illinois; and Lawrence Dennis, New York author of the book *The Coming American Fascism,* who was described by U. S. Department of Justice officials in 1944 as the "Alfred Rosenberg" of the American Nazi-fascist movement—all visited Germany, attended official Nazi gatherings, and consulted with high Nazi officials.

Other American agitators were financed by German agents and officials. William Baxter, head of the Nazi-fascist Social Republic Society of Los Angeles, California, was paid by the German agent Prince Zur Lippe, who was the liaison between American fifth columnists and Captain Fritz Wiedemann, German Consul General and Bund paymaster on the West Coast. Laura Ingalls, who organized anti-Semitic, anti-Administration and pro-Axis women's groups in the United States, was paid by Baron Ulrich von Gienanth, Secretary of the German Embassy in Washington. Frank B. Burch, an Akron lawyer who organized Nazi propaganda in the Middle West, was paid by Dr. Karl Kapp, German Consul at Cleveland, Ohio. . . .

Repeated attempts were made by Bund leaders and German agents to unify the myriad American Nazi-fascist organizations into a national American fascist political party, armed and prepared to take power by violence. Instructions to proceed along these lines were issued by Baron Manfred von Killinger, from the San Francisco German Consulate General, in 1937. Secret preparations were actually made for the launching of a fascist *putsch* against the Government of the United States. George E. Deatherage nominated the pro-Nazi Major General George Van Horn Moseley, retired, to be the national leader of the first American fascist revolution. The Nazi White Russian agent, Mrs. Fry, alias Paquita Shishmarova, wife of a former Czarist officer, served as liaison between the plotters and von Killinger. The plan called for the setting up of a General Staff of thirteen men. "The quotas I have set," wrote von Killinger, "are: three Germans (Nazi sympathy), three White Russians (anti-Soviet sympathy), three Italians (fascist sympathy), four Americans (Republican sympathy). All native-born or naturalized."

On July 28, 1938, in a letter to the Convention of the Nazi-fascist American Anti-Communist Federation, which was being held in the Bund's headquarters at the Deutsches Haus in Los Angeles, Frank W. Clark, head of the National Liberty Party, wrote that the *putsch* was to be carried in a series of steps. The first step was to be some act of provocation, such as the Nazis used in 1933 when they fired the Reichstag, which could be blamed on "the Jewish Communists." The second step would be "to establish a state of general CIVIL WAR." Finally, wrote Clark, "we will have cleaned up and cleaned out this thing we call government, having driven all enemies into the Pacific and Atlantic oceans—or else bury them here as we cannot deport them."

To create the mood of insecurity and demoralization in America, necessary as a prelude to the fascist *putsch*, German agents and their American accomplices began to make use of the same terrorist strategy with which Nazism had been promoted in Germany after 1918. Special "action squads," "phalanxes" and "guard units" of armed storm troopers were formed by the Bund, the Silver Shirts, the Christian Mobilizers and similar gangs. These squads assaulted Jewish citizens in the streets of New York, Boston, Philadelphia, Chicago and Los Angeles. They smashed Jewish store windows and painted swastikas on Jewish homes.

Many of the leaders and members of American Nazi-fascist *propagandamarsch* gangs were of the same type of human refuse, criminals and degenerates, which the German General Staff had exploited inside Germany to man its Fehmes and SS detachments.

Here are the records of five leaders of the Christian Mobilizers who terrorized New York City in the summer of 1939:

Edwin Westphal, member of the Advisory Board of the Christian Mobilizers and German-American Bund member: arrested for burglary, September 27, 1929; sentenced for burglary and grand larceny, second degree, December 13, 1929; convicted of being wayward minor and sentenced to New York State Reformatory, July 14, 1930; convicted of violation of New York Copyright Law, sentence suspended, February 17, 1937; convicted of disorderly conduct, sentenced to six months' probation, August 13, 1939.

Joseph Hartery, leading speaker for Christian Mobilizers: arrested under name of Joseph Herman, charged with offering or agreeing to receive two persons for purposes of prostitution, lewdness or assignation, pleaded guilty, sentenced to 30 days, January 7, 1932; discharged from work for attempting attack on fellow worker with an axe, December 21, 1934; arrested for threatening a man with a clasp knife and sentenced to 3 days in workhouse, December 14, 1938; arrested for defacing seats in a courtroom, sentence suspended, February 14, 1939; fined for violent statements made at street meeting, August 31, 1939.

John Zitter, Captain of Christian Mobilizers Guard Unit: arrested for burglary, admitted part in four other burglaries, sentence suspended and placed on probation for period of two years, December 4, 1934; served with court summons for inflammatory speech, August 26, 1939.

John J. Olivo, leading speaker for Christian Mobilizers, Assistant Captain of Christian Mobilizers Guard Unit, and responsible for training Mobilizers in drilling, rifle practice, jiu jitsu and general street fighting: committed to Reformatory School as delinquent after being arraigned for stealing an automobile, January 14, 1931; sentenced to penitentiary for attacking and raping a woman in Central Park, New York City, and fleeing with contents of her purse, December 10, 1934.

By 1940, almost all the Nazi-fascist organizations in the United States were directly or indirectly affiliated with the

Christian Front, the nationwide propaganda and terrorist movement founded and headed by the radio agitator Father Charles E. Coughlin of Royal Oak, Michigan. The Christian Front had some 200,000 members throughout the country, and many of them were secretly drilling with rifles, bombs and other military equipment at Bund camps and other Nazi training centers. The official organ of the Christian Front, *Social Justice,* which was not barred from the mails as seditious until 1942, weekly incited its thousands of readers to racist violence and regularly reprinted the inflammatory propaganda issued to America by Dr. Joseph Paul Goebbels, director of the Nazi Propaganda Ministry in Berlin.

On January 13, 1940, the Federal Bureau of Investigation arrested seventeen New York members of the Christian Front. According to J. Edgar Hoover, these Frontists had planned "to knock off about a dozen Congressmen." Besides these assassination plots, the Frontists also planned to seize armories in New York City, steal guns and ammunition, and stage a violent anti-Administration revolution in cooperation with the German-American Bund, the Silver Shirts, the Mobilizers and several other similar organizations. In the course of its investigations, the FBI uncovered a number of secret Christian Front arsenals containing bombs, cordite, rifles, ammunition, powder and dynamite, including arms which had been stolen from arsenals of the National Guard. The seventeen arrested Frontists hailed Father Coughlin as their "leader."

There followed one of the strangest trials in the history of the American law courts. Although the defendants were shown to have plotted a fascist *putsch* and the assassination of American congressmen, although they had been caught redhanded with the weapons and explosives in their possession, and although they openly boasted of their pro-Nazi sympathies, these followers of Coughlin were acquitted by the Brooklyn court of the charge of conspiring against the United States Government and were set free.

One of the Christian Front defendants, Claus Gunther

Ernecke, had committed suicide in his cell before the verdict of acquittal was handed down. He had been proven to be a Nazi agent.

V. *After Pearl Harbor*

On December 6, 1942, Attorney General Biddle released to the press a sixteen-page mimeographed statement summarizing the work of the Department of Justice during America's first year of war. Attorney General Biddle stated: "The Department of Justice has virtually put an end to organized sedition in the United States."

But during the war years 1941-1945 scores of organizations continued to spread the anti-United Nations, anti-war, anti-Negro, anti-Semitic, anti-Administration propaganda originally inspired by the German agents at work in America before the war.

Here are a few of the "nationalist" publications which, in the spring of 1945, still continued to flood the country with disruptive racist propaganda and demoralizing attacks on America's allies and war leadership:

Publication	*Editor*	*Locality*
The Broom	C. Leon De Aryan	San Diego, Calif.
Women's Voice	Lyrl Clark Van Hyning	Chicago, Ill.
The Cross and the Flag	Gerald L. K. Smith	Detroit, Mich.
The Defender	Gerald B. Winrod	Wichita, Kan.
The X-Ray	Court Asher	Muncie, Ind.
America Preferred	Carl Mote	Indianapolis, Ind.
America Speaks	William Kullgren	Atascadero, Calif.
Patriotic Research Bulletin	Elizabeth Dilling	Chicago, Ill.
The Green Mountaineer	Frank A. Parker	New York City
Bible News Flashes	William W. Hearstrom	Minneapolis, Minn.
The Constitutionalist	Constitutional Government League	Seattle, Wash.
The Guildsman	Edward A. Koch	Germantown, Ill.
The Malist	Henry Sattler	Meriden, Conn.
National Defense	A. Hoppel	Arcadia, Calif.
Western Voice	Harvey Springer	Englewood, Colo.

In the summer of 1943, at a time when the United States was making an all-out effort in preparation for major offensives against Germany and Japan, American war production was suddenly disrupted by a series of race riots organized in key industrial centers throughout the country by Fifth Column propagandists and agitators.

In Mobile, Alabama, on May 25, 1943, sixteen thousand Negro workers were driven from their jobs in the Alabama Dry Dock and Shipbuilding Island Yard by hoodlums armed with clubs and pieces of chain. Many of the Negro war workers were seriously injured, along with the white workers who tried to protect them. Work at the vital shipyard was drastically interrupted for two days.

In Beaumont, Texas, in the second week of June 1943, armed bands stormed the Negro quarter, killed two men, injured scores, and wrecked shops and homes. War work throughout the city was seriously interrupted for several days.

Los Angeles, New York City, Philadelphia, Boston, Jersey City, Chicago and other war production centers were the scenes of violent outbursts incited by anti-Semitic propaganda. Jewish people were attacked in the streets by armed ruffians shouting Nazi slogans. Store windows, sidewalks and residences were smeared with anti-Semitic slanders and swastika signs. Jewish cemeteries were desecrated . . .

The most violent, terrifying and destructive of all the racist outbreaks, a dreadful anti-Negro pogrom, occurred in June 1943, in America's largest war production center, Detroit, Michigan. By the night of June 21, when martial law was declared in the city, the following destruction had been accomplished:

> Thirty six persons dead and more than a thousand injured;
> the loss of more than 1,000,000 man-hours of production;
> the total disruption of the life of the most important war production center in the United States;
> property damage estimated at hundreds of dollars.

Incalculable harm had been done to the national unity and morale of the United States.

Detroit, the city in which this calamity occurred, was the headquarters of the racist propagandists, Father Charles E. Coughlin and Gerald L. K. Smith. Both of these men were carrying on their inflammatory work at the time, Smith openly in the pages of his disruptive publication *The Cross and the Flag*, and Coughlin secretly through continued contact with former members of his Christian Front.

The most important Nazi-fascist organization openly functioning in Detroit at the time of the riot was the National Workers League headed by the former labor spy and Nazi-fascist agitator, Parker Sage. Through its publication, *The Nationalist Newsletter,* Sage's organization was carrying on an intensive campaign to stir up violence against Jews and Negroes in Detroit. Sage's associate, Garland L. Alderman, called for "terror, terror, terror" as the best way of spreading the Nazi-fascist doctrines in wartime America. In 1942, Sage and Alderman had been indicted by Federal authorities for their part in fomenting an anti-Negro riot at the Sojourner Truth Housing Project in Detroit. But they were never brought into court on these charges.

One of the leading members of Parker Sage's National Workers League was the Nazi agent, Dr. Fred W. Thomas, a well-to-do Detroit physician and German-American Bund member, who was convicted on espionage charges in 1944. Dr. Thomas had been financing Sage's organization. Another member of the organization, Mrs. Therese Behrens, a prominent Detroit social worker, was also convicted as a Nazi spy in 1944. Still another of Sage's associates, Max Stephen, who owned a restaurant in Detroit where secret Nazi meetings were held, was sentenced to life imprisonment in 1944 for trying to conceal an escaped Nazi prisoner.

Nevertheless, in June 1944, when the riot occurred, Parker Sage and his National Workers League were still openly operating in Detroit.

In January 1944, Parker Sage was indicted by the Department of Justice on charges of conspiring with agents of Nazi Germany against the Government of the United States.

In the spring of 1945, still not convicted, Parker Sage remained a free man in the United States.

CHAPTER TEN

IN THE NAME OF PEACE

> "In the United States we have many of our compatriots and even more friends among the citizens of the United States who are favorably disposed towards us. Many of the latter hold important positions in political and economic life."
>
> *From a speech delivered in Berlin in 1940 by Reich Minister Darré.*

> "The best you can do is to support America First."
>
> *Instructions of the Gestapo agent, Baron Ulrich von Gienanth, to Laura Ingalls, 1941, as revealed by the United States Department of Justice.*

I. *Peace Offensives*

DURING the crucial years immediately preceding the open Axis attack and declaration of war on the United States, a strange series of lavishly financed so-called "peace" organizations appeared one after the other on the American political scene. Some "peace" organizations were founded and financed by German agents, or maintained close connections with them; others were set up and financed by American isolationists.

Here are a few of the most important of the "peace" organizations which were formed in the United States during the years 1939-1941:

The American Fellowship Forum: organized in March 1939 by Dr. Friedrich Ernest Ferdinand Auhagen, former Professor of German Literature at Columbia University and secret agent of the German Military Intelligence. The Forum was financed mainly through funds received from Dr. G. Kurt Johannsen, Nazi paymaster in Hamburg, Germany, and from Dr. Ferdinand A. Kertess, an I.G.Farben economic agent and German spy in America, who was one of the incorporators of the Forum.

The Forum, which had its headquarters in New York City, specialized in spreading isolationist propaganda among prominent businessmen in the United States. The propaganda of the Forum was spread chiefly through its magazine, *Today's Challenge,* whose Editor was Dr. Auhagen and whose Associate Editor was the Nazi agent, George Sylvester Viereck. Contributors to the magazine included Lawrence Dennis, Wall Street "theoretician" of American fascism, indicted in 1944 on charges of conspiring with Nazi Germany against the U. S. Government; Senator Ernest Lundeen, some of whose isolationist congressional addresses were secretly written by Viereck; Representative Hamilton Fish, whose Washington office later became the headquarters of a Nazi propaganda ring organized by Viereck; William R. Castle, former Under-Secretary of State in the Hoover Administration, and behind-the-scenes advisor to appeasement groups in the United States; and Philip Johnson, the "foreign correspondent" of Father E. Coughlin's pro-Nazi *Social Justice.*

National Committee to Keep America Out of Foreign Wars: organized in the fall of 1939 by Representative Hamilton Fish of New York. Shortly after organizing the Committee, with headquarters in Washington, D. C., Congressman Fish traveled to Nazi Germany. In Germany, immediately prior to the outbreak of the war, Fish met with Joachim von Ribbentrop, the Foreign Minister of the Third Reich; Count Galeazzo Ciano, the Foreign Minister of Fascist Italy; and with other Axis leaders. In a private plane placed at his disposal by von Ribbentrop, the Congressman traveled about Europe urging the smaller nations to acceed to Germany's demands. In Berlin, Fish told American newspapermen, "Germany's claims are just."

As soon as Fish returned from Europe, the activity of his National Committee to Keep America Out of Foreign Wars was greatly intensified. Early in 1940, the Committee began mailing out, under Fish's congressional frank, tens of thousands of reprints of isolationist speeches and articles.

Citizen's Keep America Out of War Committee: organized in 1940 in Chicago by the well-known isolationist businessman Avery Brundage. In 1936 Brundage had served as Chairman of the Olympic Games when they were held under Nazi auspices in Berlin, despite international protests.

The Citizen's Keep America Out of War Committee spread quantities of anti-British and anti-Soviet propaganda and held mass meetings at which Charles E. Lindbergh and other isolationist leaders denounced America's aid to nations fighting the Axis. Rallies sponsored by Brundage's Committee were arranged in cooperation with a number of pro-Nazi German-American groups grouped together in the *Einheitsfront*.

Islands for War Debts Committee, also known as the *War Debts Defense Committee,* and the *Make Europe Pay War Debts Committee:* organized in 1940 in Washington, D. C., by the Nazi agent, George Sylvester Viereck. The chief purpose of the Islands for War Debts Committee was to get isolationist propaganda inserted in the Congressional Record and to mail throughout the country, under the congressional frank, mass quantities of reprints of this material in the Record. The Secretary-Treasurer of this Committee was Viereck's Washington aide, Prescott Dennett, who was indicted in 1944 on Federal charges of conspiring with Nazi Germany against the U. S. Government.

The Chairman of Viereck's Committee in Washington was isolationist Senator Ernest Lundeen. Honorary Chairman was Senator Robert Rice Reynolds, Chairman of the Senate Military Affairs Committee, and founder of an American "nationalist" organization called *The Vindicators.* The Vice-Chairman was isolationist Representative Martin L. Sweeney of Ohio.

The franked envelopes of the following Congressmen were utilized by Viereck's Committee in its distribution of material: Senators—D. Worth Clark, Rush D. Holt, E. C. Johnson, Gerald P. Nye, Robert R. Reynolds and Burton K. Wheeler; Representatives—Philip Bennett, Stephen Day, Henry Dworshak, Hamilton Fish, Clare E. Hoffman, Bartel Jonkman, Harold Knutson, James C. Oliver, Dewey Short, William Stratton, Martin L. Sweeney, Jacob Thorkelson, George Holden Tinkham, and John M. Vorys.

No Foreign Wars Committee: organized in Washington, D. C., in 1940 by Verne Marshall, a Mid-Western isolationist newspaper publisher. The Committee launched a campaign of mass meetings, nationwide radio hookups and barrages of printed propaganda—all devoted to "warning" Americans against the "deceptionists" who were allegedly trying to involve the United States in the war in Europe. Among those who played a prominent role in the activities of the Committee was Charles A. Lindbergh.

No Foreign Wars Committee received its chief financial backing from William Rhodes Davis, a millionaire oil operator with large investments in Nazi Germany, who was a confidante of Field Marshal Hermann Goering. Davis offered $100,000 to finance a nationwide isolationist advertising campaign by Marshall's Committee.

Most of these organizations spread the same sort of propaganda throughout the United States. Through nationwide radio hook-ups, mass-circulation newspapers, magazines, bulletins, newsletters, leaflets, street meetings, businessmen's conferences, mass rallies, and by organized whispering campaigns they assured the American people:

> that the Axis powers were fighting to free the world from Communism and to save Christianity, hence the United States should give no aid to the enemies of the Axis;
> that the United States was in no way menaced by the Axis armed forces or Fifth Columns; and that participation of the United States in the war was being deliberately planned by the Administration with the ultimate aim of promoting International Communism;
> that the United States defense program and Lend-Lease were nothing more than sinister devices by which a "power-mad" President was seeking to involve American manpower and resources in an unjust and senseless war;
> and that President Roosevelt and other Administration officials were deliberately deceiving the American people and were making commitments which involved surrender of American sovereignty to Moscow and to British Imperialism.

These and similar statements, spread throughout the United States by these "peace" organizations, were repetitions of the official Axis propaganda designed to sabotage American defenses, to demoralize and disunite the American people, and to leave America unprepared to meet the coming Axis attack. Not all of the prominent "peace" spokesmen who voiced these charges were conscious of their origin in the enemy propaganda bureaus; many were the unwitting tools, no less effective because of their irresponsible naiveté, of the Axis propaganda machine.*

By far the most important of all the "peace" organizations was the America First Committee, which made its appearance in the United States just one year after Germany had launched its

* For various reasons, including the inability of most Japanese agents to operate openly and directly in America, the Axis propaganda machine in the United States was chiefly directed and supervised by German agents. In the Philippines and throughout Asia, the Japanese agents directed and supervised Axis propaganda. Since 1933, Berlin and Tokyo carried on all espionage and propaganda operations in intimate collaboration under a secret agreement, later made public as the Anti-Comintern Axis.

Second World War, and after Germany had overrun Europe and conquered France, and was secretly preparing for its invasion and conquest of Soviet Russia. . . .

The America First Committee was founded in September 1940.* It was headed by the isolationist Chicago businessman General Robert E. Wood, who publicly stated that he was willing to hand Europe over to Hitler and, if necessary, all of South America "below the bulge." Other early America First leaders included: Henry Ford, who had accepted a medal from Hitler; Avery Brundage, former head of the Citizens Keep America Out of War Committee; Charles A. Lindbergh, who had accepted a medal from Hitler and who advocated cooperation with Germany in a war against Soviet Russia; Representative Hamilton Fish, whose Washington office had been used by George Sylvester Viereck as the headquarters of his Nazi propaganda ring; Representative Clare E. Hoffman, reprints of whose Congressional speeches, one of which was sub-titled *Roosevelt Is a Judas,* were widely distributed throughout the United States by pro-Nazis and American fascists; Senator Burton K. Wheeler, whose isolationist, anti-British and anti-Soviet speeches were circulated by Nazi agents; and Senator Gerald P. Nye, who subsequently excused Japan's attack on Pearl Harbor by saying it was "just what Britain planned for us."

As soon as it was formed, the America First Committee be-

* Early in November 1940 the Toronto *Financial Post,* reported that German industrialists had opened peace negotiations through certain business circles in the United States. On December 5, 1940, reports were current that the Portuguese dictator, Antonio Oliveira Salazar was serving as intermediary between German and Anglo-American circles interested in promoting a negotiated peace in the west.

On December 26, 1940, the America First Senator Burton K. Wheeler publicly demanded that President Roosevelt undertake peace negotiations with Nazi Germany.

President Roosevelt replied to the peace offensive on December 29, 1940. The President declared there could be "no appeasement of the Nazis" and went on to warn the American public: "There are also American citizens, many of them in high places, who, unwittingly in most cases, are aiding and abetting the work of these agents. I do not charge these American citizens with being foreign agents. But I do charge them with doing exactly the kind of work that the dictators want done in the United States."

came a vehicle of German political conspiracy in the United States. Behind the public façade of American isolationism, German agents directed entire local branches of the Committee and used it to spread Axis propaganda in the United States, on a hitherto unparalleled scale of intensity and effectiveness.

German agents and American Fifth Column propagandists received direct instructions to join the Committee.

"The America First Committee is truly American and truly patriotic!" announced the Nazi Propaganda Ministry in a special shortwave radio broadcast to the United States on January 22, 1941.

In May 1941, the *Deutscher Weckruf und Beobachter,* official organ of the German-American Bund, told Bund members: "Join the America First Committee and continue to bombard your representatives in Congress with letters and telegrams in protest against President Roosevelt's foreign policy."

The pro-Nazi Detroit priest, Charles E. Coughlin, instructed his Christian Front followers to support the America First Committee with *"the one grand objective of keeping this country out of the war."*

The leaders of the Silver Shirts, Ku Klux Klan, National Workers League, Christian Mobilizers and scores of other American pro-Nazi organizations issued similar instructions to their memberships.

Paid Axis agents assumed positions of leadership in the Committee. The Nazi agent, Laura Ingalls, became the Committee's leading woman spokesman, and organizer of its many women's affiliates. The Nazi agent, George Sylvester Viereck, provided the Committee with vast amounts of propaganda and worked closely with its Washington office. The Nazi agent Frank Burch founded and headed the America First chapter in Akron, Ohio. The Bund leader F. K. Ferenz became a key distributor of America First literature in California. The Nazi economic agent Werner C. von Clemm supported the Committee financially and served as a behind-the-scenes propaganda strategist for the Committee in New York. The Japanese agent Ralph

Townsend was a leading spokesman for the Committee and a member of the editorial boards of *Scribner's Commentator* and *The Herald,* the two chief propaganda organs of the Committee . . .

The aim of the German and Japanese agents in the America First Committee was to promote nationwide isolationist, anti-British and anti-Soviet sentiment in the United States, to prevent American aid to nations fighting the Axis, and to soften up America for the coming direct Axis attack.

In Philadelphia, on the evening of May 29, 1941, sixteen thousand America First members heard Charles A. Lindbergh denounce the President of the United States and demand "new policies" and "new leadership" in America. On the platform beside Lindbergh sat the isolationist Senator David I. Walsh and other America First spokesmen and officials, including the America First women leaders Kathleen Norris, Mrs. Bennett Champ Clark and Mrs. Burton K. Wheeler. Reporters noted that box seats and reserved sections of the meeting hall were packed with prominent German-American Bund leaders, Christian Fronters and the local representatives of the German Government. When Lindbergh denounced the President, the response of the audience was hysterical. Frantic applause was interspersed here and there with shrill cries, "What are we waiting for?" "Impeach Roosevelt!" "Are we going to let the Jews run this country?" In their excitement some members of the audience jumped up and gave the Nazi salute. Observers reported that the Philadelphia America First meeting had the mood and character of the hate-crazed mass Hitlerite rallies which preceded the Nazi triumph in Germany. . . .

In June 1941, the international Nazi peace offensive reached its spectacular climax when Hitler's deputy, Rudolph Hess, dropped by parachute in Scotland and told British officials, "Take me to the Duke of Hamilton. I have come to save humanity from Bolshevism."

That same month Nazi Germany invaded Soviet Russia and the decisive phase of the Second World War was begun.

In the United States, Charles A. Lindbergh informed his America First followers that "only the British, the Jews and the Roosevelt Administration" were interested in stopping the German enslavement of Europe and Russia. On October 30, 1941, Lindbergh told an America First mass rally in New York that he had long ago decided that Germany should be allowed to expand eastward or else there would be chaos and devastation in Europe. Lindbergh said:

> "By 1938 I had come to the conclusion that if a war occurred between Germany on the one side and England and France on the other it would result in either German victory or in a prostrate and devastated Europe. I therefore advocated that England and France . . . permit Germany to expand eastward into Russia without declaring war."

Two months later, with the Nazi *Wehrmacht* apparently on the verge of taking Moscow and smashing the Red Army, Germany's eastern partner, Japan, attacked Pearl Harbor. Japan, Germany and Italy declared war on the United States.

Twelve days after the attack on Pearl Harbor, the America First Committee was officially disbanded. A number of prominent isolationists repudiated their former stand and supported the United States Government in the war against Axis aggression. Other isolationists, equally prominent, temporarily went underground, to await a more favorable time for the reorganization of the America First movement. Still others were prepared to carry on in the open under new "nationalist" façades.

II. *America First Underground*

On December 17, 1941, ten days after the attack on Pearl Harbor, a secret gathering of America First leaders was held in New York City at the Beekman Place home of Edwin Sibley Webster, Wall Street broker and former Executive Director of the New York Chapter of the America First Committee. Webster's guests included Charles A. Lindbergh and other key America First national leaders. The purpose of the gathering was to decide the future of the America First Committee.

According to New York newspaper reporters who discovered and exposed the clandestine meeting, one of the chief speakers was Horace J. Haase, former Brooklyn America First leader. Haase told the other America First leaders:

> "It is obviously necessary for leaders of America First like [General Robert E.] Wood and Webster to keep quiet. But the organization should not be destroyed. I have never been in the limelight and I have nothing to lose. I can remain active in a quiet way. I should like to offer to keep the files. We must get ready for the next attack which must be made upon this Communist Administration. . . ."

Haase spoke of the day when the America First leaders would be able to come into the open again and head a new mass movement in the United States. "If and when that moment comes," said Haase, "I feel sure that our leaders, especially the Colonel [Lindbergh], will take the leadership and lead us to victory."

A few weeks later, Haase founded a new "peace" organization in New York called *Americans for Peace.*

In January 1943, Haase was arrested in New York by the Federal Bureau of Investigation on charges of draft evasion. At his examination, Haase told United States Commissioner Cotter: "The U. S. A. is fighting on the wrong side of the war, while the Germans and the Japanese are fighting on the right side."

Only a short time before he was arrested, Haase had been in touch with the former America First Senator Gerald P. Nye. On January 14, 1943, Senator Nye had written Haase expressing his regret that the America First Committee had been officially disbanded and asking Haase to see him when he came to Washington in the course of his propaganda and organizational work. "Of course," wrote Senator Nye to Haase, "if you are coming this way I shall want to see you. . . ."

Senator Nye was not the only former America First Congressman determined to continue the America First agitation for a negotiated peace with the Axis.

"War pursued to the bitter end is a bitter tragedy, and the sooner we can stop it the better," declared Representative Clare E. Hoffman, speaking at a Town Hall meeting on the air on August 12, 1943. Hoffman indirectly called for a negotiated peace.

Senator Robert Rice Reynolds, then Chairman of the Senate Military Affairs Committee, wrote in the July 1943 issue of his new "nationalist" publication, *The National Record:*

> "I was an isolationist. That not only applies to the past, however. I am now an isolationist, and I am a thousand times more isolationist today than I was before we became engaged in this war. But that is my privilege. However, I prefer to be referred to as an America Firster, or a Nationalist."

Senator Reynolds' words were promptly reprinted in *The Cross and the Flag,* a propaganda magazine which was soon to be named by the Department of Justice as an agency used in a conspiracy to undermine the morale of the United States armed forces. *The Cross and the Flag* was published in Detroit by ex-Silver Shirter No. 3223, Gerald L. K. Smith. In the spring of 1942 Smith's magazine featured letters of endorsement from Senator Reynolds and Senator Nye.*

In 1943, Gerald L. K. Smith founded a new "nationalist" political organization. It was called the America First Party. Its activity consisted in carrying on the America First campaign for a negotiated peace with the Axis powers, and spreading Nazi-like racist propaganda in the United States. After the Battle of Stalingrad, the "peace" line of Smith's America First Party was changed to agitation for an immediate soft peace for Nazi Germany and furious attacks against United Nations' postwar cooperation.

* Senator Reynolds' letter to ex-Silver Shirter Smith, which was written on March 23, 1942, read in part: "Let me congratulate you with my full heart upon your first edition [of *The Cross and the Flag*] . . . It is just the right size; it hits the bull's eye with every paragraph; it is straight from the shoulder; it is gotten up in a conservative manner; it should have its appeal; it speaks the truth."

On March 26, 1942, Senator Nye wrote to Smith regarding *The Cross and the Flag:* "It is excellently done!"

Two other congressmen endorsing Smith and his work in 1942 were Representatives Clare E. Hoffman and Roy Woodruff of Michigan.

The America First Party held a National Convention in Detroit in August 1944. One of the speakers at the Convention was Homer Maerz, the former Bundsman, Silver Shirter and ex-convict from Chicago. Maerz introduced the following Nazi resolution on the floor of the Convention:

> "Whereas America is confronted with an acute Jewish problem which seems destined to lead to bloodshed and strife as in the case of other nations where Jews have surreptitiously maneuvered to a dominant political, social and economic status . . .
>
> "Be it resolved, by the delegates here assembled that all Jews be deported to a later designated area or voluntarily leave American shores within five years to countries of their own choosing, and
>
> "Be it further resolved, that those Jews who elect to remain in America submit to sterilization, thus solving the American Jewish problem for all time."

A few months later, America First ideology was publicly endorsed by Captain J. M. Patterson, publisher and editor of the New York *Daily News.** On October 27, 1944, the *Daily News* stated in its leading editorial:

> "When World War II broke out, a group of Americans headed by Gen. Robert E. Wood, long regarded as a sterling citizen, organized an outfit called America First. Its object was to keep the United States out of the war; to save this country from a repetition of its World War I mishaps.
>
> "We had a dynamic President, however, who kept blowing bellicose blasts at Germany and prodding Japan. Eventually we were hurled into this war, and America First disbanded. Its name was taken by Gerald L. K. Smith and tacked to a political party which Smith runs from Detroit.
>
> "Ever since Wood got his original crowd together, international-minded writers and world-savers have tried to make 'America First' a term of shame. . . .
>
> "Mr. Roosevelt gave impetus to this drive when he went out to sea in August, 1941, conferred with Mr. Churchill, and came back with a thing called the Atlantic Charter. He followed this up with the phrase 'United Nations,' which he has been trying to sell ever since as something finer than the United States.

* After the Axis attack on the U. S., the N. Y. *Daily News,* together with the associate newspapers, Colonel Robert McCormick's Chicago *Tribune* and Cissie Patterson's Washington *Times-Herald,* continued without let-up to spread America First propaganda among millions of Americans.

"We don't subscribe to that doctrine. We're still for America first . . . and expect always to be for America first."

Gerald L. K. Smith's America First Party was only one of the innumerable organizations by which disruptive agitation was being carried on in the United States as the Second World War drew to its close in Europe and the German General Staff prepared for its Fifth Column battle against victory and lasting peace.

III. *Peace Now!*

In April 1940, a few days after the *Wehrmacht* moved into Norway, a lean, sallow-faced, twenty-eight-year-old Norwegian left Oslo with a passport issued by Nazi-controlled Norwegian authorities and traveled, via Japan, to the United States. The young Norwegian's name was John Albert Collett. He was the son of Emil von der Lippe Collett, a wealthy Norwegian manufacturer of vitamin concentrates. Ostensibly, he had come to America to take over the management of a branch of his father's concern at Ossining, New York.

Collett soon left his job at the Collett Corporation in Ossining. He began a mysterious odyssey into widely separated regions of the United States. The professed motive for these extensive travels was that he had now become a "student." Within a short time Collett visited a number of colleges in different parts of the country, including Swarthmore College in Pennsylvania, Black Mountain College in North Carolina, the University of Southern California and Pasadena Junior College in California. He stayed briefly at each institution and then moved on to the next.

After Collett's strange cross-country expedition he became associated in an organization with Dr. George W. Hartmann, Professor of educational psychology at Teachers College, Columbia University, and a former leading member of the Socialist Party. Dr. Hartmann was on leave from Columbia and teaching at Harvard University. During the years 1930-31, Dr. Hartmann was a student at Berlin and Leipzig in Germany.

By July 1943, Hartmann had become the head of an organization in New York City called the Peace Now Committee. Congressional investigators later revealed that the idea of the Peace Now Committee originated with John Collett.

The purpose of the Peace Now Committee was to bring about an immediate end to the war by a negotiated peace between the United States, Germany and Japan.

The Committee's program stated:

> "We must stimulate the people to urge a negotiated peace upon the government by all possible non-violent means—petitions and letters to Congress and the President, personal interviews with congressmen, delegations to Washington, letters to newspaper editors and public meetings, demonstrations . . ."

The Secretary of the Peace Now Committee and manager of its New York headquarters was a woman named Bessie Simons. In 1941, Miss Simons had been the office manager of the Washington Branch of the America First Committee. She had also been employed by the isolationist Representative Henry C. Dworshak, whose franking privilege had been made use of by George Sylvester Viereck's Nazi propaganda ring.

The propaganda disseminated by the Peace Now Committee urged that it would be a "mistake" for the United Nations to win the war; that peace negotiations should be promptly undertaken with the Axis powers; that the war should be settled "without victory"; and that continuation of the struggle against Axis aggression was purposeless. A newspaper report quoted one of the paid officials of the Committee as declaring that "we should work with fascist Germany and Japan as equals."

In the autumn of 1943 the Norwegian "student," John Collett, took a new field trip into the Middle West to help build the Peace Now movement on a national basis. From St. Louis, Missouri, Collett reported to Peace Now headquarters in New York City:

"Quite an encouraging place on the whole. The population is very largely of German descent which may account for it to some extent."

From Des Moines, Iowa, Collett reported that he had conferred with a resident of that city whom he described as "quite active with the Japanese . . ."

In Cincinnati, Ohio, on the evening of September 23, 1943, Collett was arrested on charges of disorderly and immoral conduct. Subsequently, Congressional investigators revealed that the New York office of the Peace Now Committee paid Collett's fine, and made a false entry in the financial books so there would be no record of the transaction. Nevertheless, the story began to get around. Collett quietly dropped out of the Peace Now Committee which he had founded. The movement itself was already a national phenomenon.

Branch offices of the Committee had been set up in Los Angeles, Chicago, Boston, Baltimore and Detroit. Anti-war leaflets, pamphlets and bulletins poured from these offices. Mass mailings of special form-letters were sent to prominent businessmen, politicians, radio news-commentators, editors, educators and clergymen.

A letter addressed to leading churchmen throughout the country, read:

> "This is a direct invitation to ask you in your high office, and those in authority in your denomination, to publicly request all followers of Christ under your banner at once to lay down their arms and cease supporting this war."

A letter sent to every member of Congress stated:

> "We do not think that the defense and safety of America require an attempt to invade and conquer either Germany or Japan."

These are typical excerpts from the Committee's leaflets:

> "World War I did not end in peace by consultation or agreement. It was a dictated peace, based on 'victory'; and out of this

> peace grew World War II. 'Victory' and a new super Versailles would bring World War III on us in a few years."
>
> "Japan was begged to attack us by the Chief Executive of the United States."
>
> "To fight a war is cheap patriotism worth less than 2 cents."

The leaders of the Peace Now Committee were in close touch with former heads of the America First Committee. The Committee's Secretary, Bessie Simons, traveled frequently to Washington, D. C., where she claimed she held private conferences with Senator Wheeler, Senator Nye and other congressmen who had been prominent America Firsters. Propaganda material of the Peace Now Committee was soon being incorporated in the *Congressional Record* by Representatives Clare E. Hoffman and Jeannette Rankin.

Describing one of her first visits to Washington in the autumn of 1943, Miss Simons reported in a letter to Dr. Hartmann:

> "I had a talk with Senator Wheeler. He is not too hopeful but certainly was not discouraging. Senator Nye told me General Wood was the one to head us up and said he was expecting him this week . . . I tried to see Senator Taft, but saw him for only a minute, so wrote him a note."

In the same letter Miss Simons spoke of the progress she was making with newspapers which had formerly promoted the cause of the America First Committee:

> ". . . I had a nice talk with John O'Donnell, columnist of the *Times-Herald* and the N. Y. *News*. He gave us half a column in both these papers on Monday. . . . John is a grand man, as fine, I believe, as ever worked on a newspaper . . .
>
> "Frank Waldrop was out of town most of the time but I managed to talk with him over the phone. He is gradually taking over the management of the *Times-Herald*. . . . He is with us and is a potent force."

Former friends of the German-American Bund, the Christian Front and other Fifth Column groups flocked into the Peace Now movement. "It's not up to us to check our volunteers for possible disloyal people," Miss Simons told newspapermen. She went on to say that the Committee welcomed former members of the German-American Bund providing they were "American citizens."

"He is either an old Bundist sympathizer or a Coughlinite," wrote Dr. Hartmann to Miss Simons on October 27, 1943, regarding one applicant for membership in the Peace Now Committee, "but I think there is some chance we can use his energies constructively."

Dr. Hartmann's letter continued:

> "His suggestion about the Steuben Society is good. This is an old-line German-American social club, named after Washington's Prussian drill-master. Its members were upper class well-to-do folks. . . . If you could get hold of its officer or membership list, there is a chance of some perfectly respectable contributions, since their members must all be native born of German origin."

In the same letter Dr. Hartmann made the following reference to Edward Holton James, who had been indicted in 1942 on charges of libelling the President of the United States:

> "I seem to recall this James fellow as one from this neighborhood (Concord, Boston, etc.) who had a run-in with the FBI last year. I wonder if he is out in Colorado because he was ordered out of the Eastern defense zone? At any rate, he's a live wire; we should keep in close contact with him."*

* On January 24, 1944, Walter Winchell, who had been the first to expose the Peace Now Committee, revealed that the following persons were cooperating with the Committee: Mrs. A. E. Barker, a former follower of the American Fellowship Forum, which was operated by the Nazi agent, Dr. Auhagen; Hannah Howes, a former friend of the Bund; Irene Fox, one-time associate of Joseph E. McWilliams, head of the pro-Nazi Christian Mobilizers; Milton Meyer, who told his draft board that he preferred "sitting this war out"; and Agnes Waters, pro-Nazi propagandist among America First women's groups.

In the winter of 1943 and the spring of 1944, series of mass meetings were held under the Committee's auspices in New York, Boston, Philadelphia and other cities. The featured speaker was usually Dr. Hartmann.

The wavy-haired, heavy-set professor from Harvard was a flamboyant spell-binding orator. "Germans and Japs are no better but also no worse than Americans and British," he told an enthusiastic audience in Carnegie Hall in New York City on December 30, 1943. "One of our main jobs is to show Americans that they can have either victory or peace. They cannot have both. To win the war is the surest way to lose the peace."

At a Peace Now meeting in Philadelphia early in 1944, the guest speaker, Dr. Albert Palmer, declared:

> "Japanese soldiers are not sadists. The Japanese are the cleanest, most polite people. If you had charge of the welfare of 60 million Japanese, you would also have said: 'We must dominate China.' "

From overseas came a highly appreciative comment on the work being carried on in the United States by the Peace Now Committee. Via shortwave radio to America on January 29, 1944, Tokyo broadcast:

> "The Peace Now movement presents the war in its true light to the people who have never taken the trouble to see for themselves how they are being treated by their government. No freak organization is the Peace Now movement for it is headed by one of America's greatest thinkers, George W. Hartmann. . . . Peace Now takes up the stand that the U. S. A. must in its own interest . . . abandon the use of force and work for a negotiated peace."

In October 1944, following announcements that official investigations were pending which would look into the financial background of the Peace Now Committee, the organization closed its offices and went out of business. Leaders in the movement continued their "peace" activities under the auspices of other organizations.

IV. *Women Against Victory*

Since the drafting of millions of men into the armed forces, women have played an increasingly important role in American political and economic affairs. This has also been true of American Fifth Column affairs. The German General Staff, frantically mustering its international underground forces for the postwar struggle to save its own power, is making every possible use of its *Frauenschaften,* or women's auxiliaries, in the United States.

On December 11, 1941, the day that Germany formally declared war on the United States, the America First women's organizer, Laura Ingalls, hurried to Washington to see Baron Ulrich von Gienanth, Secretary at the German Embassy, from whom she had been receiving her money and instructions as a Nazi agent. Laura Ingalls wanted the names of persons "who can continue our work in this country." A few weeks later she was arrested on charges of having failed to register as a paid agent of the Third Reich.*

The work which Laura Ingalls had begun as the organizer of women's propaganda groups in the United States was carried on by other persons.

A nationwide network of pro-Nazi women's groups, operating under various "peace" and America First slogans, was successfully organized in the United States and supplied with constant streams of propaganda by Elizabeth Dilling, Mrs. Agnes Waters, Mrs. Leslie Fry, Lois de Lafayette Washburn and other notorious professional pro-Nazi American women agitators. These women's groups called for immediate nego-

* Laura Ingalls was not the only Nazi woman agent engaged in organizing America First and other women's propaganda groups before the open Axis attack. Another agent was Jane Anderson, alias Marquesa de Cinfuegos, who conducted a nationwide lecture tour on behalf of Generalissimo Franco of Spain, got her Nazi-fascist propaganda material reprinted in American national magazines, and organized "peace" women's groups throughout the country. In 1941, Jane Anderson, an American citizen, showed up in Berlin as the official Nazi woman propagandist over the German shortwave radio. In 1943, the Department of Justice listed Jane Anderson as a traitor to the United States.

tiated peace with Germany and Japan, fomented national dissension and racist outbreaks, demanded the "impeachment" of President Roosevelt as a "traitor," and continuously assailed the United Nations. Most of these disruptive women's organizations were still active in 1945.

Early in 1944, two years after Germany declared open war on the United States, the Cleveland *Press* published a series of articles exposing the activities of a propaganda organization called the United Mothers which was active in the midwestern States.

The articles were written by Johanna Steinmetz, an undercover reporter for the *Press* who had been assigned to join the United Mothers of Cleveland.

Miss Steinmetz reported:

> "From the headquarters of the United Mothers here flows a steady stream of propaganda branded by the FBI as Nazi-inspired . . .
>
> "The organization devotes itself to creating race hatred, disunity among the American people and distrust of our Allies . . .
>
> "I attended their meetings and was given publications written by men charged by the FBI with 'conspiracy to aid in the establishment of the National Socialist (Nazi) form of government in the United States.'
>
> "They told me to circulate stories like the one that American officers in Sicily were 'Communists who have forced Sicilian girls to walk through the streets bare.' . . .
>
> "A separate peace between Germany and America was advocated. 'Let England and Russia fight their own war if they want to.' . . .
>
> ". . . The one purpose of the semi-monthly meetings of the United Mothers of America was to instil Nazi-like propaganda and rumors in the minds of its members."

The leaders of the United Mothers of Cleveland were still carrying on this disruptive propaganda campaign in the spring of 1945. . . .

Before the war, Mrs. Agnes Waters of Chicago aided in the organization of propaganda agencies within the women's auxiliaries of the America First Committee. In Chicago, on February 24, 1942, Mrs. Waters addressed a mass women's "peace" rally. "Traitors, Jews and Communists" controlled America, said Mrs. Waters. President Roosevelt was a "traitor" and should be "impeached." Mrs. Waters charged the President with "stripping our country of its defenses" and cried, "He ought to be killed!" Several women in the audience shouted "Let's do it!" In 1944, Mrs. Waters told Patricia Lochridge, Washington correspondent of the *Women's Home Companion,* "If we cannot get these traitors out of office by peaceful legal means we can resort to shooting them out! This would be easier than to fool with elections." Mrs. Waters went on, "Let us demand this war be stopped at once. Let's keep a clothesline handy in every little back yard to hang the traitors, or a gun!" In the spring of 1945, Mrs. Waters was still carrying on this agitation among America First women's "peace" groups throughout the country. . . .

In Detroit, in the spring of 1944, the America First women's group organizer and agitator, Beatrice Knowles, head of an organization called American Mothers, was mailing out inflammatory racist and anti-United Nations propaganda to a regular mailing list of 50,000 women. On February 25, 1945, Gerald L. K. Smith announced he was going to change the name of his America First Party to the Nationalist Party. As members of his "advisory committee," Smith listed the indicted propagandist Elizabeth Dilling; the America First women's group organizers Mrs. David Stanley and Mrs. Sue Braun of the United Mothers of America; and Harvey Springer, former associate of the indicted propagandist, Gerald B. Winrod. This committee, Smith announced, would organize a new campaign against "the Dumbarton Oaks proposals" and opposing United States participation in any United Nations' postwar peace enforcement activity. . . .

In Cincinnati, Ohio, an anti-Administration, anti-Semitic and anti-United Nations organization, called the Mothers of Sons Forum, was spreading its propaganda through the mails and reaching 65,000 women. . . .

In New York City, similar women's groups were operating. Before the war, in New York, Catherine Curtis, associate of the

Christian Front leader Father Charles E. Coughlin, headed the Women Investors of America. Her organization was referred to in the July 1942 Federal sedition indictment. She was also active as an officer of the National Legion of Mothers. In 1941, Laura Ingalls wrote Catherine Curtis, with whom she was intimately associated in America First agitation: "I have always known that the best way to keep the United States out of war was to pray for and aid a swift German victory . . . Visit me in my little chalet near Berchtesgaden."

Women's groups spreading the America First propaganda line throughout the United States in the spring of 1945 included:

Mothers of Sons Forum, Cincinnati, Ohio.
We, the Mothers, Mobilize for America, Inc., Chicago, Ill.
American Mothers, Detroit, Michigan
Loyal American Mothers, Flint, Michigan
National Blue Star Mothers of America, Philadelphia, Pa. (formerly Crusading Mothers of Philadelphia)
Mothers and Daughters of Pennsylvania, Philadelphia, Pa.
United Mothers, Cleveland, Ohio
Nebraska Women of America, Nebraska
American Women Against Communism, New York City
Legion of Mothers, Boston, Mass.
National Legion of Mothers, Philadelphia, Pa.
Mothers of Minnesota, Minnesota

The chief directing organization of all these disruptive women's groups was We, the Mothers, Mobilize for America, a national women's organization, with central offices in Chicago. Dilling, Washburn, Waters and other professional women agitators were collaborating with We, the Mothers and with its national director, Mrs. Lyrl Clark van Hyning, a middle-aged ex-school teacher. The propaganda techniques of We, the Mothers set the pattern for all of these women's groups.

We, the Mothers was originally organized in 1941, a few months before the open Axis attack. One of its first activities was to mail letters to the parents of the American sailors who were killed when the U. S. destroyer *Reuben James* was sunk off Newfoundland by a German submarine. The letters declared that the President of the United States and the Secretary of the Navy were "murderers" and concluded with these words:

> "We, the mothers of war age boys, beg you to place the blame for the death of your sons where it belongs, and not to be deceived by propaganda into blaming a foreign power. In the name of justice, we ask you to call to account the real murderers of your loved one, the men who violated the Constitution of the United States by sending him into the war zone. Ask our boys—ask all of us—to call to account the actual murderers and we will bless you and the country will call you blessed."

Shortly after the Axis war declaration against the United States, Mrs. van Hyning told a secret conference of women propagandists in Chicago: "Instead of having one national organization we want to have thousands of small 'block groups.' We can then send out telegrams and other messages to the person in charge of each group telling them what to do and when to do it."

In the summer of 1944 Mrs. van Hyning's organization, We, the Mothers, sponsored a Women's National Peace Conference in Chicago. The Conference was convened on June 13, and was attended by 125 women delegates from twenty different states. After conferring for two days in sessions held behind closed doors, the Conference adopted a Resolution which read:

> "Whereas the policy of the United States and Great Britain of 'unconditional surrender' is un-Christian, and will prove futile, resulting in unnecessarily great loss of life, and
>
> "Whereas the Atlantic conflict is now merely a struggle between Bolshevism and Nazism for the domination of Europe . . . and
>
> "Whereas it is only too apparent that Germany's desire for cessation of hostilities is being ignored by Churchill and Roosevelt, for the purpose of insuring the election of President Roosevelt for a fourth term
>
> "Therefore be it resolved, That the United States of America, through its Congress and State Department, transmit overtures for an immediate armistice in the Atlantic theatre of war, as a preliminary for a six months' 'cooling-off' period for all parties concerned."

The Resolution of the Women's National Peace Conference

also proposed that a "peace conference" should be held in the United States, and that the majority of the delegates to the peace conference should be "British, American and German army men."

On October 30, 1944, *Women's Voice,* the official organ of We, the Mothers, with a circulation of approximately 20,000, initiated an anti-Semitic propaganda campaign against Secretary of the Treasury Henry Morgenthau, who had called for strong postwar measures to prevent the resurgence of German militarism. *Women's Voice* declared:

> "Morgenthau's harsh terms to Germany have cost thousands of American lives . . .
>
> "Even a weak but courageous people will fight to the death against a savage and merciless foe . . .
>
> "Mothers of America, those are your sons which Mr. Morgenthau's ultimatum condemns.
>
> "This inhuman ultimatum only bears out what we said in October's *Women's Voice.* The Jews live by the code of an 'eye for an eye'; they believe in a God of vengeance . . ."*

On January 13, 1945, with the Red Army launching its great offensive against Berlin from the east, and with the Americans and British preparing to strike their all-out blows from the west, Mrs. van Hyning sent a letter to every member of the United States Congress declaring that American soldiers were dying only because of Soviet and British "power politics" and urging that they be immediately brought home.

"More important than victory," wrote Mrs. van Hyning in her letter to U. S. Congressmen, "is to stop that slaughter as soon as possible."

* Another article in the same issue of *Women's Voice* had this to say about buying U. S. war bonds: "$100 for $75—analyze that statement . . . You pay $75, you receive a bond, a mortgage on the future earnings of producers. The $75 will be spent for destruction—killing men, women and little children, destroying their homes, their small savings. The boys who live will have to pay you the money you loaned to prolong the war. Yes, they risked their lives, they violated the moral code 'Thou shalt not kill' to use the bombs which your $75 buys . . . The living boys will envy their comrades who died on the field. . . . Wars are for profits—the profit is in the bonds. No bonds—no profit . . ."

CHAPTER ELEVEN

LEIPZIG IN WASHINGTON

"It will always remain the best joke made by the democratic system that it provided its deadly enemies with the means of destroying it."

Dr. Paul Joseph Goebbels, Nazi Propaganda Minister

DURING the last quarter of a century the world has witnessed many fantastic farce-trials of the criminals bred in Germany's military-political underworld and of their international Fifth Column accomplices. In one court after another, in Europe and America, Germany's war criminals, terrorists, assassins, political conspirators, spies, saboteurs and foreign aides were able to make a mockery of the proceedings, to turn the courtrooms into public forums for their own propaganda, and then to get off scot-free or with ridiculously lenient sentences. In 1921, there was the Leipzig trial of the German military war criminals; in 1919-23 the trials of the officer Fehme murderers in Germany; in 1924, the Munich trial of Adolf Hitler and Erich Ludendorff; in 1938, the trial of the Nazi-fascist Cagoulard conspirators in Paris; in 1940, the trial of the Christian Front terrorists in New York. At each of these trials, and at many others, an evil guardian spirit seemed to be watching over the accused, protecting them from punishment and frustrating democratic justice.

To Americans concerned with the future peace and security of the United States, the most fantastic and alarming of all of these trials was the one which took place in the summer of 1944 in Washington, D. C. . . .

On November 3, 1941, a Washington Federal Grand Jury started holding hearings on seditious activities in the United

States. For six months the Grand Jury conducted a careful investigation, during which 670 witnesses were questioned and 6,800 pages of testimony compiled. On July 23, the Grand Jury indicted twenty-eight men and women on charges of conspiracy to provoke revolt and disloyalty among the United States armed forces. In January 1943 the indictment was revised and extended to include five more persons.

Among the men and women named in these Federal indictments were:

George Sylvester Viereck, the notorious Nazi propaganda agent, who was described by the Department of Justice as "the head and brains" of the Nazi propaganda machine in the United States and who was already serving one prison sentence for his Nazi activities in Washington, D. C.

William Dudley Pelley, former head of the Silver Shirts and one of the first Nazi agents among American fifth columnists.

Edward James Smythe, head of the Nazi-fascist Protestant War Veterans, who called Adolf Hitler "The Twentieth Century Messiah."

Elizabeth Dilling, head of the Nazi-fascist propaganda organization, Patriotic Research Bureau, authoress of the *Red Network,* and close collaborator with Nazi propaganda agencies in Germany.

Robert C. Noble, West Coast fascist leader, who declared four days after Pearl Harbor, "Japan has done a good job in the Pacific. . . . I believe this war is going to destroy America."

Ellis O. Jones, leader of the National Copperheads, who believed, "The Japanese have a right to Hawaii . . . I would rather be in this war on the side of Germany than of Great Britain."

Ralph Townsend, former leading spokesman and writer for the America First Committee, who was already serving one prison sentence for having secretly and illegally acted as a paid Japanese agent.

David J. Baxter, head of the terrorist Social Republic Society of America and recipient of funds from Nazi agents in America, who in 1942 issued this secret order to his followers: "Do not neglect your arsenals. Buy arms and keep them in a safe place where they are readily accessible."

George E. Deatherage, head of the Knights of the White Camellia and the American Nationalist Confederation, who was "American delegate" at the World Congress of Nazi propagandists held in Erfurt, Germany, in 1937-8 under the official sponsorship of the Nazi Government.

James True, leading American Nazi anti-Semitic propagandist, who boasted he was the inventor of a blackjack called the "kike-killer."

Colonel Eugene Sanctuary, an associate of the Nazi spy, Frederick Joubert Duquesne, and of the Nazi propaganda agent, Peter Stahrenberg, and one of the leading distributors of Nazi propaganda material in the United States.

In the two years following the handing down of those Federal indictments, there was another Grand Jury investigation connected with the same case, a third indictment, and a trial lasting six and a half months. Hundreds of new witnesses were heard, vast quantities of new evidence were accumulated, and thousands more pages of testimony compiled.

Yet by the spring of 1945—after three years of Government investigation and court procedure involving an expenditure conservatively estimated at $70,000, *not a single one of the persons accused of seditious conspiracy had been convicted on these charges.* A few had been sentenced to jail on other charges. The rest were still at large and, in America's fourth year of war, still carrying on the same type of activities for which they were indicted during America's first year of war.

The moment the Federal indictments were handed down in the summer of 1942, it became clear that there were powerful political forces in the United States which would go to almost any lengths to discredit the case of the U. S. Government. "The fact that Representatives Hoffman and Fish and Senators Taft and Wheeler have come to the aid of the defendants, now gives our personal friends something to go on," wrote the defendant Charles B. Hudson, editor of the pro-Nazi newsletter, *America In Danger,* in 1942.

The defendant E. J. Garner circulated a propaganda leaflet

expressing his personal appreciation of the support he and the other defendants were receiving from "Senator Taft and other good Americans."

With the United States engaged in a life-and-death struggle against Germany and Japan, American citizens witnessed the astounding spectacle of certain American politicians publicly coming to the support of notorious agitators who for a decade had been spreading German and Japanese propaganda, and who had done everything within their power to undermine the morale of the American people and sabotage their defense preparations.

"They are no more guilty of conspiracy than I am, having seemingly done nothing more than I and others of us here have done time and time again," Senator Gerald P. Nye declared on the floor of the Senate on January 14, 1943.

"However misguided they may have been," said Senator Burton K. Wheeler, "I cannot believe that some of them were guilty of a conspiracy to obstruct national defense or break down the morale of America." The Senator from Montana characterized the Federal Grand Jury investigation as "one of the most disgraceful proceedings that has ever been carried on in this country."

Senator Robert Taft wrote a letter to Attorney General Biddle stating, "I feel very strongly that the methods used by the Government in their Washington indictments present a real danger to the continuation of freedom in this country."*

Representative Hamilton Fish denounced the Government case as an "utterly preposterous" attempt on the part of the Department of Justice to indict "opponents of the Administration's foreign policy, or of President Roosevelt, or anti-New Dealers, anti-Communists or anti-Semites."

Representative Clare E. Hoffman sponsored a resolution in the House of Representatives to form a new congressional committee to investigate the Government's sedition case as

* The complete text of Senator Taft's letter to the Attorney General was included in a leaflet which the pro-Nazi propagandist Gerald B. Winrod distributed to solicit funds for his own defense.

part of a "conspiracy against Congress." In a letter to the Attorney General, Senator Wheeler supported the demand for an investigation of the Department of Justice on the grounds that it had resorted to "entrapment" in its indictment of the alleged seditionists. Representative Martin Dies announced that he intended to publish a report charging "Communist," "International" and "Liberal" organizations with having plotted a "purge and smear campaign" against congressional members, a part of which was the Federal indictment of the alleged seditionists. Dies demanded a special investigation of Walter Winchell and others who had been particularly instrumental in exposing the Fifth Column propagandists.

Most Congressmen who so vigorously defended the alleged seditionists had previously been connected with the America First Committee, which was listed in the Federal indictments as one of the agencies used in the conspiracy. Some permitted their franking privileges to be used by the propagandists named in the indictments. . . .

The New York *Daily News,* the Chicago *Tribune,* the Washington *Times-Herald* and the Hearst press widely publicized the campaign of the America First politicians against the Federal indictments. The *Times-Herald* reported that an unnamed "super-defamation organization" controlling a network of spies, was "the most powerful influence behind the conspiracy indictment." The Chicago *Tribune* openly defended the indicted propagandists as "patriotic" and "Christian" Americans. The Hearst press denounced the Federal indictments as part of a "Communist conspiracy."

On February 6, 1943, after months of this campaign of incessant slander, rumor, distortion and vilification, the Department of Justice announced that O. J. Rogge, former Chief of the Justice Department's Criminal Division, was replacing William P. Maloney as special Government prosecutor on the sedition case. Maloney had been the chief target of attack by the Fifth Column network and its supporters in the press and in politics.

Shortly after taking over the prosecution of the sedition case, O. John Rogge announced his intention of seeking a new indictment. In October 1944, after six months of investigation and preparatory work by Rogge and his staff, Attorney General Biddle reported that a "considerable amount of new evidence" had been uncovered directly linking the alleged seditionists with a "Nazi conspiracy in the U. S. A." That same month a new Washington Grand Jury was sworn in.

On January 3, 1944, the new Grand Jury handed down its indictment, the third of the sedition case. The indictment named twenty-two of the persons who had been accused in the former indictments and included eight new names. Eleven of those formerly indicted were left out of the new indictment.*

The indictment charged that the defendants had plotted "with each other and with officials of the government of the German Reich and leaders and members of the Nazi Party to undermine the loyalty, morale and discipline of the military and naval forces of the United States"; that they had conspired to overthrow the government of the United States and replace it with a National Socialist form of government; and that they had participated in "a systematic campaign of propaganda" organized by the Nazi Party and its leaders "to destroy democracy throughout the world."

A furious outcry went up in those same circles which had fought the sedition case since its inception. "The citizen who is not horrified and outraged by the Government's conduct,"

* The eight new persons indicted were: Joseph E. McWilliams, former head of the Christian Mobilizers; Lawrence Dennis, leading American fascist "theoretician"; Peter Hans von Stahrenberg, former head of the American National-Socialist Party; the National Workers League leaders, Parker Sage and Garland Alderman; and the Bund leaders, Gerhard Wilhelm Kunze, August Klapprott, and Ernest Frederick Elmhurst. The individuals dropped from the indictment were James Garner, Court Asher, C. Leon De Aryan, William Kullgren, Otto Brennerman, Dr. Donald McDaniel, Oscar Brumrach, Ralph Townsend, Hudson de Priest, William Griffin and Paquita de Shishmareff. The reported reason for the elimination of these individuals from the case was that there was inadequate evidence directly linking them with Nazi Germany.

declared an editorial in the Chicago *Tribune* on January 6, 1944 "may fancy himself a believer in liberty, but he's kidding himself . . . The mass indictment is itself an offense against liberty." A few days later the *Tribune* stated editorially, "They (the American people) will find among the things the defendants are accused of having said in pursuance of the alleged conspiracy statements the substance of which is held to be true by millions of people." The Washington *Times-Herald* featured this headline: "Sedition Case Framed by Pseudo G-Men." Senator Wheeler ridiculed the idea of "a bunch of crackpots" being involved in a "Nazi plot to overthrow our government," and declared that the "danger . . . of a fascist government eventuating in the United States . . . does not emanate from crackpots but from the trend of our government toward the supremacy of the executive branch." The defendant, Prescott Dennett, who had been uncovered directly linking the alleged seditionists Viereck, confidently told newspapermen that Senator Wheeler would "ruin the case," and boasted of the encouragement he claimed he had received from Senators Reynolds and Nye, and Representative Hoffman.

As the day of the trial approached, the alleged conspirators in Washington, D. C., seemed more and more like actors who had carefully rehearsed their parts at the trials at Leipzig and Munich. They displayed incredible boldness. Some swaggered about the Federal courtroom, issued defiant statements to the press, brazenly flaunted their anti-Semitic, pro-Nazi sentiments, and indulged in a series of clownish stunts and insolent provocations designed to belittle the whole proceedings and obstruct the conduct of the trial.

Mrs. Elizabeth Dilling appeared in the courtroom carrying a false nose and mustache and wearing a badge with the words, "I am a spy." Lois De Lafayette Washburn posed for newspaper photographers on the steps of the Federal courthouse giving the Nazi salute, and shouted at the reporters, "I am a fascist!" James L. Laughlin, counsel for James E. Smythe, declared he planned to summon Rear Admiral Husband E. Kimmel and Major General Walter C. Short as witnesses in the defense of his client. "If I am ever tried on this indictment," Joseph E. McWilliams declared in an anti-Semitic statement which was prominently featured in the Patterson-McCormick and Hearst press, "I will call as my first witness one of the five most powerful men in the world. His address has been for eleven years the White House, Washington. His name is Judge Samuel Rosenman!"

When the impaneling of the jury began on April 17, the defendants on trial promptly turned the Federal court into a forum for their anti-democratic propaganda. Some noisily protested against the seating of any juror who was Jewish. "I do not think that any juror who is of Semitic blood can fairly sit upon this case," declared J. Austin Latimer, counsel for James True and George Deatherage. Another of the defendants' attorneys violently objected to the seating of a juror who was employed by a firm whose president was a Jew. These were some of the questions asked prospective jurors on the insistence of defense counsels and defendants:

"What does Jew mean?"
"Do you think the Jews are an international people?"
"What is Zionism?"
"What does international bankers mean?"
"What is meant by Mongolian Jew?"

As the impaneling of the jury proceeded, the Washington courtroom was kept in a constant uproar by the endless disruptions of the thirty defendants and their battery of twenty-odd lawyers. Ellis O. Jones and Robert Noble had to be repeatedly forced into their seats by court marshals when they refused to obey Judge Edward C. Eicher's admonition that they sit down. Eugene Sanctuary's lawyer, Henry H. Klein, after being called to order several times for his violent anti-democratic outbursts, had to be forcibly ejected from the courtroom, as he struggled with three court marshals.* Dellmore

* During the court proceedings in Washington, the lawyer Henry Klein made public a letter he had sent to members of the House of Representatives, stating: "Why do you permit a self-convicted felon who is disqualified by statute to serve as President of the United States and as Commander-in-Chief of its Army and Navy?"

Lessard, counsel for Elizabeth Dilling, introduced a motion to bar Judge Eicher from the trial.* Another defense lawyer handed out leaflets in the courtroom entitled *Impeach Roosevelt!*

Day after day, tumult and disorder reigned in the courtroom as the defendants and their attorneys interrupted the proceedings with shouts of "Mass Moscow trial," "star chamber proceedings," "trial by dictatorship," and similar outcries and demonstrations. Whenever Judge Eicher would overrule one of the defense motions, some defendants would chant, "Railroad, railroad, toot, toot, toot . . ."

"They think they are going to run this as an orderly, routine trial," the former leader of the Christian Mobilizers, Joseph E. McWilliams, told a newspaperman. "Well, they are not!"

Delayed by constant defense motions, by the adept use of legal technicalities and countless disruptions, the selection of the jury dragged on through April. By the twenty-fifth of the month only five jurors had been seated. On April 26 there was an uproar in the court when the defendant Lois De LaFayette Washburn temporarily disappeared. On the following day the defendant James True suddenly became "sick" and failed to appear. On May 1, the deadline having passed for the selection of a jury from the April lists of veniremen, Judge Eicher was forced to dismiss all the prospective jurors and start the impaneling all over again.

When the trial finally started on May 17, one month after the impaneling of the jury had originally begun, the accused and some of their lawyers turned the courtroom into a complete bedlam. As the United States prosecutor Rogge delivered his opening address to the court, he was stopped every few minutes by boos, shouts, catcalls, whistles, spurious motions of objection, and other interruptions from defendants and some of the lawyers.

"The defendants talked in terms of blood baths and of blood

* The lawyer Dellmore Lessard had formerly been the Oregon State Chairman of the America First Committee. He had been forced from his America First post by a public scandal when the American Legion disclosed the fact that he had accepted funds for the America First Committee from the Nazi-controlled *Kyffhaeuserbund* (German War Veterans).

flowing in the streets," Rogge told the jury. "One defendant said that the pogroms in this country would make Hitler's look like a picnic."

"And maybe they still will!" shouted the defendant Garland Alderman, one of the former leaders of the Nazi-financed National Workers League.

Rogge went on:

> "The Government's evidence will show that the defendants were apt pupils of the Nazi method and took all assistance that they could get from Nazi leaders. The defendants were not revolutionists in the old sense that they carried bombs under long, black capes. They were revolutionists in a much more dangerous sense; more dangerous because their technique was new, because it was always hidden behind a smoke screen and because it flourished under the very democratic system which the defendants sought to destroy . . ."

Edward James Smythe suddenly sprang to his feet. "Does this court recognize the Constitution?" he shouted.

Lois De LaFayette Washburn also jumped up. Dramatically pointing to someone seated among the crowd in the audience, she screamed, "There's another government stooge! Throw him out!"

"Is this a Moscow Trial?" yelled Lawrence Dennis, the fascist "theorist" from Wall Street.

When a motion by one defense lawyer was turned down, a number of defense lawyers would jump up and make the same motion necessitating Judge Eicher's answering each in turn.

Albert Dilling, the lawyer husband of Elizabeth Dilling, set a keynote for the defense in his opening address to the court. "Organized Jewish policies appear to conflict with gentile Americanism," he said, and went on to picture the Government's case as a "Jewish conspiracy."

As the trial proceeded Judge Eicher was repeatedly compelled to fine James Laughlin, Ira Koehne, Maximilian St. George, each a defense lawyer, for contempt of court. Finally, in the second week of the trial, Judge Eicher was able to secure a semblance of order in the court by threatening to impose jail sentences for the provocation of any further disturbances in the court. After this warning, the disturbances took a slightly more subtle, "legal" form. During the testimony of the witness Hermann Rauschning, for example, there were 189 "objections" within four hours . . .

The trial dragged on through the summer and into the autumn of 1944. The government attorneys introduced witness after witness who testified that the most intimate relations had existed between certain defendants and Nazi organizations and representatives. Some of the defense attorneys and accused employed endless devices to obstruct the proceedings and to make them seem as ridiculous as possible. In November 1944 the St. Louis *Globe-Democrat* summed up the trial in an editorial entitled: "Reducing Justice to Absurdity. . . ."

On the evening of November 29, 1944, the sixty-five-year-old Judge Eicher died of a heart attack. One week later the defendants were asked whether they would be willing to continue the trial with another judge. Most said they would not.

On December 7, 1944, Federal Judge Proctor declared a mistrial. The Washington Trial was over. . . .

The chronology of its tortuous three-year progress speaks for itself:

Federal Grand Jury begins hearings	November 3, 1941
First Government indictment announced, naming 28 men and women, and listing 30 publications	July 23, 1942
Second Government indictment announced, naming 5 new individuals	January 4, 1943
O. John Rogge replaces William P. Maloney as Government prosecutor in case	February 8, 1943
Rogge announces Government will seek new indictment	March 18, 1943
New Grand Jury sworn in	October 27, 1943
Third indictment announced, naming 22 of persons formerly indicted and adding 8 new persons	January 3, 1944
Impaneling of Jury begins	April 17, 1944
Trial opens	May 17, 1944
Judge Edward C. Eicher dies	November 29, 1944
Mistrial declared	December 7, 1944

In the spring of 1945, there were rumors that new indictments would be handed down and new proceedings started. Meanwhile, the American Fifth Column had already reorganized its innumerable fronts and underground cells in preparation for intensified activity in the postwar years ahead.

CHAPTER TWELVE

WAR BY WORDS

I. *Stoerungskern*

IN October 1943, the United States Department of Justice, after extensive researches and investigations, made public a long list of political slogans and appeals by which German agents and their Fifth Column associates sought to influence American domestic and foreign politics. The chief slogans and appeals used by the Nazi propagandists in America have been these:

> "The United States is governed, not by the duly elected representatives of the people, but by a group of alien-minded persons opposed to American principles and ideals and seeking to overthrow the Constitution of the United States."
>
> "President Roosevelt is reprehensible, a warmonger, liar, unscrupulous, and a pawn of the Jews, Communists and Plutocrats."
>
> "President Roosevelt and Congress, through a surreptitious and illegal war program against the Axis powers sold out the United States and forced the Axis Powers to wage war upon us."
>
> "Our program of giving American arms and equipment to foreign nations results in United States military and naval forces being inadequately armed and equipped and in their being exposed to terrible slaughter."
>
> "An honorable and just peace could be brought about speedily were it not for the opposition of Communists, International Jewry, and war profiteers."

The purpose of these Nazi propaganda slogans and appeals was to convince the American people that they were being deceived, misled and betrayed by their own Government; that their two chief allies, Britain and Soviet Russia, were actually their enemies; and that the war against Germany and its Axis partners was an unjust and senseless war which should immediately be halted. The underlying Nazi motive was to weaken the fibre of American democracy and to split the United Nations.

This propaganda was disseminated not only by German agents in the United States. The official spokesman of the America First Committee, Charles E. Lindbergh, had informed the American people in 1941 that only "the British, the Jews and the Roosevelt Administration" had anything to profit from a war against Axis aggression. Similar statements were repeatedly broadcast by other prominent America First spokesmen and by the America First press. Through these irresponsible elements, Nazi propagandists actually succeeded in gaining political influence in American affairs.

Nothing illustrates this more remarkably than the Nazi propaganda campaign against the President of the United States, Franklin Delano Roosevelt. . . .

At an early date, the German psychological warfare experts in Berlin decided that the key political *Stoerungskern,* or storm center, in the United States was the violent opposition which President Roosevelt's New Deal Administration had aroused among the extreme reactionary and isolationist wings of the Republican and Democratic parties. Nazi Fifth Column political activity concentrated on exploiting and intensifying this opposition in an effort to convert it into an instrument of German conspiracy in America.

In 1936, Dr. Friedrich Schoenemann, an important secret Nazi agent, was assigned to get close to President Roosevelt, to study his background, note his personality and opinions, and to transmit a confidential report to the General Staff's Psychological Laboratory in Berlin. The report was to be used as a basis for Nazi propaganda in the United States.

In the guise of a foreign correspondent, Schoenemann contrived to get aboard the presidential train which took Roosevelt on his cross-country election campaign tour that year. From

Grafton in West Virginia, through Fairmont, Pittsburgh, Dubuque, Oelwein, Hayfield, Minneapolis, the German spy followed the President to Iowa, Nebraska, Wyoming and Colorado. Subsequently, Dr. Schoenemann wrote out a lengthy report for Berlin concerning the character of the President of the United States. The German spy advised Berlin that it was vitally necessary to the "future" and "security" of German power that Franklin Delano Roosevelt be removed from the political leadership of the United States.

"The democratic ideology," wrote Dr. Schoenemann, "is the core of that crusading mood which led to American intervention under President Wilson. Under President Roosevelt it again represents a danger of the first magnitude, threatening our security and our future."

That same year, just before the German invasion of Poland, the Nazi Propaganda Minister, Dr. Paul Joseph Goebbels, published a special series of articles in the Berlin press charging President Roosevelt with seeking to "betray" the American people into an unjust war against the Axis. President Roosevelt's foreign policy, stated Goebbels, was inspired by "Jews and Communists." Goebbels' articles were headlined: "ROOSEVELT'S SHAMEFUL TREASON!" Goebbels declared that the American people should "impeach" the President as a "traitor" to the United States.

The same cry was immediately taken up by the American propagandists.*

From 1939 to 1945, the attack against Franklin Delano Roose-

* In Detroit, Father Coughlin's *Social Justice* headlined: "IMPEACH ROOSEVELT." In Wichita, *Publicity* headlined: "SAVE AMERICA BY IMPEACHMENT NOW." In Omaha, Charles B. Hudson's pro-Nazi newsletter *America in Danger!* headlined: "IMPEACH FDR." Pelley's *Liberation* headlined: "Four Million Militant Women Getting Congress Aid for Roosevelt Impeachment!" Parker Sage's *Nationalist Newsletter* stated: "The answer . . . should be impeachment of our President!" Elizabeth Dilling's *Patriotic Research Bulletin,* Gerald B. Winrod's *The Defender,* William Baxter's *Social Republic Society Bulletin,* George E. Deatherage's *News Bulletin* and every other subversive publication in America called for the "impeachment" of President Roosevelt. Others lent a sinister undertone to this campaign by incessant incitements to acts of violence against the President.

velt was the dominant theme of Nazi political propaganda in the United States. With the aim of discrediting his leadership and undermining his influence with the American people, the innumerable American outlets of the Nazi propaganda machine poured forth an incessant stream of provocative rumors and poisonous slanders directed against Roosevelt's personal character, his wife, his children, his habits of life, and his domestic and foreign policies as President of the United States. No lie was too grandiose or too mean, no vilification too obscene, for the Nazi psychological warfare experts or their American accomplices.

This Nazi anti-Roosevelt agitation reached a peak during the crucial wartime presidential election campaign of 1944. Berlin gave the signal to unleash all forces in an effort to defeat Roosevelt, who, as the key American architect of the United Nations' postwar security structure, represented a deadly threat to the secret plans of the German General Staff. Large sums of money were made available through underground sources in America to enable German agents and American pro-Nazi agitators to spread the Nazi anti-Roosevelt propaganda charges across the length and breadth of the land. . . .

At the Washington Trial, in the summer of 1944, a newspaperman noticed the indicted pro-Nazi, anti-Semitic propagandist Victor Broenstrupp, alias "Count" Cherep-Spirodovich, copying a long list of names from an official trial record book. The list had been compiled by the American postal authorities and it recorded the names and addresses of 50,000 persons in the United States who had been receiving Nazi propaganda material directly from Germany through the mails. Broenstrupp told the newspaperman that these persons would make excellent recipients for the quantities of "anti-Roosevelt material" which he was currently sending out as part of the presidential election campaign.

"There are 50,000 names here—people we didn't know existed," said Broenstrupp. "They'll be excellent prospects for my anti-Roosevelt material. I'm getting the biggest anti-Semitic army in America. We're going to organize these people when we get out. And then we're going to drive the Jews into the Atlantic and the Mississippi!*

Throughout the summer and fall of 1944—momentous months in world history, when the western world's fate literally was being decided by the American, British and Soviet armies on the giant battlefields of Europe—the United States was being deluged with Nazi propaganda aimed at convincing the American people that their war was unjust and their leadership false and traitorous.

This propaganda was not only spread by German agents and subversive American agitators. The Nazi anti-Semitic and anti-Communist charges against the President of the United States were taken up and repeated as effective "campaign slogans" particularly by isolationist anti-Roosevelt politicians who, since the tragic, premature death of Wendell Willkie, were boldly seeking control of the Republican party machine.

Wittingly or unwittingly, these elements fostered the Fifth Column agitation. They publicly repeated the Nazi propaganda which accused President Roosevelt of being "a tool of the Communists and the Jews." They charged that President Roosevelt was being secretly financed and controlled by "Sidney Hillman," who they described as a "Russian Jew," and by "Earl Browder, the Moscow agent." Radio commentators, public lecturers and columnists who were the spokesmen of American isolationism and reaction; fanatical Roosevelt-hating politicians of both parties; and such national newspaper syndicates as the McCormick-Patterson, Frank Gannett and Hearst chains daily assured millions of Americans that "a vote for Roosevelt is a vote for Communism," and recklessly jeopardized American war morale by asserting that the United States' war leadership was "corrupt," "inefficient" and "deceitful," and that the President

* In May, 1943, the official Nazi news agency, DNB, had called for "cooperation" among their anti-Semitic agitators in all countries. "Only history knows to what extent anti-Semitism among our enemies can change matters in our favor," declared the Nazi news agency. "It may even influence the future conduct of the war." As a result of the Fifth Column campaign in 1944, anti-Semitism became an issue in an American presidential election for the first time in history.

of the United States was "alien-minded," "power-mad" and "willing to sacrifice American lives to satisfy his own ambitions."

The anti-democratic and the America First networks found the finances and guidance to spring into new life throughout the country to spread the Nazi propaganda line against Roosevelt. In many cases, notorious agitators received open encouragement from certain of Roosevelt's political opponents, who exhibited an extraordinary naiveté or irresponsibility . . .

In 1942, before the FBI arrested him, the pro-Nazi propagandist Frank W. Clark had exclaimed: "When the time comes to settle the score and I'm given a reward for my patriotism, I want to be made chief executor of those guys who are now sticking up for democracy!" In the summer of 1944, while still standing trial in Washington on Nazi conspiracy charges, Clark addressed a 3,500-word communication to the Republican candidates outlining a campaign strategy to defeat Roosevelt. Governor John Bricker of Ohio, who was the Republican candidate for Vice-President, replied to the indicted propagandist: "Dear Mr. Clark: Thank you for your letter of July 15 enclosing a letter addressed to Governor Dewey. I shall see that the letter reaches him. I appreciate your suggestions and your helpfulness." Clark's letters, including his 3,500-word propaganda treatise, were thereafter inserted in the *Congressional Record* on September 21, 1944, by Senator William Langer of North Dakota.

The former Bundist and ex-convict, Homer Maerz of Chicago, later told the St. Louis *Star-Times* reporter, Harry Wohl, that he had made a special journey to Benton Harbor, Michigan, to supervise anti-Roosevelt agitation in that area. Maerz claimed he helped in the re-election of the isolationist Representative Clare E. Hoffman who, a few weeks after America was attacked by the Axis, had publicly demanded the "impeachment" of President Roosevelt for having led the American people into war by "deception." Maerz claimed that he met and dined with the Congressman during the election campaign. "We did all right," said Maerz. "Hoffman was re-elected by the biggest majority in his career. We need more like him."

William J. Grace, secretary of Citizens USA Committee and former head of a "peace" committee which held joint meetings with the pro-Nazi *Einheitsfront,* declared in a speech before his organization in Chicago on September 15, 1944:

> "He [President Roosevelt] and he alone is responsible for the murders that took place on the 7th of December, 1941. The dead boys, our sons and brothers, rise up and cry, 'We accuse you, the cigarette-smoking indefensible man!' We must continue to shout until the truth comes out and Roosevelt is thrown out of office!"

Gerald L. K. Smith, Detroit founder of the America First Party, personally attended the Republican National Convention. Subsequently, Smith conducted a special tour of the midwestern states addressing mass America First rallies at which he violently assailed the United Nations, spread divisive and disruptive propaganda, and called for the defeat of President Roosevelt in the election. The isolationist Republicans, Senator Gerald P. Nye and Representative Clare E. Hoffman, and the isolationist Democratic Senator Robert Rice Reynolds publicly gave their endorsement to the campaign activities of Gerald L. K. Smith.

In New York City, William J. Goodwin, former Christian Front candidate for Mayor of New York and leader of the anti-Semitic American Rock Party, took a leading part in the campaign. Goodwin had once defined democracy as "unadulterated slime." In April 1941 he declared, "There's nothing wrong with Fascism. Hitler has done a good job in Germany." In the summer of 1944, Goodwin became an executive officer of the so-called American Democratic National Committee to defeat Roosevelt, and distributed propaganda charging the President with seeking to promote a Communist regime in America. Goodwin's collaborator in this organization was Robert M. Harris, a Wall Street broker who had been financial adviser to the pro-Nazi Father Charles E. Coughlin. By October 14,

1944, Goodwin's organization had received $113,998.00 for its expenditures on anti-Administration propaganda.*

The campaign against President Roosevelt, as the symbol of American anti-Axis leadership, did not end with the 1944 elections. Immediately after the elections, the campaign was resumed with intensified vehemence against the President's foreign policy as represented by the Teheran Accord, the Dumbarton Oaks Agreement and the historic Yalta decisions of the Crimea Conference.

II. *The Case of Dr. Rumely*

Senator Schwellenbach: . . . "When a man comes in and represents himself as a patriotic American it is relevant to see if it is the same campaign being conducted by you as was conducted by the German Government in 1915."

Mr. Rumely (interposing): "There was not or is not one scintilla of evidence . . . I thought we were here to discuss—"

Senator Schwellenbach (interposing): "When we find the same man, who, when trouble in Europe was going on between the German Government and other governments, is engaged in propaganda activity, trying to educate the American people today, we are interested in what he was doing the last time a similar situation was existing."

Extract from Proceedings of Senate Committee to Investigate Lobbying Activities, 1938.

One of the most important and industrious of the anti-Roosevelt agitators during the 1944 presidential election campaign was Dr. Edward A. Rumely of New York City.

After the First World War, Dr. Edward A. Rumely was exposed by U. S. Senate investigators as having been used by the German propaganda machine in the United States.

In 1944 Dr. Edward A. Rumely called himself a "Public

* Other notorious persons campaigning against Roosevelt included: the indicted pro-Nazi propagandists Elizabeth Dilling of Chicago, Gerald B. Winrod of Wichita, Parker Sage of Detroit, and George E. Deatherage of St. Albans, Virginia; and the anti-labor "specialist," Joseph P. Kamp, head of the Constitutional Education League of New York. There were scores of others.

Relations Expert." He was the Executive Secretary of the Committee for Constitutional Government, which has its headquarters in New York City, and which specialized in propagandizing against the Roosevelt Administration. According to Dr. Rumely, the economy of the United States was redolent of the "perfume of Karl Marx." The United States' war against the Axis was "but a step in the revolution" inspired by Karl Marx.

Born in La Porte, Indiana, Rumely studied as a young man in Germany at the Universities of Heidelberg and Freiberg. In the early 1900's he founded the Interlaken School for Boys in Wisconsin. "Dr. Rumely," observed the *Bulletin* of the Interlaken School, "is carrying out in American form the soundest ideas of German education." The *Bulletin* added: "It is almost solely by the power of its new type of education that Germany has forged to the front in the last twenty-five years. . . ."

At the outbreak of the First World War, according to testimony before a Senate Committee in 1919, Rumely became involved with the German propaganda ring in the United States. This ring was headed by Dr. Heinrich A. Albert, the Commercial Attaché at the German Embassy in Washington, who was the brains behind German espionage-sabotage in the United States; Count Johann Heinrich von Bernstorff, the German Ambassador who was also playing a key role in espionage-sabotage work; Dr. Bernhard Dernburg, the former German Secretary of State; and George Sylvester Viereck, who received $100,000 from the Central Powers for his propaganda services during the First World War and who went to jail for his propaganda services for the Nazis during the Second World War.

Witnesses testified at the Senate hearing in 1919 that during the war Rumely had invested $200,000 in advertisements in 619 foreign language newspapers in the United States, urging that America refrain from sending munitions to the Allies. In the spring of 1915, with money secretly provided through German diplomatic channels, Rumely bought the New York *Evening Mail.* He operated the paper for two years at a total cost to Germany of $1,451,000.

On July 18, 1918, Rumely was arrested by the United States authorities. After prolonged court action, he was sentenced on December 18, 1920, to serve a year and a day in prison for making a false report to the U. S. Government under the Trading With The Enemy Act. The sentence was affirmed on appeal. Rumely, however, had powerful friends. George Harvey, the American Ambassador to England during 1921-23, wrote in his magazine *War Weekly:* "Rumely's close, if not closest friend during the past six years has been Henry Ford." Rumely served thirty days in a penitentiary. Subsequently, President Coolidge granted him a complete pardon.

For some time afterwards Dr. Rumely discreetly withdrew from public affairs. But by the early 1930's he was back in circulation. He organized an "investment concern" in Chicago and was soon engaged in various lobbying activities in Washington, D. C.

In 1933, after Hitler came to power, a young woman educator, planning a trip to Germany, asked Rumely if he could give her an introduction to any interesting personages in the Third Reich. Rumely dashed off a note on his personal stationery. The note was addressed to Putzi Hanfstaengel, Chief of the Nazi Press and then one of Hitler's most intimate aides.

In the winter of 1936, Frank Gannett, publisher of a string of isolationist American newspapers, called together a small group of wealthy men in New York City. He proposed that they establish an organization which would spread propaganda on a mass scale against Roosevelt's New Deal Administration. He had the man to head such an organization. The man's name, said Frank Gannett, was Dr. Edward A. Rumely.

The name of the organization set up by Gannett and his friends, with Rumely as Executive Secretary and Gannett as Chairman, was called the National Committee to Uphold Constitutional Government (the name was changed in April 1941 to the Committee for Constitutional Government). Lavishly financed by the Gannett group, Rumely launched an anti-Administration propaganda campaign of truly colossal proportions.

During the first six months of his Committee's existence, Rumely supervised the distribution of no less than 10,000,000 pieces of propaganda. This material was sent to editors, clergymen, business executives and educators in every part of the country. In one case when Administration-sponsored legislation was pending in Washington, Rumely sent a special telegram to 32,000 influential citizens living in states represented by key congressmen. The telegram urged the defeat of the legislation in question. The cost of the telegram was $1.27 per message, or $40,640 in all.

Sometimes, by mistake, Rumely sent his propaganda material to the wrong people. In one case, Rumely's propaganda, accompanied by a solicitation for funds, reached Secretary of the Interior, Harold Ickes. "I don't know how my name happened to get on your sucker list," wrote Secretary Ickes to Rumely's Committee, "but I advise you to spend your money where there is a greater prospect of pay dirt and a greater respect for dirt."

During 1937-1944, the expenditures of Rumely's Committee totaled approximately $10,000,000.

Here is a summary of the anti-Administration material distributed by Rumely's Committee:

82,000,000 pieces of literature, booklets, pamphlets, reprints of editorials and articles, especially addressed letters and 760,000 books;

more than 10,000 transcriptions, carrying 15-minute radio talks on national issues, besides frequent national hook-ups for representatives of the Committee;

many thousands of releases to daily and weekly newspapers; full-page advertisements in 536 different newspapers with a combined circulation of nearly 20,000,000;

350,000 telegrams.

In December, 1944 the Special Congressional Committee investigating presidential campaign expenditures requested Dr. Rumely to produce the full list of his financial supporters. Dr. Rumely refused. "Our activity is not political," he declared. The congressional investigatory body thought otherwise and subpoenaed the files of Rumely's Committee for Constitutional Government. Dr. Rumely defied the subpoena. A District of Columbia Grand Jury indicted him for alleged contempt. Rumely still would not produce his files. Moreover, he continued his propaganda activities without let-up. . . .

In the spring of 1945, a stream of propaganda violently attacking the Roosevelt Administration was still pouring from the New York offices of Dr. Edward A. Rumely.

III. *Germans Without Swastikas*

In January 1941 a confidential report was sent by Walter Kappe, chief of the Nazi *Kameradschaft USA,* which had its headquarters at Stuttgart, Germany, to all Nazi Party members and sympathizers in the United States. Kappe's message, requesting the forwarding of certain information to Germany, stated:

> "*Important to us* are reports concerning public opinion in the United States, such as the nature of the attitude of Germans, which clubs have disbanded, how the average American considers the situation, how anti-Jewish sentiment is developing, etc. . . ."

Walter Kappe had been one of the leading Nazi espionage chiefs in the United States. Kappe originally came to America, like so many other Nazi agents, shortly after the First World War. In New York, Chicago and other cities, Kappe reorganized the old Pan-German secret societies, converting them into Nazi espionage and propaganda agencies. Kappe returned to Germany just before the outbreak of the Second World War in Europe. In 1943, the U. S. Federal Bureau of Investigation announced that it had evidence that Kappe might have secretly returned to the United States as a special agent of the SS Intelligence Division. . . .

One of the important tasks which Kappe sought to accomplish in the United States was to promote Nazi influence over the widespread German-American press. After the First World War, many German-American newspapers had consistently promoted the cause of the German General Staff and attacked all American efforts to collaborate with the Allied peace-enforcement authorities in Europe. Kappe and other Nazi agents sought to utilize these German-American newspapers to create sympathy for the German cause in the Second World War, not with open pro-Nazi propaganda such as was carried on by the organs of the Bund, but by means of isolationist, anti-Roosevelt, anti-British and especially anti-Soviet propaganda.

The Nazis were confident that they could build a powerful political pressure group in the United States from certain sections of the German-American community despite the fact that the majority of Americans of German extraction were descendants of democratic German revolutionaries who had been forced to flee from their own country to escape persecution or death. In Berlin in 1941, the Nazi press chief Dr. Paul Schmidt told the American correspondent, Bernard Lansing:

> "The American race will have to recognize Adolf Hitler because it will some day feel its German heritage, which is much stronger than anything the Anglo-Saxons have given you. There are 23,000,000 Americans of German descent . . . Do you think a single one will ever forget he is a German? Never! So is it not better America recognizes in time the direction of destiny?"

After Pearl Harbor, even a part of the non-Nazi section of the German-American press, in the name of isolationism and "anti-Bolshevism," carried on incessant attacks against America's allies in the war. In the spring of 1945, these newspapers were still being circulated throughout the country, influencing the thinking of tens of thousands of German-Americans, and even being distributed among captured Nazi soldiers in American war-prison camps. . . .

A typical example was the New York *Neue Volkszeitung*. William L. Shirer, the former Berlin correspondent, radio commentator and author of *Berlin Diary*, declared in 1944 that "no newspaper under the thumb of Dr. Goebbels has been more vitriolic, more anti-Russian than the *Neue Volkszeitung*." The editor of this newspaper was the German émigré politician, Friedrich Stampfer, a one-time luminary in the German Social Democratic regime which from 1918 to 1933 served as the "democratic" and "anti-Bolshevik" façade behind which the German General Staff prepared for its Second World War.

Under the direction of the German émigré Friedrich Stampfer, the *Neue Volkszeitung* became one of the most vehement organs of German "anti-Bolshevik" propaganda in the United States. It was made available as reading material for Nazi war-prisoners in the United States. Incessantly, this newspaper published propaganda playing the western democracies against Soviet Russia.

On December 25, 1943, after the signing of the Soviet-Czech agreement which assured the future independence and security of Czechoslovakia, the *Neue Volkszeitung* paralleled the current Nazi propaganda by declaring:

> "Russia does not seek to attain collective security for Europe, but a Russian protectorate. Once Russia is securely seated in Prague, it can from there control Europe without any effort."

On January 22, 1944, following the historic Teheran Agreement between America, Britain and Russia, the *Neue Volkszeitung* declared:

> "The whole of Europe west of the Russian border will have a common interest after this war. That is, to preserve their independence in the face of their powerful Russian neighbor. This cannot be achieved without the help of England and America."

On January 5, 1944, with the American, British and Russian

armed forces relentlessly closing in on Nazi Germany, the *Neue Volkszeitung* exclaimed, "Yes, the world is endangered by Bolshevism!" This newspaper actually went on to recommend to the German General Staff a military-political strategy. "Germany should reverse its defense, be rigid in the East, elastic in the West," declared the paper. "Every political consideration should lead to a strategy which will prevent total victory in the East, but which will not irritate the West unnecessarily."

Stampfer was not the only German émigré politician spreading this sort of propaganda through the German-American press. In recent years, a number of former German political and military émigrés have come to the United States or Canada and organized extensive propaganda for circulation in the German-American press. Some of these men succeeded in gaining the confidence of American government agencies as "advisors" on German policy. They sought to convince American officials that, unless they were sent back to rule Germany after the defeat of the Nazis, "Bolshevism" would become dominant throughout Europe.

The former German U-boat commander and Freikorps leader Gottfried Treviranus presented high-placed American officials and businessmen with a plan to save Germany from "Bolshevism" and to preserve the German economy after the war.

Heinrich Bruening, former leader of the German Centrist Party; Paul Spicker, former Commissioner for Prussia; Dr. Ernst Hanfstangel, former Nazi press chief; Hermann Rauschning, former friend of Hitler; Otto Strasser, brother of Hitler's rival and co-founder of the Nazi Party, Gregor Strasser, and organizer of the German Fascist and allegedly anti-Nazi Black Front; and several other German politicians of the pre-Hitler era have been seeking to convince the United States and British Governments to send them back to Germany as officials of a German "Second Republic."

The "anti-Bolshevik" propaganda line devised by Stampfer and other German émigré politicians in the United States was not confined to the New York *Neue Volkszeitung*.

The Bismarck, North Dakota, *Staatsanzeiger* declared on January 6, 1944:

"Once Germany lies in ruins there won't be any nation left to hinder Russia from becoming the predominant power of the Continent. Maybe this will make the English realize that the calculations of the much-criticized Neville Chamberlain were not so wrong after all: he tried to keep Germany as a defense-wall against the Russian high tide."

The Chicago *Abendpost* daily repeated the same line. In January 1945, just before the Red Army launched its great offensive into the heart of Germany, the *Abendpost* declared that Stalin was staging a "sitdown strike" on the eastern front, letting America and Britain do all the fighting. Then, on January 21, 1945, immediately after the Red Army began its drive, the *Abendpost* declared: "Presumably the Russians will soon enter Berlin and Germany will be annexed to the Soviet Union." On January 28, 1945, this newspaper wrote: "In his organ *Das Reich,* Hitler's propaganda minister, Goebbels, warns of the threatening Bolshevization of Europe. This warning is apparently not unjustified."

The same propaganda was repeated by the *Detroiter Abendpost;* the Milwaukee *Deutsche Zeitung* and by German-American newspapers associated with the old Pan-German movement. On January 6, 1945, the Milwaukee *Deutsche Zeitung* opposed the punishment of what it termed the "so-called" Nazi war-criminals. A typical paragraph from this newspaper stated:

"What purpose would the punishment of war criminals serve? By punishing them do we not condemn ourselves according to Paul? Do we still punish human beings because they are sick? . . . And the so-called war criminals—including ourselves—are sick human beings whose punishment and execution does not contribute in the least to the recovery of humanity."

The only possible effect of the propaganda carried by this section of the German-American press can be to arouse doubts and suspicions among the United Nations, thereby furthering the basic aim of the German General Staff to split the Allies in the postwar period.

CHAPTER THIRTEEN

THE POLITICS OF A THIRD WORLD WAR

I. *The Hopes and Plans of Dr. Goebbels*

TO penetrate and influence the political affairs of other nations has been the classic strategy of German conspiracy. General Karl von Clausewitz, foremost theorist of the German General Staff, wrote that "war is the continuation of politics by other means." Conversely, the German General Staff has always regarded politics, including propaganda, intrigue and conspiracy in other countries, as the continuation of war by other means. Today, the continuation of the Axis war by political intrigues in other countries has become the dominant purpose of the international Nazi Fifth Columns.

"Peace?" said a high-ranking German officer in Paris whose words were recorded by *La France Libre* on July 12, 1943. "There will be no peace anywhere in the world after the guns stop firing. The battle of the Fifth Columns will take the place of the battles of the tanks and armored cars."

The German General Staff definitely counts on an increasing growth and power of its already widespread Fifth Column in the United States, not only as an instrument for provoking national dissension in the postwar period by race riots, anti-Semitic terrorism and wildcat labor-capital feuds; but also as a means of exerting direct influence on American politics, and especially on the future course of American foreign policy.

In his Message to Congress in January 1945, President Roosevelt warned the American people that the great hope and aim of the German strategists was to bring about postwar division among the Allied nations so that the German General Staff might get the opportunity to rise again and attack the world for a third time in this century.

"The wedge that the Germans attempted to drive in Western Europe," said the President, "was less dangerous in actual terms of winning the war than the wedges which they are continually attempting to drive between ourselves and our allies."

Those isolationist forces in the United States which favored collaboration with Germany in the past, and which, wittingly or unwittingly, rendered such notable services to the Nazi Propaganda Ministry during the crucial wartime presidential elections of 1944, remain a powerful factor in American politics. The Nazi leaders of Germany are fully aware of this fact and have planned to take advantage of it.

On February 22, 1945, the Nazi Propaganda Minister in Berlin, Dr. Paul Joseph Goebbels, indicated the future course of German political plans for the United States. Writing in his personal organ, *Das Reich,* Dr. Goebbels predicted that in 1948 "a Republican isolationist" would come into the White House and would immediately take steps to "withdraw American troops from the devil's cauldron of Europe." With America under isolationist control, the United Nations would soon fall asunder. A war would break out "between Great Britain and Soviet Russia." Amidst the universal chaos, Germany would be able to rebuild her might and reinstate herself as a world power. . . .

There was evidence in the United States that these hopes of Dr. Goebbels were not the outcome of mere wishful thinking on the part of the astute Nazi Propaganda Minister.

On January 19, 1945, three days before the Nazi Propaganda Minister expressed his hopes in *Das Reich* that American troops would soon be removed from Europe and war would break out between Britain and Russia, Captain J. M. Patterson editorialized in his New York *Daily News:*

> "If the Russians should knock Germany out of the war, we surmise that most of our fighting men in Europe would feel that was fine, and now how about quitting Europe. . . . We also surmise that large numbers of people on the home front feel the same way. . . . We are being drawn deeper and deeper into European

politics . . . in various imaginable clashes between British and Russian interests in Europe our boys may well find themselves in the middle."

The same issue of the *Daily News* featured a letter from an anonymous correspondent who signed herself "Soldier's Mother." It was typical of the anti-Soviet and anti-British propaganda appearing daily on the editorial pages of the newspapers published by Captain Patterson, Colonel McCormick, Cissie Patterson and William Randolph Hearst. This letter read:

> "How much longer must our boys be slaughtered in this European madhouse for the future glory of Red Russia and the salvation of the tottering British Empire? Let these Europeans solve their own problems with their own blood. Ours is too valuable to be shed every time Britain has a war on her hands."

Another typical "letter" from the same newspaper, same day, same page, same edition, signed "W. J. Smythe," reads:

> "Here is a comparison . . . George Washington crossed the Delaware and won a splendid victory. Roosevelt double-crossed the mothers and fathers at Boston. For the results, take a look at the casualty lists."

On February 12, 1945, immediately after the announcement of the Yalta decisions to smash the German General Staff and to maintain the unity of the three great powers, America, Britain and Russia, as a bulwark of lasting peace and security, Dr. Paul Schmidt of the German Foreign Office announced in Berlin that "Stalin had imposed his will on President Roosevelt and Prime Minister Churchill" and "This is an unlimited triumph for Stalin in all spheres . . . Stalin has become the governor of the three big powers on the Continent. . . ."

On February 13, 1945, the Tokyo radio declared in a broadcast recorded by the United Press that the Crimea Conference was "nothing but absolute Anglo-American submission to the overwhelming influence of Russia. The United States and Britain have been forced to play second fiddle in the game and have been obliged to recognize the dominance of the Soviet Union in the so-called postwar disposal of Germany."

On February 14, 1945, Senator Burton K. Wheeler declared in a public statement in Washington, D. C., that the Crimea Conference "is a great victory for Stalin and Russian imperialism." The Senator stated that Russia had seized control of Europe and a large part of Asia.

The New York *Daily News* editorialized on the same day:

> "If a Big One emerges finally from the current trio, it is anybody's guess who he will be. His identity may possibly be foreshadowed, though, by the fact that the previous Big Three Conference was held at Teheran, on the southern fringe of Russia, while this latest one was held in Russia itself. . . . The declaration which came out of the Crimea Conference contained considerable tosh about how this war is preparing all mankind to enjoy freedom from fear and want, as specified in the Atlantic Charter. . . . But that is Roosevelt's story, and he is stuck with it. . . ."

William P. Simms, Roy Howard's chief commentator on foreign affairs, wrote in the New York *World-Telegram:* "Under the pact signed at Yalta, in the Crimea, President Roosevelt and Prime Minister Churchill gave way completely to Marshal Stalin . . ."

Karl von Wiegand, William Randolph Hearst's special European correspondent, cabled the Hearst New York *Journal American* from Madrid: "With the impending collapse of Germany and her destruction as a dam against Communism, Spain and Portugal, a thousand miles to the west, become the next barriers to the on-rushing Red Russian flood . . . With Italy a hunger-anarchy, France a political economic chaos, Spain, peaceful and calm, is the next bulwark against the Red flood."

On February 28, 1945, continuing the attack on the Crimea Conference, Senator Wheeler declared over a nation-wide radio hook-up:

> "Let us recall what was actually decided at Yalta. . . . There was decision to partition, dismember, de-industrialize and enslave the German nation, all in the sweet name of peace!"

That is how the great, history-making Yalta decisions of the Crimea Conference were introduced to millions of Americans by certain politicians, presslords, and correspondents.

In the spring of 1945, despite the impending complete military collapse of Nazi Germany, Dr. Goebbels still had reason to be hopeful as to future developments of the German plans against the peace and security of the world . . .

II. *New Political Assignments*

The sensational Colepaugh-Gimpel case, which reached American public attention in February 1945, was widely misinterpreted as another case of German sabotage against the American war effort. But the arrival of Colepaugh and Gimpel on American soil meant that the German conspiracy in the United States had already entered a new phase of operations—the phase of new postwar political intrigue.

On the night of November 29, 1944, just after the re-election of President Roosevelt for a fourth term, two German agents were secretly landed by a submarine on the coast of Maine. Their names were William Curtis Colepaugh, alias William C. Caldwell, an American traitor, born in Niantic, Connecticut, on March 25, 1918, and Erich Gimpel, alias Edward George Green, a German, born in Merseberg, Germany, on November 25, 1910. These men were not ordinary saboteurs or German military spies. The purpose for which they were sent across the Atlantic by submarine and landed in America had nothing directly to do with the course of the military hostilities which, by November 1944, were already entering their final phase in Europe.

The German agents, Colepaugh and Gimpel, were sent into the United States to carry out special long-range political assignments on behalf of the Intelligence Division of Heinrich Himmler's SS, the chief directing organization of the new international Nazi underground.

Colepaugh and Gimpel had been carefully picked by the SS to carry out this political mission in America. Both men were intelligent, educated and politically experienced.

The American, Colepaugh, had attended a private academy in New Jersey and had studied engineering at the Massachusetts Institute of Technology. He was thoroughly familiar with

American politics, and had previously been active in American isolationist and pro-Nazi political circles.

The German, Gimpel, had operated for many years in South America on behalf of the Nazi Propaganda Ministry. His last headquarters were at Lima, Peru, where he held an executive position with the German radio corporation, Telefunken. Gimpel was also familiar with American politics. He spoke English fluently and with almost no accent.

Before being sent across the Atlantic, Colepaugh and Gimpel were thoroughly schooled in the new SS espionage and propaganda techniques at a special SS training center located in The Hague, Holland. They were then summoned to Berlin, interviewed by high-ranking SS Intelligence officers, and given a list of names and addresses of persons they were to contact when they arrived in the United States.

The two men left Kiel, Germany, aboard the U-boat 1230 on September 26, 1944. The submarine stayed under water all day, surfacing only at night, to elude British and American naval patrols. After fifty-four days, the U-boat entered Frenchmen Bay on the coast of Maine and proceeded up the bay for some seven miles to Hancock Point. Here, at 11 P.M. on the night of November 29, the two agents were rowed ashore in a rubber boat and set loose on American soil.

The SS Intelligence Division in Germany had taken steps to make it possible for Colepaugh and Gimpel to reside in the United States for many years to come. When they landed on the Maine coast, the two agents had in their possession $60,000 in American currency and a store of valuable diamonds worth additional tens of thousands of dollars. They had also been provided with skillfully forged American birth certificates; forged Selective Service registration and classification cards; forged discharges from the United States Navy; and other false identification documents. Some of these papers were dated ahead to 1946. Others were left undated; the agents had been given special marking devices to date them as required.

In January 1945, having been at large in the United States for a little over one month, Colepaugh and Gimpel were trapped by the Federal Bureau of Investigation. They had been living at expensive hotels and apartment houses in Boston and New York, posing as well-to-do young American businessmen.

"I was asked to go to the United States to find out about the political situation," Gimpel told the FBI when he was arrested. ". . . They [Gimpel's SS instructors in Germany] said they would like to have someone in the United States to make some contacts."

Before their arrest, Colepaugh and Gimpel had destroyed the list of names and addresses of their American contacts. . . .

In February 1945, the two German agents were tried before a military court, found guilty of espionage against the United States and sentenced to death.

The court sessions were held in secret for reasons of wartime security; but publicity was given to the revelation made by the Government prosecutor during the trial that "other agents," similar to Colepaugh and Gimpel, were still at large and active in the United States.

CHAPTER FOURTEEN

CONCLUSION

NAZI Germany has suffered a military defeat; but the struggle for the peace has just begun. That is the central fact of the present time. Around it revolve all questions of future security and world reconstruction.

The German General Staff is resigned to a temporary military defeat. Germany's rulers have prepared their plans to win the peace and convert it into a basis for a third world war.

The aim of the United Nations is to enforce the unconditional surrender of Germany after German armed resistance is ended, and then to go on to convert the military defeat of Germany into the final destruction of German militarism and Nazism, and the uprooting and wiping out of the German General Staff.

At Yalta, in the Crimea, early in February 1945, Roosevelt, Stalin and Churchill, the leaders of the three great powers on whose shoulders the burden of the battle and the responsibility of victory chiefly fall, announced their joint decisions and joint policy on Germany.

The three leaders of the United Nations declared:

"It is our inflexible purpose to destroy German militarism and Nazism and to insure Germany will never again be able to disturb the peace of the world. We are determined to disarm and disband all German armed forces; break up for all time the German General Staff that has repeatedly contrived the resurgence of German militarism; remove or destroy all German military equipment; eliminate or control all German industry that could be used for military production; bring all war criminals to just and swift punishment, and exact reparation in kind for the destruction

wrought by the Germans; wipe out the Nazi party, Nazi laws, organizations and institutions, remove all Nazi and militarist influences from public office and from the cultural and economic life of the German people, and take in harmony such other measures in Germany as may be necessary to the future peace and safety of the world. It is not our purpose to destroy the people of Germany, but only when Nazism and militarism have been extirpated will there be hope for a decent life for Germans, and a place for them in the community of nations."

This program must be achieved.

The world must never forget the crimes of the German General Staff.

During the past thirty years, in two world wars, a colossal price has been paid in human suffering and destruction as a result of German aggression. There must be no third world war.

On the full realization of the program outlined at the Crimea Conference, through the continued and growing unity of the United Nations, depends the future peace and security of all mankind.

THE END

The first edition of this book went to press before this country and the world were shaken by the tragic death of our great Commander-in-Chief, Franklin Delano Roosevelt. As the beloved leader of the American people and the immortal architect of the United Nations, President Roosevelt guided us to victory and showed us the way to lasting peace. Now more than ever, every American must pledge himself to the fulfillment of that victory and peace which President Roosevelt made possible and for which he gave his life.

Michael Sayers
Albert E. Kahn

INDEX

CPSIA information can be obtained
at www.ICGtesting.com
Printed in the USA
BVOW03s1447121017
497510BV00001B/8/P